BRITAIN IN EUROPE:

A losing cause

David Hannay

(Lord Hannay of Chiswick)

To Kiran and Joan

A la recherche des Temps perdu ...

David

London

June 2021

To all those with whom I travelled on this, often painful, journey. Our combined efforts may have failed; but they were worthwhile.

"Oxford… home of lost causes and forsaken beliefs and impossible loyalties!" Matthew Arnold: Essays in Criticism, First Series (1865)

"Yes, they didn't just waste their time, they wrote."
Leo Tolstoy: War and Peace.

CONTENTS

Introduction

Oxford, the university where I took an undergraduate degree in modern history a little over sixty years ago, has been described as the home of lost causes. So it is probably suitable to mention it at the outset of this book. It was there, after all, that I studied European history in the 18th, 19th and early 20th centuries. And it was there that I learned from that study how unwise, and indeed how futile, it was for Britain to turn its back on developments in the rest of Europe; and how intimately we were linked, historically, culturally, economically and politically to our fellow European countries.

Before putting pen to paper in writing yet another book (I have so far written four, three published and one self-published, on which a bit more explanation below), I did hesitate for some time. After all the politics and economics of Britain's relationship with the European Communities (now known as the European Union) have singularly failed to arouse much interest or enthusiasm in this country. Too often discussion has become bogged down in an alphabet soup of acronyms; and the contentious nature of the debate has obscured any rational consideration of the issues at stake.

Moreover the hard fact is that those who supported Britain's continued membership of the European Union, as the present author did, lost the argument, first narrowly in the in/out referendum of 2016 and then, more decisively, in the general election of December 2019. Would not anything I wrote seem like a case of sour grapes, the lamentation of a bad loser?

And I cannot pretend that, at any point in the last thirty years since I ceased to be Britain's Permanent Representative to the European Communities in July 1990, have I played a major or a decisive role in the shaping of the events I would be describing. More often I was an appalled spectator and, at most, a member of the chorus who, as in the great, classical Greek tragedies, lament the failings of the principal players on both sides and foretell the inevitability of disaster overtaking them.

That is the case for dignified silence. Against it stands the sneaking feeling that, as so often occurs, history will be written by the victors, not only by those who campaigned with many a half truth and, even more, with a lot of outright lies for our departure, but also by academic historians, whose capacity to resist hindsight is often limited, and who may be inclined to treat Britain's exit from the EU, which it had joined late and reluctantly, as inevitable, as at best an accident waiting to happen, even what Sellars and Yeatman in their wonderful book "1066 and All That" might have categorised as "a good thing". In my view such a fate would be a travesty of what actually occurred.

And then along came Coronavirus, providing me with a period of enforced isolation while the memory of the events of recent years remained fresh in the mind. So, on both substantive grounds and those of opportunism, the case was made.

The most important initial decision was when to start the story and when to conclude it. In my earlier books, most particularly in "Britain's Quest for a Role", but also in "Cyprus: The Search for a Solution", in "New World Disorder: The UN after the Cold War" and in the self-published book I wrote for my family and friends "The Tale of a Grandfather" there is a good deal about European diplomacy and my long years spent in Brussels (1965/77 and 1985/90). So some overlap with the present book cannot be avoided. But, by starting this book in 1990, when I moved from close to the centre of Britain's European policy making to its periphery in New York I have tried to avoid too much of that overlap. As to the end point, January 31st 2020, the day Britain left the EU was an obvious choice even if it does deprive the reader (and the author) of the delights of following the post-Brexit negotiations over Britain's new, external relationship with the EU, which have since ended in a lamentably thin and second-rate outcome.

Prologue

I offer no apologies for starting this account with a repeat of the valedictory despatch which I sent to the Foreign Secretary when I left Brussels on 28 August, 1990, heading off to New York where Saddam Hussein's invasion of Kuwait and the international community's response to it were already erasing most of the old Cold War landmarks and taboos (it appears also on pps. 157/172 of "Britain's Quest for a Role").

I do so because, at the time, I assumed this would be my professional farewell to the European Communities, to whose business and its relationship with Britain I had devoted almost all of the previous twenty-five years. So I tried to pull together some wider and more profound thoughts than would usually have found their way into a document of this sort.

I do so also because what I wrote then benefits from no sort of hindsight and seems to me to have stood the test of time reasonably well. And I do so because this despatch was written at what turned out to be a climactic moment both in the history of the European Communities, when German re-unification was under way and the creation of the Euro was on the horizon and in the history of Britain in Europe when the split in the Conservative Party which followed Margaret Thatcher's removal from office was only a few weeks away.

Here it is:

I am leaving Brussels almost 25 years to the day after first being posted here to the small delegation we maintained during the period between our first and our second applications for membership of the European Communities and almost five years after being appointed Permanent Representative. Of the 25 years since I first came into contact with the European Communities 21 have been spent dealing with their affairs.

In these last five years I have prepared and attended a dozen European Councils, over 100 meetings of the Council in its other manifestations, and 200 or so meetings of COREPER; and UKRep has sent rather over 20,000 telegrams to the Department. These figures alone show how hard it is for any of the main participants in Community business to maintain a view of the wood as well as of the trees which crowd around them week in, week out. They also illustrate graphically how easy it is to become obsessed by issues of negotiating technique and procedure to the exclusion of a wider view of policy; and they highlight one of the besetting weaknesses of the Communities that they often seem to outsiders to be organisations designed by bureaucrats for bureaucrats.

So a sense of perspective is an all-important attribute for handling Community business. The widest perspective sets it in the framework of European, and indeed world, history in the twentieth century, with the collapse, disintegration and destruction of so much, and so many of the inhabitants, of our continent in the first half of the century, contrasting vividly with the prosperity and security achieved within a framework of cooperative effort and the rule of law which has characterised the second half. A somewhat narrower perspective contrasts 1965, the year I came to Brussels, with the present day.

In 1965 the Community of Six seemed set to stay that way, the UK having been on the receiving end of De Gaulle's 1963 veto and appearing to have no stomach for another attempt. The Community was in any case dead in the water, crippled by a French boycott of its meetings; no Council met, not even COREPER. As an external force it was negligible except in Africa and in the Kennedy Round of trade negotiations. Now we have a Community of Twelve which has come successfully through three successive enlargements, with another imminent and further accessions before the end of the century more likely than not; a Single Market is being created not just in the meeting rooms of Brussels but by economic operators, and it is transforming the economies of Europe; the Community is regarded as an important, if hesitant and unsure, actor from one end of the world to the other. To sharpen the focus still more one can contrast the first half of the 1980s with the second, the former characterised by stagnation and internecine quarrelling over the need to right the inequity of our budgetary contribution, the latter a period of unprecedented development both internally and externally. These exercises in perspective are not tricks, but they do conceal much. There have been plenty of failures, there are plenty of weaknesses and there are tensions, some of them set up by the very speed of the developments in recent years. Recent success has owed as much to the substantial economic growth following the hard decisions taken by national governments earlier in the last decade as to any Brussels alchemy.

The main landmarks: 1985/90.
My early months as Permanent Representative were entirely absorbed in the negotiation of the Single European Act. This strange animal, whose name epitomises the Community's capacity to reduce even the

most significant developments to almost meaningless mumbo-jumbo, was denounced at the time as a meaningless mouse and subsequently as a federalist trap. In truth it is neither. It was a compromise between those who sought much more wide-ranging constitutional reform and those, like ourselves, who, while sharing the main objectives of achieving the Single Market and strengthening Political Cooperation, saw no need to change the basic treaties to do so. Its substantive content fell a good deal closer to our end of the spectrum than to the other. That judgement need not be taken on trust; an analysis of the decisions taken since then on matters falling under treaty provisions switched from unanimity to qualified majority voting by the Single European Act, shows the UK voted down only very seldom, much less often than a number of other member states. But the episode demonstrated that our own strong preference for proceeding pragmatically and step by step, without too much thought about, and too much definition of, the final objective, was in conflict with the views of all other member states which felt the need to reflect substantial developments in Community policy in new treaty provisions.

Close on the heels of the Single European Act came the accession of Spain and Portugal. This third enlargement went more smoothly than the previous two. Fears at the time of a prolonged bout of indigestion proved misplaced. Spain, in particular, made its mark with a notably successful first Presidency. Contrary to much conventional wisdom, this enlargement tended to reinforce the Community's centripetal rather than its centrifugal tendencies, majority voting being more widely practised where it was provided for in the original treaties but had long been in disuse, it being generally recognised, even before the Single European Act came into force, that conducting the business of a twelve

11

member Community on the basis of consensus was going to be impossibly difficult.

1987 was the year the Community ran out of money and when even creative accounting could no longer conceal it. Profligate spending on the Common Agricultural Policy despite earlier attempts at reform, linked with the ambitions of the poorer member states, the Commission and the European Parliament to boost structural fund and other spending, dragged the member states back into another major budgetary negotiation only three years after they had wearily concluded the previous round at Fontainebleau. Like all such negotiations, this one was long, arduous and bad-tempered. But the final outcome was a clear advance from our point of view. Not only were we able, with the bare minimum of fracas, to carry over our two thirds rebate provision into the new budgetary arrangements. But, for the first time, serious progress was made on CAP reform. Overall limits on agricultural expenditure were buttressed by individual product stabilisers. Since then, and thanks admittedly in part to the effects of two years of drought in the US, agricultural spending has been well below the limits set and most of the main products in surplus have been subject to effective penalties. A price had to be paid in the form of the doubling of structural funds; but, given the effect of the Fontainebleau mechanism on our own contribution and the support that was gained from the poorer member states for the Single Market programme, that could be considered an acceptable trade off.

When the Milan European Council in 1985 set the 1992 deadline for achieving the Single Market and gave a broad blessing to Lord Cockfield's White Paper laying out what would be necessary to bring it about, few would have ventured much money on its fulfilment. After all, the history of the Community was littered with *the whitening skeletons of such promises; the procedures for taking the decisions were laborious in the extreme and, although they were about to be facilitated by the introduction of Qualified Majority Voting, they were also about to be complicated by giving the European Parliament a greater say in the process. Most member states had not suddenly been transformed into fervent partisans of a liberal, economic approach but rather were being dragged reluctantly towards such policies. So, the legislative programme which has ground its way remorselessly through innumerable Council meetings since then and is now well past the two-thirds mark was certainly not condemned to succeed, as most historians will now, no doubt, say that it was. It owes much to our own support, assisted by a scanty band of like-minded member states, and the effective determination and hard work of the Commission. Most important, we have together been able to ensure that the legislation reaching the statute book is generally of an open and deregulatory kind and to resist the attempts of a number of member states to make it no more than a further layer of regulation piled on top of existing ones. Fortress Europe has been comprehensively seen off.*

As the Single Market programme took shape, the pressure began steadily to build up for progress towards Economic and Monetary Union and now that issue dominates the Community's current agenda. It presents us with many problems. As a non-participant in the Exchange Rate Mechanism, I feel we have tended to underestimate the forces propelling our partners towards a treaty commitment to the final stages of EMU. Having committed themselves to maintaining a stable relationship with the strongest currency in the Community, the Deutschmark, most dramatically in the case of the French who tore up their previous interventionist and expansionary policies to achieve this, they see little political or economic merit in fighting to maintain a national autonomy of decision-making on monetary policies which is widely regarded as a mere facade. This analysis has, quite fortuitously, been reinforced in their eyes by the imminence of German unification. Acquiescence in the DM zone, as opposed to what they hope will be a system in which decision-making will be genuinely shared, becomes that much less acceptable as general concerns about excessive German strength lurk close to the surface.

The previous landmarks have all concerned the internal development of the Community and, in truth, those internal issues have dominated the agenda for much of the last five years. They have, however, influenced the Community's external relationships quite notably. The Single Market programme in particular has exerted a powerful external influence, at first arousing considerable alarm lest it be fundamentally protectionist and, more recently, as those fears receded and as the successful completion of the programme became more likely, acting as a kind of magnet. Thus, the Community's responsibility for, and stake in, a successful outcome of the Uruguay Round has become more evident. And the EFTA countries seek a relationship amounting to a kind of country membership of the Single Market and going well beyond the simple free trade arrangements they concluded when we joined the Community. Meanwhile the United States has clearly re-appraised its view of the Community's significance and potential usefulness and, since President Bush took office, has sharply upgraded it.

But the external development which has wrought a sea-change in the Community and in its external policies has of course been the collapse of communism in Eastern Europe, bringing in its train the unification of Germany and thus the inclusion of the GDR in the Community, the emergence of democracies and putative market economies in the Soviet Union's former satellites, and the Soviet Union's own remarkable shift from outright hostility towards the Community to a somewhat bemused anticipation of its emergence as an exemplar and a source of much-needed material support. With the Commission propelled overnight at the Paris Economic Summit of July 1989 into the role of coordinator of all free-world assistance to Eastern Europe, the Commission has risen well to the challenge; emergency food aid, longer term assistance and, in the case of Romania, firm political action when it was needed, has been forthcoming. But a long and expensive road lies ahead; and choices no doubt less clearly black and white than those of the past year will have to be made.

A glance to the future.

Prediction of future developments in and of the Community is always a chancy business, especially when it is, as now, in a period of rapid evolution and lies close to the centre of upheavals, to its east in particular, which are bound to have an important influence on it. Some major issues, German unification, two Inter-Governmental Conferences on Political Union and Economic and Monetary Union are likely to come to a head in the latter months of this year or in the course of 1991; others, such as further enlargement, the completion and dynamic effects of the Single Market and the budgetary review of 1992 lie further off, but certainly not over the horizon.

The Community dimension of German unification will come first. It looks like being a rather messy affair as a result of unification being advanced from December to October. A more orderly and systematic process with a December timetable would have been preferable. But the outcome is not in doubt nor is the detailed content

15

likely to be much altered; nor should it be unduly costly, though some net costs there will be. Neither the derogations needed from the immediate application of Community law in the GDR nor the costs are likely to be as substantial as would have been the case if the GDR had formally acceded to the Community, the former because so much of FRG law will simply apply in the GDR without more ado, the latter because the FRG seems itself to have set its face against expensive solutions financed from the Community budget.

None of this addresses the concerns that have arisen since the Berlin Wall came down about the economic, political and military strength of a united Germany and the purposes to which that strength might in the future be deployed. These concerns are felt throughout the Community and beyond, even if their articulation and the response to them differs widely. All suffered to some degree from the events of the first half of the century. Most see the problems of that period as lying not so much in the economic strength of Germany but in the combination of that strength with a footloose and erratic foreign policy and a willingness to apply Clausewitz's dictum about war being an extension of other means in a singularly irresponsible and destructive way. In this view the right response is to sustain and to strengthen the multilateral disciplines and capacity for collective action of the Community and NATO, with the former playing the central and most durable role, given its readier acceptability to all shades of political opinion in Germany itself. German economic strength cannot in any case be gainsaid, based as it is now on a pluralist democracy and a free market economy. I find this analysis convincing. The thesis that a unified Germany will come to dominate the Community and thus be able to bend it to its will, I find much less so. After all Germany has been the dominant economic force in the

Community for a long time now; it bears by far the heaviest budgetary burden; and yet it still punches below its weight in the conduct of Community business. Nor does the Community, its processes and its institutions, lend itself to domination by one member state, as the French found to their cost in the 1960s. So I would argue firmly that we should treat the Community as part of the solution to this problem, not as an extension of the problem itself.

The Inter-Governmental Conference on Political Union is not something we would have ever gone out of our way to look for, but now that we are landed with it, I believe we can put it to purposes consistent with our own approach and can contain the pressures for the sort of changes we wish to resist. The perception that this negotiation is designed to produce a kind of Single European Act Mark 2 and not a futuristic charter for a federalist Europe is now general, whatever the rhetoric of the maximalists to the contrary. Some extension of majority voting - on environmental issues, for example - may make sense; but we will need to resist it on social matters, where the pressure will be strong, and on fiscal matters where it will be less so. The European Parliament and its chief protagonists among the member states will keep up a noisy clamour for more powers. Our own ideas for strengthening its control over the executive - that is the Commission - may help to channel this pressure in a helpful direction. The awakening awareness of national parliaments to the fact that the European Parliament is as much a rival as a partner may also prove useful. But we shall face some difficult choices at the end. The least predictable area is that covered by the Franco-German call for a common foreign and security policy. So far, the two authors have failed to put flesh on the bare bones of their April initiative; it is hard to believe that either is really willing to accept the

17

full implications of their rather opportunistic move. But other, smaller member-states will have few qualms. It is all the more important therefore that we should ourselves come forward with a set of sensible and evolutionary changes to strengthen Political Cooperation; this would be the right move tactically, even if it were not also, in my view, the right approach in strategic terms given the trend of recent events, the shifting of international forces and the reinforcement of Germany's weight.

The outcome of the Inter-governmental Conference on Economic and Monetary Union is a good deal less easy to foretell. The gap between the approach broadly favoured by the other eleven member states and the Commission and our own preferred approach has narrowed but it has not disappeared. It has narrowed because the original idea in the Delors Report for elaborate, centralised decision-making on budgetary and fiscal policies has faded; and because our own recent proposals for a "hard" ECU and a European Monetary Fund in the next stage are seen as a clear step forward. But it has not disappeared because the other member states appear determined to write into the treaty a commitment to a single currency and a central banking system to manage a single monetary policy, while we are equally determined to avoid any automaticity as to a move beyond the next stage and to ensure that any such shift, if it does eventually come about, results from an evolutionary process and is not pre-determined in advance. Can this gap be bridged? It is too soon to say. There are major advantages to all if it can be; and serious risks if it is not. Our partners are less keen to go it alone than they sometimes let the press suppose but they are determined to press ahead. We on our side need to weigh carefully the downside consequences - for the City and for inward investment to mention only the most direct ones - if it does go that way.

The further enlargement of the Community is not an issue for 1991 but it is an issue for the 1990s. It is hard now, with four declared applicants and others speaking freely of their future applications, to see the Community reaching the end of the century as a Community of Twelve. Our present policy of stating a general welcome to accessions by democratic European states which can assume the full obligations of membership while keeping clear of specific commitments on the timing and detail seems likely to serve well for some time to come. In particular it offers the East European countries the maximum incentive to stick to the stony path leading to stable democracy and a flourishing market economy. We are wise to be cautious about the specifics. There are plenty of snags. Enlargement could be expensive if it involved the East Europeans, all likely to be substantial beneficiaries from the CAP and the structural funds and modest contributors to the budget. We can certainly not afford to assume that enlargement will lead to looser, more flexible institutional links. Putting off the evil day when the Community has to explain to Turkey that there is no room at the inn must surely be a plus. All these tricky problems will be easier to handle tactically if we ourselves have not shown too much zeal in the cause of enlargement in the meantime; accession terms tend to be shaped by those who hold back than by those who dash forward.

The Single Market will remain a constant and crucial theme through the 1990s. The process neither begins nor does it end on 1 January 1993. We still have a substantial amount of unfinished business, on financial services and transport in particular, on which we have to keep up the pressure. But things are moving the right way and the Commission are solid allies. In two difficult areas for us, taxation and frontier controls, we are not out of the wood yet, although our tactical position has considerably improved over the last year. A system which will permit the abolition of fiscal frontiers without the bureaucracy of Lord Cockfield's clearing house approach and without elaborate measures of tax harmonisation should be agreed by the end of the year. But there will remain strong pressure from other member states to complement that system at the very least with a minimum VAT standard rate as a safety-net provision to avoid the risk of competitive ratcheting down and we will have to decide whether we can live with that. The frontiers question remains a delicate one but there is now a better understanding that the different geographical characteristics of member states justify quite different solutions; and the rising political pressures generated by the domestic sensitivity of Third Country immigration in virtually every member state are beginning to cause them to take a more cautious view of the sweet simplicities of the Commission's "Europe without frontiers" approach. If we play our cards well, it should be possible to achieve a substantial reduction in the present controls on business and individuals without sacrificing the essential checks needed to maintain our defences against drugs, terrorism and illegal immigration.

As the legislative thrust of the Single Market programme tapers off, so will the twin issues of implementation and enforcement come to the fore. The former is already moving sharply up the agenda as result of the initiatives we have taken. Peer pressure is beginning to have some effect; the threat of Court action, particularly if new treaty provisions can be devised to give the Court more bite, should do the rest. Enforcement will be a slower, messier business but one in whose success we have just as great a vested interest. We will be sure to face some dilemmas in that, as with fraud, it is the Commission that will have to set the pace. In some instances that is bound to mean giving them more powers and authority which will be criticised as intrusive. But the Commission is the only heavy roller available and, if we want a level wicket, then we will have to be ready to make use of them.

Some lessons learned.

The European Community is no simple, tidy organisation, conforming to a recognisable pattern of multilateral international activity and proceeding towards clearly defined objectives. Nor is it any embryo of a sovereign state. It remains today and for the foreseeable future a construction sui generis, operating somewhere between these two extremes. Moreover, it is shot through with paradoxes and criss-crossed with historical fault lines which do much to explain the tensions which invariably surface when major decisions are imminent, as they are now.

A fault line which runs as deep as any is the different historical experience of its member states in the first half of this century. Broadly speaking one can classify them into two categories; the first consists of countries whose national institutions - government, parliament, civil service and judiciary - foundered comprehensively in the maelstrom of that period; the second consists of countries whose national institutions survived that experience and indeed helped to carry them through intact. It is striking how often the instinctive reaction of each country to a further development of the Community runs along that fault line. In the first category the tendency, when a new problem arises or an old one gets out of control, is to look for a Community solution; the proposition that a national solution makes more sense gets short shrift, given the fundamental lack of confidence in national institutions. Countries like Italy and Belgium fall quite obviously into this

21

category; but so, to some of extent, do countries as inherently nationalistic as France, whose flirtation with a Gaullist approach to Europe is now receding into the past. In the second category the tendency is the opposite, to turn towards a national solution unless it can be shown very clearly that a wider approach will make more sense. The UK falls quite obviously into that category, as do the Netherlands and Denmark. The second category is much less numerous than the first. It is not difficult to categorise aspirants to membership, Austria and the East Europeans in the first, the other EFTAns in the second.

There are plenty of other paradoxes around. Some are almost semantic but they are none the less real. For a German federalism means decentralisation, the avoidance of a unitary state; for us it means almost the opposite. To most member states the word union is a gloriously loose and imprecise concept that can mean all things to all men; to us it contains very precise connotations, the Acts of Union with Scotland and Ireland being characterised by the abolition of the parliaments of those two countries. Some paradoxes exist within our own policy. We recognise the crucial role of the Commission in bringing about the Single Market, in working to reform the CAP, in negotiating the Uruguay Round; as a member state in a smallish minority on all these issues we know that we would get nowhere without them. But, at the same time, we resent and oppose the Commission's pretensions to greater power and are reluctant to give them a greater degree of democratic legitimacy.

It is quite clear that the Community cannot simply resolve these paradoxes or erase these fault lines. They are too deep seated for that. But nor can it simply camp on them. So, it has to try to soften them, to build bridges across the fault lines. In recent years it has been

22

reasonably successful at that. The exercise requires a lot of pragmatism and a commitment to an evolutionary approach, two concepts which we hold dear but which I have sometimes felt we preach more actively than we practise.

The increase in majority voting following the 1986 enlargement and the Single European Act underlined but did not create the need to seek allies in Community negotiations. Although in some cases it is bearable, and indeed in the case of our budgetary contribution it was necessary, to be in a minority of one, this is something to be avoided if at all possible because it is not easy politically to sustain it and, if you cannot sustain it, you may end up failing to influence the outcome as well. Making allies in the Community is not simply a matter of seeking trade-offs; indeed, that sort of crude horse-trading is not all that common and is certainly not desirable. It consists much more of identifying our important interests on any issue and then making common cause with other member states with similar interests or whose interests can be met with solutions similar to those we are seeking. We are rather better at identification than we are at making common cause. What is essential, however, is to pursue an active, alliance-building approach, and that requires the cultivation of a complex network of contacts between capitals.

There are, however, no permanent allies for us in the Community or permanent adversaries. We may make common cause with, for example, the Dutch over a wide range of issues - CAP reform, trade policy, budgetary questions - but we will also differ on some such as EMU or the UK rebate. The only exception that appears to prove this rule is the Franco-German partnership, the handling of which presents us with almost as many unsolved questions as when we first joined the Community. We can have no illusions that it is about to disintegrate, less still that we could bring that about, even if it was desirable to do so. We can also have no illusion but that it has from time to time a formidable, almost irresistible, influence on Community debates, limited, fortunately for us, by the difficulties the two have in agreeing on the details and substance of individual issues. In the future, with a more powerful Germany, this influence can only be greater. So, I draw the conclusion that we must redouble our efforts to strengthen our links with both of them at every level and on every aspect of Community business. Even that will probably not spare us a few nasty surprises. But it will keep them to the minimum. And there is no doubt that the quality of our relations with France and Germany crucially conditions the attitude towards us of the other member states and their willingness to cooperate with us.

Meetings of the European Council are not life-enhancing occasions, let alone pleasurable ones. They are poorly prepared, often chaotic and they are all set to become once again too frequent. But they are now an essential part of the governance of the Community. Past are the days when a bout of bad-tempered wrangling in the European Council could simply lead to the abandonment of any conclusions at all and the Community could more or less proceed as if nothing serious had happened. We need therefore to update constantly our techniques for handling these meetings and develop on each occasion a systematic tactical approach designed to maximise our influence at them.

It would be remiss, although perhaps prudent, to avoid a direct comment on Britain's role in Europe, contentious as that has been both within parties and between parties ever since I first began to deal with these matters. In my view we have in fact travelled a long way in the last decade towards a mature and successful role in the conduct of Community business. Of course, you cannot have everything your own way in such a venture; but we are getting steadily better at furthering and securing our interest and at doing so in a way which is consistent with the overall Community interest. There remains, however, some way to go. Our caution, scepticism and rigorous analysis of Commission proposals are widely appreciated by those in the know, but more widely less so. We do need to be more selective about taking up the cudgels on particular issues and to ensure when we do so that our criticisms are directed principally at the policies we oppose and not in a blanket way at the institution, Commission or Parliament, or at the member state which proposes them.

I have been struck and a little saddened by the number of people who have said to me in recent months "you must have had a terribly difficult time defending our corner these last few years". I do not in fact feel I have had a terribly difficult time of it. But it cannot be healthy that there should be so fundamentally negative and defensive a perception or what the British Permanent Representative is up to in Brussels. I am not among those who believe we should be trying to vie with the Italians or others in our Community rhetoric; if we did so we would merely make fools of ourselves and convince nobody. The reality it sometimes seems to me is that, just as there is a large gap between the rhetoric and performance of a number of our partners to their considerable discredit, so there is in our own case a gap in the opposite sense, not to our discredit but to our disadvantage...

David Hannay

*   *   *

Of course, this despatch does not contain all my thoughts about Britain in Europe. Valedictory despatches were often used (some would say abused) by retiring ambassadors to unburden themselves of a list of grievances against the administration of the Diplomatic Service or against the government (a particularly well-aimed salvo from the Ambassador in Rome some years later led to their abolition by the then Foreign Secretary, Jack Straw - truly a case of throwing the baby out with the bath water). And I was not a retiring ambassador, so a certain sense of caution, or at least of self-preservation, prevailed.

There were two main omissions. One was the idea I had pioneered, and which had the support of the Foreign Secretary (Douglas Hurd) and of the Chancellor of the Exchequer (John Major), which would enable the UK to sign up to what became the Maastricht Treaty on, among other things, a single currency while retaining complete, treaty-based control over Britain's right to decide whether, and if so when, to join such a currency. This idea had already been rejected by Margaret Thatcher and I had no wish to precipitate prematurely another destructive exchange of views. In the event the idea survived and found its place in the Maastricht Treaty, ensuring complete freedom of action for succeeding British governments. The second omission was any reference to the misgivings I felt about the way Margaret Thatcher's communications strategy towards the European Communities was sowing the dragon's teeth of Euro-scepticism, in her own party in particular. During the 1980s the Thatcher government had pulled off a series of negotiating successes (the Fontainebleau budget rebate, the Single Market, enlargement) which made our membership more comfortable and which brought Britain substantial benefits. I had participated in every one of these negotiations and supported them all wholeheartedly. But each negotiation was accompanied on the home front by an orgy of Euro-bashing, often orchestrated from N° 10 by the Prime Minister's formidable Press Secretary, Bernard Ingham. And every time one of these Euro-bashing orgies took place (Margaret Thatcher's Bruges speech in September 1988 and the way it was spun was a prime example) support in Britain for our membership dropped sharply. Similarly in quieter times it rose. So I concluded that there was a real risk of sacrificing Britain's long-term interest for short-term political applause. I do not think this analysis was wrong. But it was way outside the area of responsibility of an official serving abroad. So I held my tongue.

Chapter 1

Europe seen from the other side of the pond (1990-1995)

My arrival in New York in the first week of September 1990 saw me flung into the deep end of the UN pool, with no previous UN experience and the existential crisis caused by Saddam Hussein's invasion and seizure of Kuwait in full swing. There was little time for backward glances or thoughts about European policy issues. And that remained more or less the case throughout the five years I served as Britain's Ambassador at the UN and representative on the Security Council. Crises and challenges followed each other in rapid succession - the liberation of Kuwait and the post - conflict settlement imposed on Iraq, the largest ever peacekeeping operation mounted by the UN (in Cambodia), other peacekeeping operations in Mozambique, Angola, Somalia, El Salvador, the seemingly endless wars of the Yugoslav succession, the launch of the global effort to combat global warming with the signature in Rio de Janeiro of the Climate Change and Biodiversity Conventions, genocides in Rwanda and at Srebrenica - often overlapping and thus increasing the sense of overload.

But, even so, Europe could not be ignored, tempting as it was to try to keep events and their handling in separate silos, an approach to a country's external policies which was doomed to failure. The first major European event came a few days after my arrival in New York, with the British government's much contested and much delayed decision to join the European Exchange Rate Mechanism on 5th October 1990 at £1=DM2.95.

I had never, even when I was in Brussels, been anywhere near the decision making on this which had tested Margaret Thatcher's government to destruction from 1985 onwards. Nor did my expertise lie in the arcane fields of economic and monetary policy (unlike my predecessor as Permanent Representative, Michael Butler, and my successor in the job, John Kerr). I had nevertheless been part of the collateral damage from the confrontation between Nigel Lawson and Geoffrey Howe on the one hand and Margaret Thatcher on the other at the time of the Madrid European Council meeting in 1989 which doomed my chances of being appointed Permanent Under Secretary at the FCO and Head of the Diplomatic Service. When the decision was taken to join the ERM in 1990, I registered that it was both too late to influence the negotiations on what became the Maastricht Treaty on Economic and Monetary Union; and that we had almost certainly joined at an exchange rate which it would prove difficult, if not impossible, to sustain. And when, two years later, Britain was knocked out of the ERM, I deplored the futile row with Germany over interest rates which precipitated that and the failure to pursue other courses of action by remaining in the ERM at a lower central rate for sterling or, like Italy, to allow our currency to move within much wider bands. One thing was clear and that was that the events of "Black Wednesday" had done serious damage to British public attitudes towards the European Communities and had emboldened the Eurosceptic rebels within the governing Conservative party.

The second European policy shoe to drop was Margaret Thatcher's resignation. I was in fact in London, recalled to brief the Leader of the Opposition, Neil Kinnock, on the probable course of events over Iraq and the likelihood of the UN Security Council authorising the use of force to expel Saddam Hussein from Kuwait. The members of the Cabinet were being consulted, one by one, following the Prime Minister's failure to defeat Michael Heseltine's challenge in the first round. So, I saw none of them; but the direction of travel was not in doubt. The Prime Minister's "no, no, no" outburst in the Commons which had brought matters to a head, although often, then and later, misinterpreted, clearly set us on a collision course with the other European Community member states, which would, in my view, have been an act of folly, all the more so since it was unnecessary given the possibility of negotiating a legally water-tight opt - out from the single currency for the UK.

*　　　　　　　*　　　　　　　*

The next European stone thrown into the New York pond was on the day following the referendums in Denmark and France to ratify the Maastricht Treaty. The referendum in Denmark was lost (but subsequently reversed after some deft repair work by John Kerr and others); in France it was won by a whisker on 20th September 1992. Since the Foreign Ministers of the European Community member states were all at the time in New York for the UN General Assembly, they decided, exceptionally, to hold a Council meeting there on 21st September and to re-affirm their collective intention to proceed with the ratification of the Maastricht Treaty. No longer myself a part of the Council, I sat in the margins of the meeting as an observer, my feelings as sombre as those of most participants and not in any way lightened by the performance of Roland Dumas, the French Foreign Minister and an old sparring partner from the negotiations over Britain's budget rebate, telling the assembled company that the only reason for France's narrow escape was not being sufficiently enthusiastic about European integration, which must now be pursued at full speed. I could see that these thoughts did not enthuse Douglas Hurd; he sat, pretty glum, contemplating the intensive warfare in the House of Commons which was now certain to break out over Maastricht ratification.

*   *   *

Quite apart from these moments of high drama, there was plenty of routine European business to be conducted in New York, particularly as the strengthening of the European Community's (in future to be called the European Union) role in foreign and security policy was one of the main themes of the Maastricht negotiations and treaty. I found the whole issue of European policy coordination at the UN in pretty bad shape. For one thing Britain and France, as Permanent Members of the UN Security Council, had for years been preventing any serious discussion of Security Council business at the weekly coordinating meetings of EU ambassadors. That exclusion might have been just about tolerable to the others during the Cold War when the Security Council had, for much of the time, been paralysed, but it was much less so now that the Security Council was at the centre of the effort to reverse Saddam Hussein's aggression in Kuwait. Moreover, it seemed to me that we (and the French) were thereby failing to make use of our positions as Permanent Members of the Security Council to shape EU policy on the increasing range of issues coming to the UN for policy decisions. Another problem looming on the horizon was that some of the more grandiloquent foreign and security policy texts for the Maastricht Treaty being floated in Brussels risked causing us real problems in New York if we did not ensure in advance that the management of our (and France's) responsibilities as Permanent Members was properly recognised.

Having discussed both these issues with the FCO and found that they saw them as I did, I was sent off to Paris on my next visit home to try to convince the French. The Secretary-General of the Quai d'Orsay, François Scheer, had been my French colleague in Brussels and needed little convincing about changing the Anglo-French exclusion policy. And Elisabeth Guigou, then Secretary-General for EU policy coordination was persuaded that we did need something in the Maastricht Treaty to ensure that increased prominence of EU foreign policy activity did not undermine our freedom of action in the Security Council. After some complicated haggling over drafting in Brussels this second point was satisfactorily settled by John Kerr, working with Philippe de Schouteete, my Belgian colleague from Brussels days.

From then onwards, and for the rest of our EU membership, it proved possible to work on this basis, often through periods of considerable strain when the EU member states were at odds over policy issues, as in my time they were over Bosnia. It has always seemed to me that action at the UN was a prime example of how Britain could use its EU membership to increase its global influence; and why we needed to be more positive and imaginative about how to make the most of that asset rather than being obsessed by the risks to our role as a Permanent Member. The spectre of Britain and France being replaced on the Security Council by an EU seat, much discussed at seminars and conferences, was never a realistic one, the UN being an intergovernmental organisation composed of sovereign states; which meant that for there to be an EU seat either its member states would need to surrender their independence or the rest of the UN would need to open the floodgates to other international organisations such as the Arab League or the Organisation of Islamic States having seats too. Neither of those eventualities was ever going to happen.

Chapter 2

Dipping my toe back into the European water (1995-2000)

By the time Gillian and I got back to London at the beginning of September 1995 from our long post-retirement odyssey through China, Pakistan and Uzbekistan, the immediate crisis within the governing Conservative party, triggered by the ratification of the Maastricht Treaty and reaching its climax with John Major's resignation as party leader in July 1995, was over - or more precisely it was over for a while. John Major had been re-elected and the Maastricht rebels temporarily crushed (but Tory unity on Europe was never restored). Moreover, that most debilitating of European crises, over Bosnia, which had been met with divided counsels within the EU, and which had caused tensions also within NATO, in particular between the US and its European partners, was on the way to some sort of a solution at the Dayton peace conference that autumn. Neither of these relaxations of tension was durable but both contributed to a somewhat calmer international atmosphere.

Within six months of my return I had been recruited by Malcolm Rifkind, now Foreign Secretary, to be the government's Special Representative for Cyprus, a new post which was supposed to be a part time one, but which, over the seven years I did the job, became closer and closer to being a full time one. My task was to work with the UN and the EU to try to harpoon that most elusive of international Great White Whales, a solution to the Cyprus problem so that, when Cyprus joined the EU in the next wave of accessions, which had already been conceded, it would do so as a re-united island not as the divided one it had been since 1974. The full story of that negotiation and its eventual failure when the Greek Cypriots rejected the Annan Plan in a referendum on 24th April 2004 is contained in my earlier book "Cyprus: The Search for a Solution". The experience certainly brought home to me that, whatever the EU's shortcomings and weaknesses in execution, it was a crucial player in every one of the many disputes which stretched in an arc of instability around its southern and eastern boundaries; its influence might sometimes be exercised as much by omission as by commission but it was real. And Britain, which had important assets at stake in Cyprus in the form most obviously of the two Sovereign Base Areas of Akrotiri and Dekhelia, needed to be an active part of the international team effort to get a solution.

*　　　　　　*　　　　　　*

Also soon after my return I was recruited by Michael Welsh, a Conservative MEP, who I had come across frequently on my visits to the European Parliament sessions in Strasbourg between 1985/90, to join a group, The Action Centre for Europe, more a virtual one than one which actually met, which was publishing booklets explaining the workings of the EU, setting out ways in which it could be improved, and seeking to counter the mass of Eurosceptic propaganda which was by then in full flood, not least from the pen of the Daily Telegraph's Brussels correspondent, one Boris Johnson, whom I had known since he was about eight years old, when he arrived in Brussels with his father Stanley, for whom I had found a Commission job in its environmental department in the first wave of British recruits after our accession in 1973. I wrote a booklet in October 1996 entitled "The EU's Common Foreign and Security Policy: A menu for reform". The main recommendations were first that the EU needed a High Representative for Foreign and Security Policy who would pull together the disparate strands of its external policies and reduce, if not eliminate, the endless turf fighting which hampered the efforts called for in the Maastricht Treaty to strengthen the CFSP. The second was that the daily running of the CFSP needed to be entrusted to a new Political and Security Committee (often loosely known as COREPER 3 - standing alongside COREPER 2 which prepared the General, the Economic and Monetary, the Development and the Energy Councils and the overarching European Council of the Heads of State and Government, and COREPER 1 which prepared the Internal Market, Budgetary, Fisheries and other Councils). Both these recommendations eventually found their place in the new structures for CFSP which emerged from the Amsterdam Treaty in 1997. I also wrote an introduction to a booklet by Dick Taverne, a former Labour, then Independent and then Liberal Democrat MP and peer, on majority voting. I argued that increased majority voting, which had opened the way to the construction of the EU's Single Market, was not something to be frightened of and could usefully be extended into other areas even if some decisions (on Treaty change, on new accessions, and on increases in the overall ceiling on financial resources) would still need to be taken by unanimity. Again that proved to be the direction of travel in the Amsterdam, Nice and Lisbon Treaties.

*   *   *

I also joined at its foundation the Advisory Board of the Centre for European Reform (CER), which was set up in 1998 by Ralf Dahrendorf, a former German European Commissioner and then head of the London School of Economics and of St. Antony's College, Oxford, and by Nick Butler, a close adviser of John Browne, the CEO of BP. Brilliantly led, then as now, by Charles Grant, whom I had known when he worked for The Economist in Brussels in the late 1980s, the CER has produced a stream of research papers and articles and held seminars and conferences in every corner of the European Union and indeed beyond (for example in Turkey and in Washington). Its multi-national researchers, its offices now in Brussels and Berlin as well as in London, and its even more multi-national advisory board have ensured that the CER is not an exclusively British organisation but one devoted to projecting a critical but positive view of how the EU should develop. That it has done so with considerable success through its nearly twenty-five years of existence owes a huge amount to Grant and his team; and it has enabled me too to keep abreast of the wider European picture even when many of us were being sucked into the vortex of Brexit.

*   *   *

The relative calm on the European front of the last two years of John Major's Conservative Government were however considerably troubled by a seriously mismanaged handling of the crisis over Bovine Spongiform Encephalopathy (BSE) which led to the banning by the Commission of exports of beef from Britain to the rest of the EU on human health grounds. The British government's response to this action, which might well have been less drastic if the Ministry of Agriculture had worked more closely and in a more trusting way with the Commission, was absurdly over the top as well as being particularly ineffective. The government announce on 21st May 1996 that Britain would block all EU decisions which required unanimity, irrespective of whether it supported them in substance or not (by this time there were not nearly as many such decisions as there had been in the past). Decisions taken by Qualified Majority Vote Britain could not block. Altogether this was more of a storm in a teacup than a real crisis. But it occasioned more outpourings of Eurosceptic bile; it showed how easily the Eurosceptic wing of the Conservative party could wag the governmental dog, whose parliamentary majority had by then reduced to vanishing point; and it diminished British influence in Brussels in the negotiations for treaty change, which emerged as the Amsterdam Treaty, since ministers were unable collectively to decide what Britain's position should be.

These negative developments were, however, overshadowed by the prevalent assumption - in Brussels, Westminster and Whitehall - that the election which was due at the latest in the spring of 1997 would bring Labour to power for the first time since 1979. And there was little doubt that a Blair/Brown Government which would in that event take office would be more pro-European and less riven by internal divisions over the future direction of its European policies than its predecessor had been. I had myself gone with Gordon Brown to a lunchtime speaking engagement in New York in 1995 and heard him speak with enthusiasm about the prospects for a single currency and for Britain's being part of it. So far as Tony Blair was concerned, I had been invited in 1996 by Jonathan Powell, his chief of staff, to join a group (including others such as Rodric Braithwaite, formerly Ambassador in Moscow and John Major's Diplomatic Adviser, Ray Seitz, former US Ambassador in London, Robin Renwick, former Ambassador in South Africa and Washington and Laurie Freedman, Professor at King's College) which met regularly in Blair's Islington home to brief him on foreign policy and security issues. We did not in fact spend much time on EU business (partly because neither Gordon Brown nor Robin Cook were part of the group, but also because Blair made it clear at the outset that he was a firm pro-European and intended to lead a government which would set out to repair the self-inflicted damage of recent years). The week before the Labour Party Conference in the autumn of 1996 Jonathan Powell telephoned me late one evening saying that Blair wanted to announce that I was to be Robin Cook's adviser on Europe. Was I willing? I pointed out that I could not possibly play that publicly announced role and at the same time serve as the Conservative government's Special Representative for Cyprus; and having only committed myself to Malcolm Rifkind a few months earlier I was not prepared to let him down in that way. Powell agreed but was still anxious to proceed with appointing a former British Permanent Representative in Brussels as Robin Cooke's Adviser. I suggested he approach my predecessor, Michael Butler, and that was subsequently agreed and announced. Our advisory group did meet once more, after the 1997 election, which brought Blair into office with a huge majority. We met in the cabinet room at N° 10 (which I knew reasonably well from briefing sessions with Margaret Thatcher) and went over the ground for the upcoming Amsterdam European Council on treaty change. I knew that we would not meet in that way again as the walls of officialdom closed down on the new Prime Minister. But at least things had got off on the right foot.

When it came to making the appointments to the posts foreseen in the Amsterdam Treaty (a High Representative for Foreign and Security Policy and a new, beefed-up Secretary-General of the Council) I was asked whether I would be happy for the government to run me for either post. I agreed; and in the event my name was put forward for both (to take account of the possibility that the European Council would want to appoint a politician to the first of the two jobs - as they did when they chose Javier Solana, who had been Spanish Foreign Minister and Secretary-General of NATO) I suspect it was a tactical error to go for both; and, from long experience, I did not have much confidence in the capacity of any British government to lobby for top international positions. So I ended up with neither, which, given the subsequent deterioration in my wife's health, was a blessing in disguise.

Chapter 3

A false sense of security (2000-2010)

The thirteen years of the Blair and Brown governments (1997/2010) were a period when there appeared to be no immediate threat to Britain's EU membership. Three successive Eurosceptic leaders of the Conservative party (William Hague, Iain Duncan Smith and Michael Howard) tried their different prescriptions on the electorate and twice, in 2001 and 2005, lost general elections by a substantial margin. The fourth Conservative leader during that period, David Cameron said that his objective was to stop his party "banging on about Europe". Meanwhile the Liberal Democrats, by far the most pro-European of the main parties, steadily gained both votes and seats in Parliament. Within the EU Britain played a significant leadership role, although any hope of consolidating the crucial France/Germany/UK relationship went overboard as a result of the disagreements over the invasion of Iraq in 2003. In the handling of Kosovo in 1999, in the response to the 9/11 terrorist attacks in New York and Washington in 2001 and in the management of the global financial and economic crisis in 2008/9 Britain was very much in the European mainstream, a crucial player though not a member of the Eurozone.

But opportunities were missed to consolidate support for the EU. It was striking how many of Blair's best European speeches were made elsewhere in Europe and not to British audiences (one of the few exceptions to this was his speech at the University of Birmingham on 23rd November 2001 when, as chair of the Council, I persuaded him to open our new European Research Centre). Cameron, in his bid to outflank his main leadership rival, David Davis, committed himself to pulling his party out of their alliance with the European Peoples Party (the Christian Democrats in all but name) in the European Parliament, a move which was to cost him dearly when he most needed help after he became Prime Minister and moved towards a renegotiation and an in/out referendum. The EU itself spent far too much time and effort haggling over institutional reforms in a seemingly unending series of series of Inter-Governmental conferences (Amsterdam, Nice, the Constitutional Treaty, Lisbon). Whatever the merits of the reforms introduced, and there were plenty, the process left the majority of its citizens cold, or even alienated, as was shown by the rejection of the Constitutional Treaty in both France and the Netherlands. And, when it came to dealing with the global financial crisis, effective short term stabilisation actions masked the electoral aftershocks stemming from the policies of fiscal austerity and led to the rise of Eurosceptic populist parties in many member states of the EU.

*　　　　　*　　　　　*

The arrival in office of the Blair/Brown Government in

1997, with a massive parliamentary majority, inevitably brought the focus of public and parliamentary attention sharply onto the issue of the Euro and Britain's possible participation in the single currency which was in the later stages of its preparatory process across the Channel. Whereas there had been no chance of a Conservative Government joining, the same was not the case for Labour. And when, in October of that year, Paddy Ashdown, the leader of the Liberal Democrat Party, who was known to have a close working relationship with Blair, speculated that a decision to join was imminent, the London stock market rose by three figures. Since all three main parties were committed, in one way or another, to holding a referendum on any decision to join the Euro, the need to build a cross-party alliance, including not only Labour and the Liberal Democrats but quite a few senior pro-European members of John Major's outgoing government, became urgent. It was on that basis that "Britain in Europe" (the same name as the organisation which had successfully contested the 1975 referendum) was soon established.

Britain in Europe had plenty of expertise in electoral politics and in the dark arts of communications spin but it was singularly lacking in any practical knowledge of how the EU worked and what it actually did on a day to day basis. It was also strongly overweight in Labour supporters - natural enough given Labour's domination of the political scene but not ideal for an organisation which had to reach out beyond party lines. So Michael Butler, who was advising Robin Cooke on European policy, was asked to pull together a group with EU expertise to prepare briefing material for Britain in Europe, plugging the gap between the domestic political scene and the reality of Brussels politics. I agreed to join the group from the outset and so an eclectic bunch of former Permanent Representatives, former senior civil servants and former Commission officials began to meet on a regular basis and to produce material for use in the campaign if and when it got fully under way.

Neither Britain in Europe nor our briefing group ever operated at that stage very effectively. The former was hamstrung from the outset, once it became clear that there were real tensions between N° 10 and Gordon Brown's Treasury team over the direction and the speed of travel and indeed over whether any decision should be taken at all at this stage about joining the Euro. There were also tensions with the pro-European Conservatives (people like Michael Heseltine and Ken Clarke) who were reluctant to take a step which would inevitably lead to open conflict with their party's new leadership, unless it was part of a campaign which was firmly committed to Britain joining the Euro. Finally, after much delay, and endless backing and filling, a launch event was held in the sepulchrally gloomy setting of the IMAX cinema close to Waterloo Station on 14th October 1999 with most of those from all three main parties who needed to be there present. But by then Blair and Brown had definitively locked horns over this issue (as over much else) and the campaign never really took off. With the publication of Brown's four conditions for Euro membership, backed by massive tomes of econometric obfuscation, it became clear that the four conditions were highly unlikely ever to be met and certainly not while Brown was at the Treasury. Both political and financial support for the campaign dried up and it then went into abeyance.

The problems for our briefing group were more functional than political. The main campaign team never seemed at all clear what sort of material they wanted from us and what use they would put it to. Briefly (very briefly) there was some clarity when the communications between us were managed by Danny Alexander (who was subsequently to become Chief Secretary to the Treasury in the 2010 coalition government and one of the two Liberal Democrat members of that government's steering group). When the campaign came to an end, our group decided to continue to meet and to systematise our production of briefing material, still under the chairmanship of Michael Butler and soon with the inestimable assistance (from 2005 onwards) of Nick Kent who had in the past worked as a political adviser to Ken Clarke; and we moved the meetings of what now called itself the Senior European Experts Group (SEEG) to the Commission's and European Parliament's London Office in the former Conservative Party headquarters in Smith Square - the Commission was generous in giving us meeting space but they had nothing whatsoever to do with our output, which we circulated to a number of parliamentarians of all parties, to political advisers, to journalists and think tanks and to the European Movement, at first by e-mail and then with our own website.

At no stage in our work for Britain in Europe did we really grapple with the pros and cons of Euro membership, which was probably fortunate because opinions were divided in our group (as they had been in the group which gave advice to Tony Blair when he was Leader of the Opposition, with Robin Renwick and I, the two principal EU experts, being respectively against and for). Michael Butler himself, having devised the "hard ÉCU" scheme, which was designed to be a way station on an evolutionary route towards a single currency, was very dubious about the big bang approach being pursued in Brussels. What we were all agreed about was that, if the government did decide to go ahead, then the referendum would inevitably be fought as an in/out campaign and that it would thus need to be won if we were not to find ourselves on a slippery slope leading towards exit from the EU (a glance at the list of those who were at the heart of the campaign to keep sterling showed that they shared exactly the same view). And that rationale continued to prevail even after the Euro was no longer at the centre of public debate.

*   *   *

In April 2001, during the unexpected postponement of the general election campaign on account of the outbreak of foot and mouth disease, my appointment as an independent (cross-bench) member of the House of Lords, one of the first batch of 14 names put forward by a cross-party Commission, was announced. And in June, following the election, I took my seat on the red benches. While not entirely unexpected (there had been much filling in of application forms and a lengthy interview with members of the cross-party Commission), this development was to change my life, not least because of the extent to which the parliamentary agenda in the years ahead came gradually to be dominated by Britain's future relationship with the EU.

Within a few weeks I was co-opted onto one of the sub-committees of the Lords main EU Committee. For the next 13 years (2001/14) I served on three of these sub-committees (the one dealing with Economic and Financial Affairs, the one dealing with the EU's external relations and the one dealing with its home affairs, the latter of which I chaired for several years); and I was also on the main EU Select Committee from 2002/06 and from 2008/14. The terms of reference of the Lords EU Committee and of its sub-committees were wider and more flexible than those of our opposite numbers in the Commons, so, during that period we not only scrutinised all Commission legislative proposals but we took evidence and published reports on the ones of greatest interest - in my case ranging from the operations of the recently established European Central Bank, through relations with Russia, the issue of future enlargement and the role of national parliaments in the shaping and influencing of EU policy and legislation. These Lords reports and their recommendations were generally recognised, right across the EU, as we were often told by our colleagues at the bi-annual meetings of the national parliaments' EU committees, as the paradigm of parliamentary scrutiny. They suffered, however, from two fundamental weaknesses. The first was that the government was under no obligation to accept their recommendations and often did not do so - although they were required not to agree to any proposal in Brussels until the scrutiny procedure had been completed. The second was that, although the reports contained a mass of valuable evidence and tended to demonstrate how consistent with Britain's national interests most of the EU legislation coming forward in Brussels was, public awareness of them and thus any impact on public attitudes towards the EU was close to zero. The predominantly Eurosceptic press was not interested in good news stories about the EU and the style and length of Lords reports does not appeal to people whose main interests lie elsewhere.

The EU Select Committee was not directly concerned with the work of the Convention of parliamentarians meeting in Brussels and laboriously putting together what came to be known as the Constitutional Treaty, since the House of Lords, like the House of Commons, was represented on the Convention. However on one issue, the insertion in the new proposed treaty of detailed provisions enabling a member state to withdraw from the EU and laying down how that should be negotiated, I instantly took alarm as soon as I heard of it (the original Treaties of Paris and of Rome containing no such provisions - and nor does the UN Charter). No one seriously doubted that, if a member state did decide it wanted to leave, then that wish would be honoured and negotiated. At the time of our own 1975 referendum, which could have given rise to such circumstances, there had been no problem raised about the absence of such a provision. Normalising the process of withdrawal, as was now proposed, would, in my view make it more likely to happen and would smooth the path of those who sought to do so. It was as if the shadow of the graveyard had fallen across my path. So I took the matter up with Peter Hain, at the time Minister for Europe at the FCO and a member of the Convention, and for whom I had worked closely on Cyprus. His response was that, while he shared many of my misgivings, it was too late to do anything about it. So it went into the text of the Constitutional Treaty and thence, after that Treaty's demise, into the Lisbon Treaty, where it became the infamous Article 50 with which everyone is now all too familiar.

*   *   *

During the Blair/Brown governments there were four European treaties which potentially required parliamentary endorsement before they could be ratified by the UK since they contained provisions which necessitated alterations to our domestic law - Amsterdam, Nice, the Constitutional Treaty and Lisbon. Amsterdam and Nice passed through both Houses without much trouble, partly because their provisions were not particularly ambitious and also because the government had a massive majority in the House of Commons and had the support of the Liberal Democrats in the House of Lords. The Constitutional Treaty was more substantial and was likely to be a bit trickier. But the government's majority in the Commons was clearly sufficient to see it through there. And my own view and that of David Williamson (Lord Williamson of Horton, formerly my co-negotiator of the Single European Act and Secretary-General of the Commission) who both followed these matters closely, was that it would pass in the Lords comfortably too, with Liberal Democrat and some cross-bench support (and that view was subsequently validated when the Lisbon Treaty, which contained many of the same provisions did indeed pass the Lords reasonably comfortably). Imagine our dismay, therefore, when, in the spring of 2004, Blair announced that the treaty would be put to a referendum; and when it leaked out that he had done so because he had been advised that it would not pass in the Lords without a referendum. Where he got that advice from remains to this day a mystery, Blair having cast no light on it in his memoirs. Valerie Amos, who was at this time the Labour leader in the House of Lords told me she was not consulted. It could have been Jack Straw who was Foreign Secretary but who was not well placed to make such a judgement. But I noted that Bruce Grocott, who was the Labour Chief Whip in the Lords at the time, and who had been Blair's Parliamentary Private Secretary, had ardently Eurosceptic views. In any case the damage was done. Blair's announcement helped to tip the balance in both France and the Netherlands in favour of holding referendums; and both were lost by substantial margins, leaving the Constitutional Treaty dead and thus not needing to be put to either House of Parliament in the UK, or for that matter to a referendum. As a minor footnote, at about that time, I participated in a debate in the Oxford Union on the Constitutional Treaty which ended with a vote narrowly backing the treaty. That was certainly not attributable to any eloquence on my part but rather to the silver tongue of Ken Clarke and to the flagrant jingoism of Frederick Forsyth (author of "The Day of the Jackal") who led on the other side. In retrospect another of those lost causes for which Oxford is renowned.

The EU's response to the loss of the Constitutional Treaty was, while dropping some of the more blatantly "constitutional" parts of it (flag, anthem, motto) to re-package much of its content in a different sort of treaty which, instead of replacing the original founding treaties and subsequent ones like the Single European Act, worked by amending those treaties where necessary. An unspoken objective of that approach was to avoid the need for approval by referendum (although that could not completely be avoided in cases like Ireland whose Supreme Court had long since ruled that pretty well any change to the EU treaties had to be approved by a referendum). The discomfort this all caused to the Brown Government was on full display in the contortions the Prime Minister went to in order to avoid participating in the collective signature ceremony in Lisbon on 13th October 2007. This was odd indeed since the Lisbon Treaty dumped some of some of the provisions in the Constitutional Treaty which we had, after all signed, but which we disliked, and retained the useful reforms which we considered (rightly in my view) to be in our interest. As so often we managed to get the worst of both worlds, both at home and abroad.

The legislation clearing the way for the UK to ratify the Lisbon Treaty went through the Commons without difficulty, given the substantial Labour majority there and Liberal Democrat support, though the Conservative opposition, not surprisingly, called for a referendum on the treaty. The process in the House of Lords was less straightforward, given the open-ended nature of debates there (no guillotine available) and the huge number of amendments, some simply vexatious, some wrecking, that were tabled by the Conservative opposition and by the UK Independence Party's standard bearer in the Lords, Malcolm Pearson. In the case of an international treaty, such as Lisbon, any amendment which would have required the government to re-open the text of the treaty was regarded, correctly, as being a wrecking one and there were plenty of those. This was my first immersion in the full legislative process for a lengthy and complex piece of legislation; and I set to with a will, aiming to rebut amendments by reasoned argument. It was an arduous process taking, in all, 72 hours of debate on the floor of the House. But, as David Williamson and I had predicted in the context of the Constitutional Treaty, the process was successfully completed, with the only amendments being ones designed to strengthen Parliament's scrutiny of future EU legislation. There was however one moment of maximum danger when, in the middle of a long afternoon's wrangling over the Bill, the news came through that the Irish referendum on Lisbon had rejected the treaty (a rejection subsequently reversed when the possibility that Ireland might find itself without a Commissioner, a sensible reform designed to deal with an EU heading towards 28 members in which there would not be enough viable jobs for each to have a Commissioner, was removed). The opposition immediately demanded that our own ratification process be suspended. And Cathy Ashton, the leader of the House, as promptly said (whether or not with the authority of N° 10, which was dithering, remains a little obscure) that there would be no suspension, that our ratification in no sense depended on that of other member states, and that we would take the Bill through all its stages to completion. And that was what transpired. Much later, and after the Lisbon Treaty entered into force, David Cameron dropped his party's, almost certainly legally unviable, commitment to withdraw our ratification of the Lisbon Treaty pending its submission to a referendum. So the UK went into the 2010 general election with no major issue of European policy requiring decision and none in the offing; and with opinion polls indicating, as usual, that the EU was pretty low among most electors' priorities. But it was the calm before the storm.

Chapter 4

Coalition chaos (2010-2015)

The outcome of the 2010 general election - the Conservatives the largest party in Parliament but without an overall majority, and the formation of a Conservative/Liberal Democrat coalition government - was a surprise to me, as to most others. My own view was that the Liberal Democrats took the right and patriotic decision to participate in a coalition given the extraordinarily challenging economic and financial prospects facing the country following the 2008/09 global crisis. The punishment meted out to them by the electorate at the next general election in 2015 only reinforces that view. Less praiseworthy was the hasty, piecemeal way a coalition agreement was put together in a few days. Any consideration of the many continental European precedents for forming coalitions after elections would have pointed towards a much more measured, detailed inter-party negotiation. In Germany and the Netherlands, not two particularly unsuccessful democracies, it often takes months to form a coalition and the legislative and policy programme for the incoming government are thrashed out down to the last detail. But when did British politicians ever pay much attention to precedents set by others? So we were saddled with a programme for the coalition government shot through with the unresolved contradictions between the two parties forming it - a series of accidents waiting to happen.

Nowhere were those contradictions more evident than over policy towards the EU. The Conservative party, both in Parliament and the country, was increasingly Eurosceptic, disinclined to follow the advice of their leader and to stop "banging on about Europe". The dragon's teeth sown by Margaret Thatcher's fiery rhetoric had produced a new generation of politicians. The Liberal Democrats, on the other hand, were by a long way the most pro-European of the three main countrywide parties. How were those postures to be reconciled? The honest answer to that is they could not be. But in the short term a common basis of government was found in a Bill requiring there to be a referendum before any further significant transfer of responsibilities from Westminster to Brussels could take place; and there was to be something called rather unmemorably "A Review of the Balance of Competences", part of which would be a widespread public consultation as to whether or not Brussels already had too many powers.

The Bill the coalition government brought forward in some haste - known in the demotic, quite tellingly, as "the Referendum Lock Bill" - was touted by its principal protagonist, the Minister for Europe, David Lidington, as a means of warding off demands from the UK Independence Party and from the Eurosceptic wing of his own party for an in/out referendum on our membership. I do not doubt the sincerity with which he held this view - I had known

Lidington when he was one of Douglas Hurd's special political advisers and respected him as a skilful negotiator - but it certainly did not turn out that way. The Bill did not simply require a referendum to be held in the event of the government wishing to agree to a significant further transfer of responsibilities to the EU but set out a long and detailed list of all the changes which would trigger a referendum, ranging from the obvious (joining the Euro) to some obscure and far-fetched ones. As David Williamson rightly pointed out when the Bill reached the Lords it was not so much a prescription for a referendum as for what he called a "neverendum", since it was hard to envisage the circumstances in which Britain would sign up in Brussels to a treaty change which would trigger a referendum that it would be far from certain to win.

My own views on the use of referendums in the European context had been formed in the 1970s when the issue first arose of holding one on the terms of our accession to the European Communities. And they were firmly negative. For one thing referendums, once called, tended to slip away from the question being asked to more general debates about the popularity of the government in office (which is what had happened in France over the Constitutional Treaty). For another a majority in a referendum was likely to fall far short of a majority of the electorate (in 2016 the Leave majority represented only 37% of the electorate). And the idea that holding a referendum was a sovereign remedy for healing the divisions in one of the main parties was fanciful (as the Labour experience after the 1975 referendum had demonstrated and the Conservatives were to demonstrate after 2016). The argument that the EU had changed a lot since 1975 was true; but so had the UN since we joined it in 1945 and NATO since 1948 - and no one believed we should be having a referendum on them. On wider constitutional grounds I simply did not believe that referendums were a higher form of democracy than the representative parliamentary model which we had achieved after centuries of conflict and debate. When the House of Lords, in the previous session, debated a report from its Constitutional Committee on the use of referendums, I had deployed these arguments and been accused by Charlie Falconer, speaking from the government front bench, of a "rant". Maybe, but surely one which showed some foresight?

The Bill had an easy passage through the Commons, since coalition discipline held up. But in the Lords there were deep misgivings, even if there was no stomach to go for the nuclear option of rejecting the Bill outright. So I moved an amendment which would have stripped out a lot of the detailed circumstances triggering a referendum, thus leaving the government a good deal more flexibility over how to play the hand in Brussels. This amendment passed with substantial support from pro-European Liberal Democrats such as Shirley Williams. But, when the Bill returned to the Commons the government refused to relent; and the Lords did not try to insist.

*   *   *

The Review of the Balance of Competences did not have a parliamentary dimension and my own attempt to get the

EU Select Committee to offer evidence to the review failed on the grounds that it was not a piece of EU legislation and it thus fell outside our terms of reference. But the review was taken seriously by the Cabinet Office and the FCO, and by the numerous trade associations, trade unions, think tanks, academics and others who submitted evidence to one or more of the sectoral studies into which it was divided. Angus Lapsley, a talented FCO official working then in the Cabinet Office, came to a meeting of the Senior European Experts Group (whose chair I took over in 2014 following Michael Butler's death) and encouraged us to contribute to the review. I was quite dubious about doing so on two grounds. The first was that it would absorb a great deal of our exiguous resources in the period ahead. The second was that I did not believe that the Conservative wing of the government (the review was very much a Liberal Democrat project, headed up by William Wallace, the coalition's FCO minister in the Lords) would pay the slightest attention to its findings nor that it would have any traction with public opinion (its title was hardly very sexy). Having said all that, we nevertheless agreed to contribute to the best of our ability and in fact submitted 12 papers on different policy areas for which we were publicly thanked by the Minister. The broad overall thrust of the contributions from all quarters to the review was very clear. There was no general perception that too many competences had been transferred to the EU. Some evidence called for more EU activity (on trade in services and digital); some called for great caution in going any further (on social policy). And there was also a general perception that the present balance of competences served

British interests well. Not surprisingly these conclusions were catnip to the Conservative wing of the government, which had by that stage been committed by David Cameron's Bloomberg speech to a re-negotiation and an in/out referendum. As a result it proved impossible to agree any government conclusions to the review, and the mass of material which had been accumulated was finally furtively released into the public domain and effectively smothered by the N° 10 spin machine.

$$*\qquad\qquad*\qquad\qquad*$$

Nor did the coalition government have anything like a trouble free ride in EU negotiations in Brussels. In December 2011 David Cameron precipitated a humiliating rebuff over his attempt to block a new treaty commitment by the Eurozone member states to tighten up fiscal discipline. Cameron sought to get agreement on some complex and ill-prepared proposals covering Single Market legislation on financial services as the price for agreeing to the fiscal changes. His proposals were rejected and the other member states simply decided to proceed with the fiscal changes outside the formal EU treaty framework, precisely the by-pass we had feared might occur in the 1990s had the UK refused to accept what became the Maastricht Treaty on Economic and Monetary Union. Not for the last time Cameron and his team demonstrated an unsure touch when it came to handling the grinding detail of an EU negotiation; and also demonstrated over-reliance on his personal relationship with the German Chancellor,

Angela Merkel, on whose influence he relied to pull the chestnuts out of the fire on his behalf.

A rather similar sequence of events occurred in the summer of 2014 when Cameron tried to block the appointment as President of the Commission of Jean Claude Juncker, the Prime Minister of Luxembourg. On that occasion the UK was simply voted down, since the treaty provided for majority voting. But unjustified over-reliance on Chancellor Merkel's support was again in evidence.

Both these episodes made more difficult the task the Prime Minister was contemplating setting himself of winning an in/out referendum.

∗   ∗   ∗

And then in June 2013 the first in/out referendum Bill found its way onto the parliamentary order paper in the form of a Private Members Bill tabled in the Commons by a Eurosceptic Conservative MP, James Wharton, who had by chance come top of the list of those entitled to table such private legislation. But this was different because the Conservative wing of the government quickly lent it their support in both Houses. The Bill was in fact totally inadequate as a basis for holding a referendum, since, under British constitutional practice, such legislation has to be free standing and to set out all the electoral minutiae of the proposed vote; and this Bill was lacking most of that. But that was not its real purpose, which was to increase the pressure on the Conservative leadership to bring forward its own, fully-fledged in/out referendum legislation. The

Bill passed in the Commons but, when it came to the Lords, it quickly became clear that it was in for a rough ride. As a private member's Bill it had to be piloted by a back bencher, and Michael Dobbs, a recently appointed Conservative peer (best known as the author of the television series "House of Cards") took on what was to prove a pretty thankless task, not helped by his own inexperience in the complex niceties of Lords parliamentary practice. So, for a series of Friday sessions (the only day on which private members' bills are debated, with a cut off time of 3.00 p.m.) the House worked its way through the text of the Bill, with amendment after amendment being voted through by an alliance of Labour, Liberal Democrat and cross bench peers against fairly feeble Conservative opposition. After several weeks of this, and when the House voted to refuse to extend the sitting beyond 3.00 p.m., the government, in the person of Joyce Anelay, the Conservative Chief Whip in the Lords, threw in the towel and the Bill died, never to be seen again. But in truth this was something of a Pyrrhic victory because the authors of the Bill had succeeded in their main objective of ratcheting up the pressure for an in/out referendum on their own leadership. It did, however, for the first time bring into being the cross-party alliance in the Lords opposed to Britain leaving the EU which was to cause the government plenty of problems in the years ahead.

*   *   *

I must confess that, when I came onto the EU Select Committee's Sub-Committee for Home Affairs in 2008, I had never even heard of Protocol 36 of the Lisbon Treaty, let alone been aware of its implications for Britain's relationship with the EU. That state of ignorance and personal detachment did not long survive the arrival in office of the coalition government. When the EU first became active in what came to be known as Justice and Home Affairs (JHA) legislation at the London European Council in December 1986 (whose conclusions I, as Britain's Permanent Representative, had some part in shaping), it was established that cooperation should be purely inter-governmental, that all decisions should be taken by unanimity, that the Commission should have no oversight over member state compliance, and that the European Court of Justice should not have jurisdiction. Since those early days EU involvement in JHA had grown rapidly, driven by the increasing challenge from serious international crime - drugs, money-laundering, human trafficking, child pornography and, above all, by the threat from international terrorism following the 9/11 attacks in New York and Washington. The need for law enforcement across the EU to be handled internationally became almost axiomatic. Two new EU agencies, Europol (for police cooperation) and Eurojust (to assist prosecutions across jurisdictional boundaries) were set up. Several Europe-wide data bases were established - the European Criminal Record Information System (ECRIS), the Schengen Information System, the Prum decisions (exchange of DNA and of number plate information), Passenger Name Recognition Rules (for air passengers); and, most important of all the European Arrest Warrant (EAW) which cut through the many layers of legal delay and obstruction which had made the extradition of suspected criminals a matter of months and sometimes years. The UK was one of the member states which made the most use, and derived the most benefit, from this network of law enforcement cooperation.

By the time the Lisbon Treaty came to be negotiated there was near unanimity among the member states that JHA legislation needed, in the jargon, to be "communitarised" i.e. to be decided by qualified majority vote, to be subject to Commission oversight and to come under ECJ jurisdiction. Only the Blair government held out against this, clearly worried about a possible backlash in Parliament (oddly enough the Home Secretary of the day, Charles Clarke, told me that he had favoured acceptance of the changes). To break this deadlock the UK was given a way out, albeit a singularly unattractive one, in the form of Protocol 36 of the Treaty; under this provision for five years after the entry into force of the Lisbon Treaty "communitarisation" would not apply to the UK's pre-Lisbon JHA legislation (although it would apply to post-Lisbon legislation for which the UK had an opt-in/opt-out choice for each individual piece of legislation, to most of which we were in fact opting in). At the end of the five years, that is to say by November 2014 the UK had either to accept the "communitarisation" of all pre-Lisbon JHA legislation or lose the lot. This appalling booby trap now lay waiting for the coalition government.

At an early stage Peter Bowness, the chair of the Justice Sub-Committee, and I realised that Protocol 36 and its implications needed careful, evidence-based scrutiny; and, since the EU's JHA legislation crossed the dividing

64

line between our two committees, we persuaded our colleagues that a joint enquiry by the two was the only sensible way to proceed (an unprecedented approach, by the way). We had hoped to have our enquiry well under way before the coalition government declared its hand. But that hope was frustrated when in September 2012 David Cameron, on an official visit to Brazil and speaking against the spectacular backdrop of Rio de Janeiro's sugar loaf mountain, announced that the UK would be leaving all pre-Lisbon JHA legislation at the end of 2014. It rapidly transpired that Cameron had not consulted his coalition partners before making this announcement; so there then ensued a prolonged bout of Conservative/Liberal Democrat infighting, in particular over what, if any, of the pre-Lisbon legislation we should seek to re-join, a route out of the "all or nothing" provisions of Protocol 36 which was neither prescribed by it nor forbidden. That route was all the more appealing since quite a lot of the pre-Lisbon legislation was now either out of date or had been overtaken by subsequent legislation. But that did not make the choices any easier, since the Eurosceptic Conservative MPs, to appease whom the Rio announcement had been directed in the first place, were campaigning for a full pull out. The prolonged warfare over this behind not very effectively closed doors in Whitehall was in fact a boon for our enquiry which for once was both timely and consequential.

The evidence we took was revealing and largely consistent. Witnesses from within the law enforcement community (the Crown Prosecution Service, the Association of Chief Police Officers, the legal wings of the

Scottish and Northern Irish governments - the Irish dimension being particularly important because the JHA legislation had done so much to de-politicise using the EAW extradition procedures between the two parts of the island) all asserted the value to Britain of the main JHA agencies and instruments and wanted to retain them; so too did the Bar Council and the Law Society and many legal academics. And the Commission and the European Parliament demonstrated how these institutions were moving to remedy some of the defects in the early legislation, in particular by introducing Euro-bail provisions to help avoid Britons indicted in other EU countries being held on remand in poor conditions for a lengthy period. There were voices raised for dumping all the pre-Lisbon legislation, most notably by Dominic Raab, then a backbench Conservative Eurosceptic, who argued we should be getting out not only of the pre-Lisbon JHA legislation but also of the post-Lisbon legislation which we had opted into. But these views were few and far between. When we had a marathon evidence session at the end of the enquiry with the Home Secretary (Theresa May) and the Justice Secretary (Chris Grayling) they presented a marked contrast in both style and substance - May guarded, cautious, giving nothing away about how much JHA legislation the government would try to re-join, Grayling taking a slash and burn approach which did wonders to persuading the Conservative members of the two sub-committees to come to some robust conclusions. These were that the government would have been entirely justified in agreeing to accept the "communitarisation" of all the pre-Lisbon legislation (but of course we had no illusion that the government would actually do that); and that, if they did decide to proceed as the Rio announcement suggested, then they should seek to re-join all the main JHA agencies and legislation (many of which we listed) including the European Arrest Warrant. Not altogether surprisingly the government failed to respond to these recommendations within the two-month period laid down for such responses; they were still fighting amongst themselves.

The deadlock within the coalition government over how many and which pre-Lisbon JHA measures to seek to re-join lasted many months, with only the occasional leak revealing how the debate was going. Then in July of 2013, no doubt driven by the realisation that the time to negotiate in Brussels over the list of measures to re-join before the 2014 deadline expired was shrinking, the government sought parliamentary authority to trigger the Protocol 36 withdrawal provisions and, at the same time published the list of the JHA agencies and measures it would seek to re-join. The list of some 30 agencies and measures to re-join was reasonably satisfactory and close to the indications given in our committee's report and included the EAW; but, crucially the government did not seek Parliament's approval of the re-join list, thus avoiding a confrontation with those of their supporters who wanted the re-join list to be shorter or not to exist at all. This tactic worked in the Commons, which gave the government the authority it sought, but not in the Lords. With the support of our two committees and of the Labour opposition, I tabled an amendment suspending consideration of the government's request for authority until such time as they published their much-delayed response to our original report and amended their own resolution to include explicit approval of the re-join list. It was pretty clear that my amendment would pass, in which case the government would not be able to begin negotiations in Brussels on the re-join list. I had some tense dialogues with Joyce Anelay, the Conservative Chief Whip in the Lords, in which I made clear that I would only withdraw the amendment if both the conditions in it were met. She then put her foot down within the government; the government response to our report was published with a few hours to spare; and the government motion was amended to give explicit approval to the re-join list to be negotiated in Brussels. The government then got its business (although Labour - but not me and the members of the committees - voted against it). It had been a close-run thing.

The rest of the Protocol 36 process was much less exciting. Detailed negotiations went ahead in Brussels, with the Commission on the whole responding positively to the re-join list (although there were divisions there too, with Viviane Reading, the Justice Commissioner, causing a good deal of difficulty and Cecilia Malmstrom, the Home Affairs Commissioner - with whom I had had some useful discussions - being unfailingly supportive). By the autumn of 2014 there was agreement on the re-join list, which had not changed much but contained a few additional measures which were linked to those already on the UK list. And the government went back to the Commons to receive authorisation of the agreed re-join list which they got with a massive cross-party majority, with only 20 or so

Eurosceptics voting against it. It was the last pro-European victory for a long time to come.

*   *   *

In the meantime there had been a much more fundamental development in the Conservative wing of the government's European policy with David Cameron's Bloomberg speech in January 2013 promising an in/out referendum, preceded by some renegotiation of the terms of our membership if a Conservative government took office after the election due in 2015. While this capitulation to the Eurosceptics in his party was wrapped up in a large amount of broadly pro-European rhetoric, there was no doubt there had been a seismic shift in British politics. The move, which was principally designed to ensure that the Conservative party did not split over Europe and to minimise the size of the UK Independence Party vote, in fact achieved neither of those objectives except in the very short term. It rang up the curtain on six years of volatility and turmoil, not only in Westminster but right across Europe; and its consequences came to dominate my own life in the period ahead. David Cameron had decided to play Russian roulette with one of our main national assets.

Chapter 5

A botched renegotiation
(2015-2016)

The Bloomberg speech hung like a black cloud over British politics for two years. With the Fixed Term Parliament Act in place, it was hard to see that hiatus being cut short; and it was not. But, until it was known whether the Conservatives had an overall majority, it was impossible to tell whether renegotiation followed by an in/out referendum was going to remain an aspiration in the party's manifesto or was about to become a reality. No other party, apart from UKIP, was signed up to going down that particular road; and the assumption was therefore that, if there were to be another hung Parliament, which seemed quite possible, the aspiration would remain just that. There have subsequently been indications that some of the Conservative Leadership, especially those who were doubtful about the wisdom of holding a referendum, could have lived with that without too much suffering.

The outcome of the 2015 general election put an end to that uncertainty. The Conservatives won a small, but manageable, overall majority; and the Liberal Democrats suffered massive losses in seats. David Cameron decided to push ahead with his renegotiation and in/out referendum strategy on a tight timetable, no doubt following the usual calculation that getting difficult issues out of the way early in the new Parliament was the best way to proceed. But, with June 2016 soon emerging as the chosen date for the referendum, that left precious little time for renegotiation and none at all for the sort of grinding process through several successive meetings of the European Council which is usually the best way to get good results. Moreover the French and German domestic political timetables were not propitious. But, as usual, such considerations counted for little in the calculations at Westminster.

In any case, without waiting for renegotiation to get under way, the government needed to get a fully-fledged Referendum Bill - nothing like the Wharton Bill - through both Houses of Parliament, ready for it to be implemented once the Brussels part of the process was over. Getting the Bill through the Commons presented no great difficulties, although in the process the government accepted the advice of the Electoral Commission to substitute for the original choice of a "Yes/No" question (such as had been used in 1975), a choice between "Remain" and "Leave", which experts in these matters felt sure would be disadvantageous to the pro-Europeans. In the Lords the process was a good deal longer and more difficult, although the application of what is called the Salisbury Convention (under which the Lords accepts legislation which has figured in the election manifesto of a party which wins an overall majority in the Commons) precluded the sort of radical treatment meted out to the Wharton Bill. There was no stomach either to insert a minimum threshold requirement which, in the circumstances of 2016 would probably have invalidated the result. But there were major debates over the franchise. The extension of the right to vote to 16- and 17-year olds was one such (which would have brought in two of my grandchildren - entirely appropriately in my view, but not that of their parents!); this had been the rule in the Scottish independence referendum in 2014, which many believed had been a worthwhile innovation, had broad cross-party support and was voted through by a substantial majority. Lifting the 15-year absence limit on those living elsewhere in the EU had less support (despite the fact that it was actually included in the Conservatives' own manifesto). And there was, shamefully in my view, no general support for giving the vote to EU citizens living in the UK, who had the right to vote in our local elections and whose status and rights were going to be fundamentally affected by the outcome of the referendum. The Commons rejected extension of the vote to 16- and 17-year olds; and in the end the government got its Referendum Act, with only minor tweaks to some of the technical provisions.

*   *   *

My heart sank when I realised that David Cameron had not only nailed his colours to holding an in/out referendum but also to preceding that with a renegotiation of Britain's relationship with the EU. Not because there was nothing wrong with the EU; there clearly were plenty of reforms needed. But sailing under the banner of renegotiation, which no other member state would recognise as politically legitimate (if one member state could renegotiate its relationship, why not all of them?), was simply not the best way of doing it. I had lived through one renegotiation in 1974/75, had seen it produce slim pickings, and had noticed that the outcome of that renegotiation had had little, if any, effect on the referendum campaign that followed it. At that time I had been working in the Commission as chef de cabinet to the senior British Commissioner, Christopher Soames. My main contribution had been to write a paper for the two British Commissioners entitled "Renegotiation without tears", advising that the Commission keep well away from the whole exercise and leave the UK to see how far it could get with its fellow member states. That advice had been followed. The last thing needed in 2015/16 was a repeat of that not very glorious episode.

Moreover the jewel in the crown of David Cameron's renegotiation was the pretty worthless and totally unnecessary objective of getting Britain's exemption from the preambular reference in the EU's founding treaty to the objective of an "ever closer union" - incidentally that referred not to a union of its member states but of its peoples, a much vaguer concept. The reason it was unnecessary was that a preambular, and not an operative, reference in a treaty had no binding legal force; and it never had been used, nor could it be used, as the basis for legal decisions on further integration. It really was one of Don Quixote's windmills. Nevertheless it was considered to have great totemic significance within the Conservative party - David Cameron's Deputy Chief of Staff, Kate Fall, in her book "The Gatekeeper" said it was regarded as a commitment to a federal United States of Europe. I deployed these arguments over a convivial dinner at the

Danish Ambassador's house to Kim Darroch, the Prime Minister's National Security Adviser and, earlier, my fifth successor as EU Permanent Representative. He said that, while my arguments might have some validity, this issue was way above his pay grade; and the Prime Minister was not going to change his mind on its centrality.

The rest of the renegotiation package was an eclectic mixture of the highly technical and the unrealisable. Among the technicalities were provisions to ensure that the UK, whose capital city was also the financial services capital of the EU was not marginalised by the Eurozone countries when single market measures on financial services were under negotiation. The financial services provisions in the package were what should have been achieved back in 2011 when Cameron messed up his attempt to block the EU's Fiscal Treaty, with which the other member states then went ahead outside the formal EU structures. They were achievements, but not ones that anyone outside the City would either have understood or appreciated. The unrealisable was the attempt to tinker with one of the four basic freedoms on which the EU was based - goods, services, capital, people. There was much loose talk about an emergency brake on immigration from the rest of the EU; and, when that could not be achieved, which was inevitable from the outset, it looked like a major defeat. Meanwhile, as a number of us tried to point out through probing questions in Parliament, the government was not even making full use of powers it had under EU law to return EU immigrants to their own country if they could not find a job within a specified period (Belgium did this and had not fallen foul of the Commission).

But the main arguments against the renegotiation approach were political and not technical or legal. The first was that, as in 1975, renegotiation and the results obtained by it were never going to be of any real significance once the referendum campaign got under way. In 2016 the shelf life of the results of the renegotiation was a matter of days, not weeks or months. The second was that renegotiation ensured that the six months before the referendum campaign kicked off were entirely filled with adversarial negotiations, depicted in the press as "Britain v. Europe". It was not easy to pivot in February 2016 from gladiatorial combat to warm embrace on the back of the underwhelming outcome of renegotiation. And the third was that renegotiation enabled those who decided, either for opportunistic or ideological reasons, to throw in their lot with the Leave campaign, to mask their motives behind arguments about the inadequacy of the renegotiation package.

Most of these considerations were in plain view in 2015. A study of the 1974/75 experience would have brought them into sharper focus. But for politicians and advisers brought up in the 24/7 news cycle, that was ancient history.

Chapter 6

Referendum (2016)

The early months of 2016 saw the renegotiation process reach its climax (in February) and the referendum campaign get under way with the declarations from Michael Gove and Boris Johnson that they would be campaigning for Leave, joining the even harder line Eurosceptics who had been urging that course for months and in some cases for years. The Conservative Party was split and its formidable vote organising machine was stuck in neutral gear for the duration; the Labour Party was led by Jeremy Corbyn, at best a tepid Remainer who refused to appear on any platform with members of other parties campaigning for Remain; it was a far cry from the referendum campaign days of 1975 when cross-party teams from all three main parties spoke from the same platforms from one end of the country to the other.

The official Remain campaign organisation, known as "Stronger In" had as its director a bright but relatively inexperienced Will Straw (Jack Straw's son) and was made up of a bevy of mainly Labour and Liberal Democrat enthusiasts. But the Labour cohort tended to be drawn from the ranks of Blair and Brown supporters and thus out of tune with Labour's new leadership - and Alan Johnson, who headed up the Labour Remain campaign was cold-shouldered by the Corbyn team. The head of the overall

Remain campaign was Stuart Rose, formerly CEO of Marks and Spencers and a Conservative peer, whose appearance at the campaign launch in an East London brewery was distinctly underwhelming and whose subsequent failure during a TV interview to remember the name of the campaign he was meant to be leading resulted in his playing no further public role in its activities. As we had done with "Britain in Europe" some fifteen years earlier the SEEG offered our services to produce briefing and to vet campaign material relating to the EU dimension and to developments in Brussels and elsewhere in Europe. But no use was made of this offer.

On the other side of the battlefield two main organisations, vied for primacy, the Nigel Farage/Arron Banks "Leave EU" team and the official "Vote Leave" campaign headed up by Gove and Johnson, with Dominic Cummings and Matthew Elliott as their sorcerers apprentices - or, as gradually became clear, as the sorcerers themselves. From the outset the Leave campaign poured forth a mendacious mix of half-truths and straightforward lies. But, as time went on and the Remain campaign's rebuttals simply bounced off their armour-plated assertions, it became clear that we had moved into a "post fact" or "alternative fact" world, in which the nemesis that in the past had overtaken political campaigns that relied on straight lies, was no longer the rule of the day.

*   *   *

At about this time my own involvement in the debate over Europe underwent a fundamental shift. Early in the new year of 2016 I was asked by Rachel Franklin, who had done some work for SEEG, whether I would be prepared to contribute material to a web-site being set up by Hugo Dixon, a former Financial Times and Reuters journalist. This web-site, known as InFacts, whose mission statement was "to make the facts-based case to stay in the EU" published two or three articles a day, each of 500/700 words enlivened with cartoons, either by way of rebuttal of Leave campaign propaganda or of promoting the main themes of the Remain campaign. It went out to a wide variety of politicians, journalists and businessmen. I did not hesitate long. I had in fact already done a little casual journalism of a similar sort for an outfit called "British Influence" run by Peter Wilding, a former official of the Conservative Group in the European Parliament. I was not too dismayed by the challenge of converting from diplomatic reporting to journalism, two professions with considerable overlap.

What of course I did not realise then was that, over the next four years, I would write 215 such articles - a rate of roughly one a week but, in busy periods, a lot more than that. Having just about mastered the capability to use an iPad and with WiFi connections almost everywhere I went - my favourite base being the Café des Voyageurs et des Touristes in St. Céré, near my house in France but I did also file articles from Bali, Bhutan, Hanoi and Albania at different times - I did not get much time off. Hugo Dixon was a wonderful editor, identifying or responding, discussing and agreeing the topics I was to write about and seldom amending my copy, except to use his editor's privilege to write the headlines. I attended many strategy meetings at Hugo's mews house just the other side of the A40 flyover from the Grenfell Tower in North Kensington; and helped him with a number of fund-raising dinners. InFacts brought together a plethora of talent in addition to Hugo himself - Quentin Peel, whom I had known when he was the FT correspondent in Brussels, Bill Emmott, former editor of the Economist, Denis MacShane, one of Tony Blair's Ministers for Europe, Will Hutton, writer for The Observer and head of an Oxford college, Luke Lythgoe, Hugo's deputy editor, and Nick Kent, my own research director at the SEEG, to name but a few.

Naturally much of the material we produced during the referendum campaign was in rebuttal of claims made and lines taken by the Leave campaign and its supporters. Here is the very first such article and my own first contribution to InFacts, dated 13ᵗʰ March, 2016:

10 of Vote Leave's half-truths and untruths.

If you have ever wondered what sort of nightmares Eurosceptics have when they have eaten too many toasted cheese sandwiches before going to bed, you need only look at Vote Leave's recent offering entitled "43 years, 43 broken promises". Here is a vintage collection of half-truths, quarter-truths and untruths, lovingly polished and embellished over the years; a gallery dedicated to paranoia. Space does not permit a full analysis of every one of those 43 allegations of broken promises; but here are a few thoughts on ten of the choicest ones.

1. Have we irretrievably eroded our essential national sovereignty? No. We have pooled the exercise of some of it, as we did when we joined NATO, the UN and other international organisations, because we believed we could put it to more effective use that way than by hoarding it. Parliament can take it back by withdrawing from the EU. That is what the vote on 23 June is about.

2.   Has Brussels forced us to put VAT on food? No. There is VAT on a few marginal food items (like potato crisps). But in every case that was because successive Chancellors of the Exchequer wanted more revenue, not because of a diktat from Brussels.

3.   Are we being forced into an Economic and Monetary Union? No. Britain's opt-out from the Single Currency is enshrined in the Treaty and was further entrenched by the February 2016 package of reforms.

4.   Are we being pulled into a federal super-state? No. The agreement reached in February makes it clear that we are not bound by any reference to "ever closer union"; and in any case that formula has no legal force, nor is it a basis for EU law.

5.   Have we lifted our border controls and lost our veto on immigration issues? No. Our opt-out from the Schengen passport-free travel zone is enshrined in the Treaty; as is our right to decide ourselves whether or not to join any legislation affecting immigration.

6.   Could we be forced to accept a European Public Prosecutor? No. Britain's opt-out from this is in the Treaty.

7.   Is the UK budget rebate secure? Yes. It would have been more honest if Vote Leave admitted that, since 1985, the rebate has spared Britain £82 billion (and still counting); and that in 2013 Britain was ninth in the contribution league table by head of population.

8.   Is there a European army? No. There is no such thing. What Presidents of the Commission may have said about this is neither here or there as such an army

is not in the gift of the Commission. Security policy issues are a matter for member states to decide by unanimity, so Britain has a veto.

9.   Could we become responsible for bailing out the Eurozone or one of its members? No. The February reform package makes it clear that Britain has no liability for Eurozone bail-outs.

10.   Does the February reform package have legal force and will it lead to Treaty change? Yes is the answer to both of those questions. It is a legally binding international agreement (which is why depositing it at the UN has more than just symbolic importance); and it will be inserted into the treaty when this is next changed. This kind of post-dated commitment was used for Denmark and Ireland in the past; in both cases it was honoured in the letter and the spirit; and no attempt was made by the European Court of Justice to question or to overturn those commitments in the period before they were incorporated in the Treaty.

All in all Vote Leave's "43 Years, 43 Broken Promises" is a shoddy piece of work, beefed up with selective quotations and inaccurate analysis and taking no account of the February 2016 reform package. It does however serve one useful purpose. It makes clear that Project Fear was not something invented by the Remain campaign in the last few weeks; it has been a standard operating procedure for Eurosceptics over the last 40 years. So this really is a case of the pot calling the kettle black.

And here is another dealing with that jewel in the crown of the Leave campaign's claim that an independent trade policy would bring massive benefits to the UK, dated 18th March 2016:

Trade fantasies.

Regular listeners to the BBC's invaluable Today programme are, quite rightly hearing a lot about Brexit. And quite rightly too they are hearing from both sides of the debate. So on 18 March there was an interview with Peter Hargreaves, a prominent financier, who favours Britain leaving the EU.

Most of the interview was taken up with Hargreave's preferences for alternative trading relationships in a post-Brexit scenario. He thought it would be perfectly straightforward to retain our trade access to the EU "Just pick up the telephone to Angela Merkel and it will be fixed". As to our trade outside the EU, Hargreaves said we should negotiate a free trade deal with the Commonwealth which would be easy because "we all speak English". The first of these assertions rests on the flimsiest of foundations and the second is simply unfounded.

How can anyone be "quite sure" that we would be able to preserve our access to the Single Market, where by far the largest proportion of our exports go? Have those who make these assertions spoken to the representatives of the 27 other member states? If Hargreaves took the trouble to speak to leaders of these other countries he would find out that they are focused on their own national interest in a post-Brexit scenario. Their priority will be to discourage anti-EU parties in their own countries. They therefore will not want Britain to leave without suffering negative consequences.

Meanwhile Hargreaves's Commonwealth option is pure fantasy. The Commonwealth does not negotiate as a trade bloc and is never likely to do so. Moreover Britain already has a free trade relationship with the majority of Commonwealth countries - all those in the African, Caribbean and Pacific regions - which we would sever if we left the EU and then have to negotiate all over again.

The largest developed country in the Commonwealth, Canada, already has a free trade agreement with the EU which again we would relinquish if we left. And the EU has plans for free trade negotiations with India, Australia and New Zealand. Britain is more likely to improve its access to these markets if it remains part of the EU, since negotiators in all three of these countries may prioritise negotiations with the EU over the far smaller UK.

All of which goes to show that the Brexit debate is shot through with wishful thinking. Unless this changes we risk waking up on 24 June in cloud cuckoo land.

An early article was directed specifically at one of Vote Leave's leaders, later to become in 2019 Prime Minister and at the end of January 2020 to take the UK out of the European Union. It is dated 6th April, 2016:

Boris's fantastic frog.

Boris Johnson began by suggesting that a vote to remain in the EU on 23 June would be a green light for the EU to charge ahead in a federalist direction. Now we are told that Britain would be like a helpless frog in a saucepan of water being boiled by those same Brussels federalists. Here's why this overheated metaphor bears no relation to reality.

First does today's EU actually look as if it is preparing for a great federalist leap forward? If so, why is it struggling so hard to find a response to the migration crisis which is threatening to unpick the Schengen passport-free travel zone? And why is it finding it far from straightforward to plot a coherent course through the Eurozone's problems? Britain of course has no part in either Schengen or the single currency. If the EU's direction of travel really is towards a super-state, is it not a trifle odd that it has just agreed that treaty language about "ever closer union" does not apply to all member states?

Second, every capital in the EU is well aware that the terms of our European Union Act, 2011 mean that any further transfer of power to European institutions would require another European referendum. Are they really likely to try to cajole a reluctant British government into a course of action which could result in the treaty changes they want being blocked indefinitely, and perhaps lead to the Brexit they are all clearly keen to avoid? Not a very realistic scenario.

Why do Leave campaigners ignore the fact that the agenda the European Council has actually approved is one which successive British governments have wholeheartedly supported? The priorities are to strengthen the Single Market, create a level playing field for the digital economy, negotiate freer commerce with our main trading partners, build a Capital Markets Union and enhance energy cooperation.

Why too do they refuse to recognise that Britain's voice will be influential in shaping the EU's response to the many foreign policy challenges it faces? We will carry much less clout if we spurn the advice of our friends and allies and opt for Brexit.

Better surely to forget the frog fantasy and pursue these positive policy objectives which could do so much to improve our security and prosperity.

And now one other trade policy rebuttal, dated 12th April, 2016:

1960s show post-Brexit trade deals won't be easy.

Supporters of Britain leaving the EU are pretty coy about the trade relationships we would be able to build up from the outside, perhaps because they cannot agree amongst themselves what they want. But they do assert with the greatest conviction that it would be alright on the night. With the rest of the EU we would be like kittens in a basket with free trade assured; third countries would rush to do deals with us; our role in the world would be enhanced not damaged.

The experience of the 1960s, the last decade when Britain operated on its own, is hardly encouraging. We tried then to negotiate a European free trade area instead of joining their customs union and were rebuffed. We tried to cooperate on sectoral issues like patents and went round and round in circles getting nowhere. In the big multilateral trade negotiation, the Kennedy Round, we had to hover outside the door as the deals were cut between the main players (the US, the EEC and Japan) and then had to accept those deals with little chance to alter them. And that was a Britain responsible for a higher proportion of world trade and the world economy than it is now.

Fast forward to 2016. Is it really likely that 27 EU member states, themselves considerably damaged by our decision to leave and extremely anxious not to encourage their own Eurosceptics would hand us a free trade agreement tailor-made to our requirements? And why should third countries, many of them already negotiating free trade deals with the EU, the largest single market in the world, give any kind of priority or special treatment to a medium-sized, mature economy which could no longer offer a gateway into the EU and which had just spurned their advice to stay in the larger grouping?

No doubt this kind of assessment will be dismissed as yet another example of Project Fear. It is not. It is simply the sort of risk analysis which any company or other institution would carry out before even contemplating a fundamental shift in its business model. What makes the Brexiteers think they are exempt from that.

But there were also plenty of articles which were not simply rebuttals. Here is one on the implications of Brexit for the union of the United Kingdom, dated 18th April, 2016:

The referendum vote on 23 June will determine whether Britain remains in the European Union or leaves it. The negative consequences of leaving that union are being hotly debated. But less attention has so far been given to the negative consequences of such a decision on that other union which joins together the peoples of England, Scotland, Wales and Northern Ireland in a United Kingdom.

Perhaps the issues are less clear-cut and less immediate. They are not, however, less real; and they do need to be thought about, particularly by those who are deeply attached to the continued existence of the United Kingdom but are contemplating voting to leave the EU.

The case of Scotland is relatively obvious. On the assumption that Scotland votes to remain in the EU - and with pretty well every party in Scotland except UKIP campaigning to remain, that must look highly probable - an overall UK vote to leave would pose a major constitutional contradiction. Would this trigger a demand for a second referendum on Scottish independence? It would seem a little foolhardy to assume it would not.

Moreover the possible difficulties in Brussels over a Scottish bid for accession would look rather different than they did at the time of the Scottish independence referendum since the proposition would be that Scotland should remain in the EU rather than be forced to leave against its democratically expressed will.

The case of Wales is less obvious given that support there for independence is so much lower. But the assumption that there would be no negative consequences for the unity of the UK if a Welsh vote to remain was overridden would seem a little rash.

And then there is Northern Ireland, where the possible negative consequences do not hinge exclusively on whether the people of Northern Ireland themselves vote to remain or to leave. If a UK vote to leave were implemented by any trading arrangement other than the UK joining the European Economic Area and thus retaining its access to the Single Market, then there would need once again to be customs controls on the border between Ireland and Northern Ireland.

Moreover, if Britain leaves the EU much of the underpinning of cooperation on Justice and Home Affairs which has enabled that cooperation to be de-politicised by processes like the European Arrest Warrant would be at risk. To assert that the Good Friday agreement would emerge from all that upheaval unscathed would seem little short of the heroic.

The sensitivity of all these issues is not in doubt. But that is a bad reason not to debate them calmly and rationally.

A key part of the messaging for the Remain campaign was that the EU was fully capable of introducing reforms and had a good record of doing so. Here is an article dated 6th May arguing why it was better for Britain to be in the EU, pressing for reforms:

The EU's long record of reform.

One of the accusations frequently deployed by the Leave campaign is that the EU is unable to adapt to new challenges and is resistant to all reforms. True or false? Do words and phrases like "sclerotic" or "shackled to a corpse" make sense? Or are they just another myth? Here are five years samples which give the lie to the suggestion that the EU is incapable of changing.

First, it became clear in the 1980s that the original construct of a tariff-free customs union was failing to maximise economic gains due to the continued existence of hundreds of national non-tariff barriers to trade. Under the leadership of Margaret Thatcher and Arthur Cockfield the Single Market was created and those barriers were gradually dismantled, increasing prosperity across the EU Much remains to be done - completing the Single Market in services, creating a level playing field for the digital economy, building an energy and capital markets union. But every one of those objectives is now agreed by the European Council. The task is to put them into effect.

Second, the word "environment" is nowhere to be found in the original Treaty of Rome. But over the years, as the need for transnational action to deal effectively with environmental damage has become more evident, the EU has forged a policy which has brought us cleaner air, drinking water and beaches as well as better habitats for wildlife. The EU has also taken a lead in combatting climate change, culminating in last

December's global settlement in Paris. The commitments made then were recently enshrined in a binding international agreement, and the EU will be a key player in ensuring they are implemented.

Third, in the 1990s, when the Soviet Union collapsed and the countries of Central and Eastern Europe regained their independence, the EU spearheaded the massive Western response of aid and technical assistance which enabled these countries to complete successfully and peacefully their transition to democracy and a market economy. In due course the process was crowned by welcoming them into the EU as members - hardly the handiwork of a corpse.

Fourth, the EU's competition policy, originally designed to break up cartels and to prevent market dominance by international companies and government monopolies, has developed over time into a new instrument for dealing with new challenges. It is abolishing roaming charges on mobile telephones, getting to grips with international tax avoidance and clamping down on illegal government subsidies.

Fifth, as international crime burgeoned around the turn of the century, the EU devised ways to cooperate against new cross - border menaces, including terrorism, cybercrime, human trafficking and child pornography. Agencies such as Europol and Eurojust help national law enforcers tackle the growing transnational dimensions of crime; the European Arrest Warrant facilitates the extradition of criminals; the exchange of information through the European Criminal Records System and the Schengen Information System helps bring criminals to book even when they cross international boundaries.

That leaves one other claim by the Leave campaign - that the EU is a ratchet mechanism geared solely to amassing more powers and blocking reforms. But is that

true? The reform of the Common Agricultural Policy
may not have been a complete success but the production
subsidies which created butter mountains and wine lakes
are a thing of the past; and the share of the EU budget
absorbed by the CAP has fallen from 70% to 40%.
The reform of the Common Fisheries Policy will end the
discarding of unwanted catches and will result in many
management decisions being made regionally rather than
centrally. A larger share of the EU budget is going
towards research and innovation, which
disproportionately benefits UK research establishments
and universities. And a system has been agreed for an
annual review of progress towards simplifying legislation,
avoiding excessive regulation and reducing burdens on
business - perhaps not a complete answer yet to the
charges levelled against "Brussels bureaucrats", but firm
evidence nevertheless that the EU is indeed capable of
adapting and reforming.

Here is an article on the tensions between generations posed by the pressure to leave the EU, dated 13th May, 2016:

> *Brexit will deny the young the chance to go out into the*
> *world.*
>
> *The mathematical near-certainty that the younger half of*
> *the British electorate will have longer to live with the*
> *consequences of that vote next month than older*
> *generations has hovered around the debate over Britain's*
> *EU membership. And yet, should those consequences be*
> *negative, the implications will be far-reaching indeed, not*
> *least by alienating the younger generations from any*
> *respect for, or the desire to participate in the political life*
> *of the nation.*

This issue did briefly come into focus late in 2015 when a substantial majority in the House of Lords voted in favour of giving the franchise on this occasion to 16- and 17-year olds, as was done in the Scottish referendum on independence. In a whipped vote in the Commons that move was rejected.

Now, as opinion poll after opinion poll shows a substantial inter-generational disconnect over the EU membership question, the matter is, rightly, getting more salience again. The younger half of the electorate appears to be heavily in favour of Remain; and the older half in favour of Leave. This would not be so significant if it were not for the evidence that the older half has a much higher propensity to vote than the younger half.

Should this inter-generational tension worry us? I would have thought it should, all the more so as this is by no means the only source of that tension around. Think tuition fees, the protection of pensioners' income, the continuance of subsidies for winter fuel and television licences for even the well-off elderly.

Moreover a successful Leave campaign would cut the younger generations off from one of the main benefits Britons have enjoyed for decades now, the possibility to go out into the world in search of work, study, experience and indeed a wider vision of what life has to offer. Determined to cut immigration into the UK from other European countries, we would lose our rights to move freely around the 27 other member states (30 if you include the members of the European Economic Area), with health and employment rights safeguarded.

It would be no good hoping that those traditional havens for British emigration, Australia, Canada, New Zealand and the United States would take up the slack. Just glance at those countries' current immigration rules and you will see how unlikely that is to materialise. As to the rest of the world, which our

91

forebears did so much to develop, the demographic trends make a liberal development of their immigration rules rather unlikely.

There is clearly no methodological or legislative solution in the time scale of this referendum to the conundrum of a rising inter-generational conflict of interests. So what remains are two possibilities. The first is to encourage the younger half of the electorate to register and vote in proportions closer to those of their elders. The second is to stimulate a more fruitful and tolerant dialogue between the two halves of the electorate, as appears to have taken place in Ireland at the time of their referendum on same-sex marriage.

And then, not long before the 23rd June referendum, I wrote an article on the gaping hole in the Leave campaign, the absence of any indication as to what would happen next in the event of their winning. In a way it proved to be a curtain-raiser for much of the debate over the next three years at the end of which, almost unbelievably many of the questions posed had not been answered. Here it is, dated 7th June:

Vote Leave's unanswered questions.

Before general elections each party sets out a manifesto of policy proposals for the next five years - and their commitments are intensely scrutinised by political opponents and objective commentators. A party which cannot defend and promote its proposals loses credibility. Ironically, the EU referendum debate so far seems to have escaped that iron discipline, even though the outcome could affect national life for much longer than five years. Here are just a sample of the questions the

Vote Leave campaign trails behind it - questions they need to answer.

1. How will falling tax revenues be met? Most economic forecasts - such as those by the Bank of England, the International Monetary Fund and the OECD - foresee both a short-term shock and a longer-term negative impact from leaving the EU. If borne out - at least in their general thrust - then government revenues will suffer, which would need to be matched by deeper spending cuts, tax rises or increased borrowing.

2. How would the fall in inward investment be compensated? Britain depends on inward investment from other EU countries and global multinationals. Many of those making those investments have said they are predicated on Britain's Single Market membership and hence could be lost after we left.

3. How will withdrawal negotiations proceed? Will the Article 50 negotiations provided for in the EU Treaty be engaged without delay? Or, will they be spun out, with the likely consequence that our departure from the EU will also be postponed?

4. How will we trade with the EU? 44% of Britain's exports go to the EU. How are we to retain that trade, assuming that our refusal to permit continued free movement of people will rule out the access we currently enjoy - free of tariff barriers and customs inspections? How will the complex supply chains British companies have with other EU countries be protected from damage?

5. How will we trade with the rest of the world? The EU already has free trade agreements agreed or in effect with the likes of South Korea, South Africa, Canada, and many countries in the African, Pacific and Caribbean regions - and is in negotiation with the US, India, Japan and the Mercosur countries of South America. How would Britain persuade those countries to give priority and a better deal for our market of 60 million, compared to the EU's 450 million?

6. How will we protect financial and other services? Roughly 80% of our economy is in services, and we are world leaders in areas such as finance and law. How can we improve our access, when UK firms may lose their passport to operate in the EU, and most other countries are reluctant to open up?

7. Will we match EU budget spending? Will the government match the support and protection offered by the Common Agricultural Policy - and how will it retain our growing EU export markets for food and beverages? What about EU support for the UK's poorer regions - Cornwall, West Wales, Cumbria, the Scottish Highlands and Islands and Northern Ireland? And for science and innovation, from which UK universities and research establishments gain disproportionately?

8. How will we fight international crime? Leaving the EU could mean losing membership of EU crime fighting agencies Europol and Eurojust, the rapid extraditions offered by the European Arrest Warrant, the European Criminal Records System and the Schengen Information System for dealing with illegal immigration. How will Britain compensate for this loss in the fight against terror, cybercrime and human trafficking?

*   *   *

What were my own views as the campaign progressed about the likely outcome? They did not change much from beginning to end. I thought it would be a tight race; and that Remain would win by a narrow margin. I never believed for one moment that we would replicate, or even nearly replicate, the 66/33 victory of 1975. There had been just too much bad publicity and bad mouthing from the predominantly Eurosceptic press over too long a period of time for that to be a realistic possibility. But I did think, mistakenly as it turned out, that the blatant lies that the Leave campaign was propagating, about the sums of money sent to Brussels each week, about the whole of that mythical sum being available to the NHS, about the imminence of Turkish accession, about immigration - much of which from non-EU countries was already under our control and yet was steadily rising - and many more would return to haunt their campaign when people came to vote. Some of the bitterness I felt over those lies was summed up in the following excerpt from an InFacts article on 20th June: *"It is often said in the Middle East that, if you are going to tell a lie, then it had better be a big one since then more people will believe you. In its handling of the issue of Turkey's application to join the EU the Leave campaign has certainly shown that it has learned to adopt and to apply that cynical piece of advice. The claims that Turkey could be a member of the EU by 2020 and that Britain has no control over the process are simply untrue."*

Did I think mistakes were made on the Remain side? Of course I did. The failure to mount a genuinely cross-party campaign of the sort we had had in 1975 was one of them. The fact that in the latter stages N° 10 virtually took over "Stronger In" certainly did not help. In 1975 Harold Wilson and James Callaghan stood well back from the fray, playing a muted and secondary role, thus reducing the temptation for Conservative voters to give them a black eye, was in sharp contrast to the 2016 pattern, as was the role played by Margaret Thatcher then and by Jeremy Corbyn now.

I did not myself think that the negative arguments about the likely costs of Brexit - Project Fear as it was cleverly labelled by the Leave campaign - could or should have been avoided or played down, although George Osborne's warning of the need for an emergency budget if Leave won was clearly a damp squib. But these costs were real and we have seen them accumulating every day since June 2016 - in lower growth, in loss of inward investment, in declining global influence. In any case the Leave campaign was running its own Project Fear in the shape of dire predictions of a federalist United States of Europe and its exaggerated claims of loss of control; but the Leave campaign was not called out in the same way.

Where I did consider the Remain campaign went awry was in failing to make a full-throated case in favour of EU membership - not, I hasten to say, a purely emotional case, since that would not have worked, but a bit more empathy towards the EU would have helped. Above all the positive case for remaining was there in the EU's most recent policy platform, endorsed by all member states in June 2015, a heavily British-influenced document likely to bring substantial benefits to the UK. So we could have done with a bit more Project Hope.

Could some additional concessions by the EU on immigration, either in the renegotiation or at the last moment before the vote, have tipped the balance? This was a favourite trope of Cameron supporters in the months after the referendum; and it seems that a last-minute appeal to Angela Merkel was contemplated but not pursued. I really doubt whether that would have worked. I have already set out in the preceding chapter why I thought that pretty well everything coming out of the renegotiation was discounted as soon as it was revealed. I suspect this would have suffered a similar fate, even if it had been achievable, which I doubt it was.

On the evening of 23rd June I made my way to the "Stronger In" party on the South Bank. It had been deluging with rain all day in London, which certainly did not help the turn out nor lighten my mood as I dodged my way round massive puddles and was soaked by passing cars. At the reception I fell in with Paddy Ashdown, normally as incurable an optimist as I tend to be. He was far from confident; and, as soon as the Sunderland result was announced, he predicted a bad night for our side. I took the same view and, although not averse to drinking warm white wine at a celebration, I saw no reason to do so at what was all set to become a wake. So I made my way back to Chiswick and listened to the results being declared in a mood of despair. It is not much fun watching a good part of your life's work going up in smoke.

Chapter 7

Triggering Article 50 (2016-2017)

The morning after the referendum David Cameron resigned as Prime Minister and Leader of the Conservative Party. Despite all Cameron's assurances ahead of the vote that he would stay on and that the referendum was not a vote to get rid of him, I had more confidence in Ken Clarke's reading of the race to the effect that Cameron would not last 30 seconds if the referendum vote was lost. The immediate consequence of his resignation was a complete hiatus in any Brexit activity while a new leader (and thus a new Prime Minister) was chosen; and the hiatus was all the more total since Labour too was plunged into a leadership contest as the result of a challenge to Jeremy Corbyn. I had, of course, no role in, and no influence over, either contest. But, having seen a certain amount of Theresa May in action during the long Protocol 36 saga (see Chapter 6), and particularly once the contest was narrowed down to Andrea Leadsom (described to me as the worst junior minister the Treasury had ever had), I had no doubt that May was the least bad option.

Theresa May's first cabinet appointments, which included the creation of two completely new departments of state, one for Exiting the EU (DexEu) and one for International Trade (DIT), however sowed the seeds of the dysfunctionality and confusion that characterised the government's approach to the Article 50 negotiations. Creating new departments is always a recipe for turf-fighting in Whitehall and so it was on this occasion, compounded by the fact that Britain's trading relationships were split between two different departments, one (DexEu) responsible for by far the bigger part of our overseas trade which was with the EU, the other (International Trade) for the rest. Moreover the Prime Minister ignored the precedent of our European Community accession negotiations in 1970/72 which had been directed by a small group of the key ministers (Treasury, Business, FCO, Agriculture and Fisheries) under the Prime Minister, underpinned by senior officials from each of these departments which would have the main roles in implementing the terms agreed; and that precedent had delivered an outcome in 18 months. The temptation for the main executive departments to stand back and watch DexEu floundering was not resisted.

In addition, May aggravated the problem by her own management style and the structure of her involvement - secretive, unwilling to give a clear lead and robotic in her public presentation. All communication had to pass through her two gatekeepers, Nick Timothy and Fiona Hill, neither of whom had any EU knowledge or experience; and Ollie Robbins, her Special Representative for the negotiations, who was not so handicapped, having started double-hatted as also Permanent Secretary of DexEu, fell out with David Davis, the Secretary of State, and thereafter depended solely on his role in Nº 10. The choice of the three key ministers (David Davis at DexEu,

Boris Johnson at the FCO and Liam Fox at International Trade) did not help either. All three were ardent Brexiters, partisans of a hard Brexit, none was good at detail, an essential ingredient of any EU negotiation. I had known David Davis when he was Minister for Europe in John Major's government (and I was starting my stint as Special Representative for Cyprus). There was plenty of surface charm and bonhomie but a distinct lack of willingness to roll up his sleeves and make hard choices. Boris Johnson I had known since he was 8, arriving in Brussels with his father Stanley, for whom I had secured a post in the Commission's environmental department as part of the first wave of British officials joining after our accession; subsequently our paths had crossed when he arrived back in Brussels in 1989 as the resident correspondent of the Daily Telegraph. There had been no doubting his ambition and upward mobility but a certain carelessness with the facts was evident from the outset. As Foreign Secretary, in 2016, far from advancing the government's Article 50 negotiating objectives, he spent most of his time roughing up the foreign ministers of the EU 27 with whom any deal would have to be concluded and convincing them, rightly or wrongly, that he was not a serious or trustworthy player.

*   *   *

My own first reactions to the outcome of the referendum came a lot quicker than the end of the leadership hiatuses. To all those with whom I was in contact - by e-mail or face to face - I took the line that there was no short cut back to the pre-referendum world where we were a full member of the EU in good standing. We would now have to go down into the valley of despond (a literary reference to the Article 50 withdrawal provisions) and only once we had trudged through that painful process would it be possible to assess whether there was a politically viable alternative to Brexit. A lot would depend on the outcome of the withdrawal negotiations, and, even more, on those for our future external relationship with the EU, referred to in Article 50 as something which needed to be taken into account as part of the withdrawal process. So, while I was angered, but not unduly surprised, by the evidence that gradually emerged of the dirty tricks and dubiously legal devices resorted to by the two Leave campaigns, I never believed there was any possibility of invalidating the referendum result.

In the short term my activities, writing regularly for InFacts and speaking in Parliament were focussed on two objectives, arguing the case for what came to be labelled a "soft Brexit" and seeking to persuade the incoming May government to make a generous, unilateral offer with respect to the post-Brexit status of the 3 million or so EU citizens in the UK. So far as the first objective was concerned the following article dated 2nd July, 2016 lays out the scene in general terms:

What could be saved from the shipwreck?

Anyone who doubted that Brexit would be a leap in the dark and that those who claimed it was were simply scaremongering must surely by now have lost any such illusions. Neither the government nor the leading figures in the Leave campaign seem to have the faintest clue about what they want to happen next, about when they want it to happen, nor about what the shape and content of Britain's new external relationship with the EU should be.

It clearly is sensible, even if there was not leadership turmoil in both main parties, to take a bit of time to fill that policy vacuum. But that pause will only make sense if it is used to conduct a hard-headed, evidence-based analysis of the various options, and then to make a choice which is not just a string of slogans like "take back control" and unattainable objectives like getting immigration down to "the tens of thousands". Here are three areas which will surely need to be covered – trade, foreign policy and crime.

The trade relationship is obviously going to be fundamental. The first step will be to give a crash course to the new Prime Minister and incoming ministers on the difference between continuing to be a part of the Single Market and merely having a limited free trade agreement with the EU along the lines of the one Canada has. So far the debate over this has been infantile. Slippery and ambiguous phrases like "access to the Single Market" are bandied around as if they were absolute truths. Of course the US has access to the Single Market. But they do not sell many cars there; and their banks (and Swiss ones too) have massive establishments in London so as to obtain the crucial Single Market passport. Of course Japan has access to the Single Market. But their car companies have made huge investments in Britain because we are a gateway into the Single Market and provide tariff and non-tariff barrier free involvement in the trade in components. If the outcome of that analysis is that it is strongly in the national interest to remain part of the Single Market, then at least we will know where to start the negotiation.

On foreign policy issues ranging from economic sanctions to global climate change negotiations, the risk is that Britain will become a "me too" country, waiting outside the door until the EU has made up its mind on a particular course of action, or until the EU, the US and China have cut a deal, and then just falling into line.

It will not be easy to avoid that major loss of influence; and it will not be possible at all if we nurture the illusion that we can remain part of the EU's decision-making structure while being outside the organisation. There will need to be a good deal of goodwill and flexibility shown by both sides; which is one reason for stopping loose talk about encouraging a revolution in the EU or even its break up.

And thirdly there is the need to strengthen, and not to scrap, our cooperation in the fight against international crime, whether it be terrorism, cybercrime or human trafficking. It was only two years ago that our own parliament voted by overwhelming majorities in both Houses, that it was in the national interest to retain our full involvement in the European Arrest Warrant, in Europol and in many other law enforcement activities of the EU. Once again, as with foreign policy cooperation, it will not be straightforward to maintain those policy commitments when we cease to be a member; but it should not be impossible given the mutual interest in doing so between the EU and ourselves.

The gap between the benefits from full EU membership and those from an external relationship with those three components will still be wide. But without them it will be a yawning one.

And a more detailed article on the foreign policy implications appeared on 15th August, 2016:

UK faces uphill battle to retain foreign policy relevance.

One can already hear the protests from ministers and senior officials disputing the fact that Britain's influence on the major foreign policy issues of the day has been diminished by the 23 June vote to leave the EU. The mantra runs something like this - fifth largest economy in the world, Permanent Member of the UN Security Council, member of the G 20 and the G 7, leading member of NATO, what rubbish to suggest that our role in shaping foreign policy has in any way been adversely affected.

And that is about where the story ends, as if such international status symbols were like a row of silver cups on a shelf which one shows to visitors to demonstrate how important one is (or once was). But foreign policy influence is not just about the clubs to which one belongs - although that does matter - but also about a country's ability to shape the decisions which are taken collectively within those clubs. For the last 40 years Britain's influence within them has been enhanced and multiplied by the fact that it was at the same time a key player in the EU and had a capacity to make its voice heard in Washington. Both parts of that equation have been undermined, perhaps destroyed, by the decision to leave the EU. Take as an example Britain's permanent membership of the UN Security Council. It is not axiomatic that that position bestows great influence on the holder of it. Chiang Kai Shek's China was a permanent member for more than two decades and was not notably influential. Britain could easily become a "me too" member of all these clubs, waiting for deals to be struck between more powerful members of them and then falling in behind.

What can be done then to avoid falling into a situation where that mantra is trotted out to convince ourselves that we still matter but no one else believes it or treats us as a significant player? Well one remedy to be avoided is deliberately to stake out positions which are different from those of our principal Western allies, the US and the EU. That was General de Gaulle's remedy and over time it brought nothing but friction and marginalisation. Cosying up to the two major authoritarian powers, China and Russia will bring few, if any, dividends and would be a betrayal of our values and of our interest in promoting a rules-based international community. The Commonwealth, valuable though its links are, is not a viable entity in terms of power politics and will not become one just because we want it to. So we end up almost where we began, attempting to reconstruct an intimate foreign policy relationship with our erstwhile EU partners and to operate effectively in Washington, albeit from less promising platforms than we had before.

It could be that can be made to work. It would be easier if the Foreign Secretary had not, during the referendum campaign, damaged his chances of being credited with integrity and professionalism. But in the end the big foreign policy decisions are likely to be taken by the Prime Minister, who does have those two essential qualities. It will however be an uphill battle - and, do not forget, an unnecessary one.

The implications of Brexit for the union of the United Kingdom were spelled out in an article on 16th August, 2016 which identified for the first time after the June vote the salience, and the extreme complexity, of the issues relating to trade and movement both between the two parts of the island of Ireland and between both parts of Ireland

and Great Britain, an issue which was to bedevil the negotiations for withdrawal and for a future UK/EU relationship in the years which lay ahead and which still do so at the time of writing:

Did electorate really vote for break-up of the UK?

It's time to take the debate about the unity of the United Kingdom a bit more seriously. During the pre-referendum debates the consequences of the vote for the future unity of the United Kingdom itself were generally treated, if they were considered at all, in a cursory and superficial manner. Brexiters dismissed any such discussion as a mere extension of Project Fear and refused to engage. The complexities of the situation in Northern Ireland were such that virtually none of the protagonists was prepared to weigh them up; no representative of Northern Ireland (nor for that matter of Wales) was present on the platform at Wembley. If this was democracy British style, it was a pretty odd form of it.

Now all that has changed. Both Scotland and Northern Ireland have voted to remain in the EU in proportions which have handsomely exceeded those of the overall vote in favour of leaving. These are simple democratic facts that cannot be wished away and which create a fundamental contradiction. To refuse even to consider the implications of those two votes, simply to charge ahead into the Brexit negotiations waving a fatuous banner inscribed "Brexit means Brexit" would be the height of irresponsibility. Saying that does not entail claiming that either Scotland or Northern Ireland has a veto over those negotiations. They do not. But they do have a right for their specific interests to be given full weight in determining the overall UK position.

The case of Scotland is perhaps the simpler of the two. The impetus the contradictory votes over EU membership has given for a second independence referendum is obvious. The likelihood that a Scotland that voted for independence would be welcomed in Brussels as an EU member, for all the grumbling from Madrid, has improved. But whether or not the Scots (in effect the SNP) decide to chance their arm again in the face of the considerable economic and other disadvantages of independence will surely be influenced by the nature and content of the UK's relationship with the EU post-Brexit. A relationship which involves the loss of all the benefits for the individual of EU membership and, in addition, results in limits on immigration from the EU and in customs controls and non-tariff barriers and perhaps even, if the UK ends up with the WTO option, tariffs on trade between Scotland and the EU, could well tip the balance towards another independence referendum and make it winnable.

The equation in Northern Ireland is even more complex. If there were to be controls on immigration into the UK from the EU it is not easy to see how the Common Travel Area with Ireland can be sustained and controls between the two parts of Ireland or between the whole of Ireland and the rest of the UK can be avoided. A customs border may be needed too. But re-imposing that border is not just a minor, technical tweak; it would be a step fraught with adverse political consequences for the future of the province. And so would be the disappearance of the whole panoply of EU Justice and Home Affairs cooperation, including the European Arrest Warrant, which has done so much to de-politicise law enforcement cooperation between the two parts of the island. No doubt it is considerations such as these which have led the Northern Ireland First Minister who *campaigned for Leave to raise the alarm over the risks of Brexit.*

Given the fact that remaining in the EU is, for the moment, not a viable option, the simplest way of minimising the damage of Brexit to the unity of the UK is to base any new relationship on maintenance of the EU's four freedoms. To state flatly, from the outset, that this is unthinkable because the rather skimpy majority for leaving was heavily motivated by concerns over immigration, is to risk ending up with a judgement that controls on immigration are of more value than avoiding the break-up of the United Kingdom. Is that really the view of the electorate?

The second short term objective, persuading the government to make a generous, unilateral offer on the status of EU citizens in the UK, brought together an unexpected alliance of Brexiters and pro-Europeans. But it was no more successful than the first. The government dithered and prevaricated, arguing that it would be wrong to make an unilateral offer without reciprocity for UK citizens in other EU countries (despite the groups representing Britons elsewhere in the EU saying that a unilateral offer would be the best way to unlock their own status); and finally launched a fruitless effort to do a deal ahead of the start of the Article 50 negotiations despite having been warned by the EU 27 that a deal on a complex issue like this could not be settled ahead of the withdrawal negotiations themselves. An InFacts article on 1st December, 2016 tells the tale:

Fiasco over right to remain can be repaired.

If the government's tactical handling of this week's botched attempt to settle the issue of the "acquired rights" of EU citizens currently living and working in the UK and of our citizens currently living and working in the other member states ahead of the negotiations for withdrawal is anything to go by, then we have plenty to worry about when the negotiations get under way next spring. Our national team at the Brexit ministry have shown themselves to be a bunch of amateurs. They have discovered the hard way that you can tot up a lot of "yeses" in EU capitals and still get a "no" in Brussels, particularly if you fail to square the capital of the member state which mattes the most in today's EU, Berlin.

Was this miserable outcome predictable? Entirely so. After all the EU had warned us in July that no aspect of the withdrawal negotiations could be settled ahead of the triggering of Article 50; and we had chosen ourselves, quite justifiably, to postpone that decision until the spring of 2017. That warning had been repeated any number of times since then. We chose to ignore it.

Was this fiasco unavoidable? Certainly not. We had ourselves largely created the problem we tried to resolve by hinting, not very subtly, that the status and rights of those four million or more citizens spread across Europe was a matter for negotiation. Liam Fox had said as much at the time of the Conservative Party conférence in October. Not surprisingly those hints created a lot of anxiety and alarm.

Having created the problem unilaterally, we could have taken a large step towards resolving it in the same way. All that was needed was a unilateral UK statement that we did not intend for our part to take any steps to question or reduce the acquired rights of EU citizens in the UK so long as our citizens in other member states were treated similarly. This approach was put to the government several times in recent exchanges in the House of Lords. They chose to ignore it. Such a unilateral statement would have engendered a considerable amount of goodwill across Europe and possibly plenty of matching statements. It would not have settled the matter there and then; but it would have ensured that, when negotiations do begin next spring, there was a good chance that it would be settled at an early stage.

Would such a unilateral statement have prejudiced the chances of British citizens across Europe getting a fair deal? It would not. It would actually have made it more likely they would get one by making it clear that any action by other member states to deprive them of their rights, of which there has in any case so far been no sign, would invalidate our own unilateral statement.

Is the situation now irretrievable? Probably not. If the government makes clear its own approach to the problem in the terms set out above, it should be possible to reduce people's anxiety and to get the eventual negotiations off on the right foot when they start next spring. But, if the government chooses to sulk and to exchange ill-tempered accusations of responsibility across the Channel, then a bad situation will only be made worse. And a negotiation, which will need a lot of goodwill if it is not to descend into acrimony, will get under way under the worst of auspices.

*   *   *

While Theresa May's support in the opinion polls rose steadily in her early months as Prime Minister (assisted in all probability by the re-election of Jeremy Corbyn to the leadership of the Labour Party), she began to make a whole series of strategic and tactical errors which were to characterise her handling of Brexit from beginning to end. It all began with an attachment to gnomic and metronomically repeated mantras of which "Brexit means Brexit" was the first and "no deal is better than a bad deal" came to be the most often used. The first major errors were made in her speech to the Conservative Party Conference in October 2016. On that occasion, without apparently having consulted her cabinet, she set her face against any possibility of remaining in the EU's Single Market and Customs Union and began the demonization of the European Court of Justice which greatly complicated the negotiations which lay ahead. It was in this speech that she used the aggressively negative phrase "citizens of nowhere" to describe legal immigrants who had come to the UK, including those who had come under the free movement provisions of the EU Treaty. From that point on she was on course for a "hard Brexit". My own reaction to that is set out in an InFacts article on 26th October, 2016:

Accentuate the positive ahead of the Brexit talks.

So far every indication which has seeped out of the government machine preparing for the Brexit negotiations, every reply by ministers in Parliament, the Prime Minister's speech to her party conference, have been unremittingly negative. No to free movement of people. No to any jurisdiction of the European Court of Justice. No to any continuing role for the Commission. No to staying in the Single Market or the Customs

111

Union. No to giving Parliament a proper say in the decision to trigger Article 50 and on our opening negotiating position.

This litany of negativism is tactically and strategically misguided and doomed to repeat the mistakes made by the government in the period preceding the June referendum. It is tactically misguided because it provokes an equal and opposite reaction from the 27 member states and the EU institutions, with whom we will be negotiating, before the negotiations even begin. Listen to the recent statements of Hollande and Merkel if you do not believe that. Moreover, it closes off pre-emptively any number of elements of a new external relationship between the UK and the EU which could be in the UK's wider economic interest before there has even been a chance to discuss them.

It is strategically misguided because, by creating an atmosphere of adversarial confrontation, it will make it far more difficult for the government to gain public and parliamentary support for the compromises that will need to be struck and for the degree of continuing cooperation in a range of fields which it will be in our interest to secure. Look for example at internal and external security - and the distinction between the two is less and less meaningful. Are we really contemplating walking away from the whole network of law enforcement machinery and cooperation which has been built up in recent years to combat the threats from terrorism, illegal immigration, drugs, human trafficking, child pornography, cybercrime and much else? Are we going to scrap our membership of Europol and Eurojust, of the European Arrest Warrant, the Schengen Information Service and the Passenger Name Recognition arrangements for air travel? Or, are we going to seek to build these instruments, which were recognised as being essential to our own security and which were endorsed by massive majorities in both Houses of Parliament as recently as 2014, into whatever new relationship we negotiate?

Look too at external security where the EU's soft power instruments are an essential matching element to NATO's hard power. Are we going to walk away from the EU's anti-piracy operations off the Horn of Africa or its operations against illegal immigration in the Mediterranean? Are we going to withdraw from its stabilisation efforts in the Balkans and Ukraine? Are we going to put at risk the commitments for combatting climate change which the EU entered into at the Paris conference last December? Are we going to abandon our joint approach to a whole range of human rights abuses around the world? Or are we going to try to establish the closest possible working arrangements between us to enable all those endeavours to be continued and enhanced in the years ahead?

The answers to all these questions are obvious. But they need to be brought out into the open and actively advocated. If the government just goes on feeding morsels of negative rhetoric to make their more extreme anti-European supporters happy, it will prove that much more difficult to get broad support for a more positive agenda. The Prime Minister's appeal in Brussels this week for a more positive approach to the Brexit negotiations was welcome. But, without specifics, generalities like that will have little influence either on her backbenchers or on her EU partners. What is needed is to put some flesh on the bones of policy fields where we want to go on working with the EU in the closest partnership obtainable.

*   *   *

In those same early months, the government picked a completely unnecessary quarrel over whether or not it was legally empowered to trigger Article 50 using the royal prerogative or whether it required parliamentary authority to do so. The quarrel was an unnecessary one because there was never the slightest doubt that Parliament would authorise the triggering of Article 50 (as it subsequently did in March 2017). The government lost the case in both the Court of Appeal and the Supreme Court, following some compelling advocacy by David Pannick, one of the small group of cross-benchers with whom I worked closely following the referendum (and also as a result of arguing that triggering Article 50 was irrevocable - which a later case brought before the European Court of Justice ruled it was not!). The government's two defeats in the courts led to a huge, and quite disgraceful, outpouring of rage among Brexiters and the tabloid press. My own view was contained in an InFacts article of 4th November 2016 after the ruling in the Court of Appeal:

Judgement unleashes Brexiter vitriol against MPs scrutiny.

It should surely be welcomed that the High Court has upheld that we are a representative parliamentary democracy where parliament has the final say, and has confirmed that we have not suddenly switched to a fully-fledged plebiscitary form of government. After all Brexiters said they were campaigning to leave the EU in order for our own parliament to recover its sovereignty.

With its decision to appeal to the Supreme Court, it was a pity the government was not able to accept the High Court ruling and press on with drawing up a document setting out its approach to the Brexit negotiations as a basis for it to seek parliamentary authorisation for triggering Article 50. Instead the government will waste another month or more fending off the probably inevitable need to give Parliament a say in the Article 50 decision.

In January 2017 Ivan Rogers, the UK Permanent Representative to the EU (and, incidentally, my sixth successor since I left Brussels in 1990) resigned; and he made quite a splash of it since his lengthy, and forensically pretty devastating, communication to his staff not too mysteriously found its way into the press. Rogers was clearly an angry man, and he had plenty to be angry about, his advice on the handling of Article 50 having clearly been systematically ignored. Did he jump just before he was pushed? Quite possibly. I did not know him at all well, but the one, long conversation we had, in the run-up to re-negotiation, had left me with a feeling that he was about the most Eeyore-ish individual I had ever come across. And experience had taught me that most ministers prefer a "can do" attitude to that of Eeyore. But his advice, which was to not trigger Article 50 until the government had a clear game plan of the divorce arrangements and the new, external relationship with the EU it wanted, was spot on. After his resignation Rogers surfaced from time to time to give lengthy, dense and often brilliant exegeses of what was wrong with the government's negotiating strategy (or, more often, lack of one). These critiques might have been more effective if he had occasionally said what he thought the government should be doing or if he had come off the fence on whether things had gone so badly wrong that a route to withdrawing the Article 50 notification was now the best option; but he did neither. Rogers was replaced by Tim Barrow, previously Ambassador in Moscow, a competent professional diplomat whose previous experience of the EU had been largely confined to foreign and security policy, a field in which the game was played by different rules to those applying to Article 50. There is no evidence that he had either a significant negotiating or advisory role in the period ahead. Indeed, the fact that he was still there on the day we left the EU at the end of January 2020 rather indicated the contrary.

By the beginning of 2017, as it became ever clearer that the government was going to lose its case in the Supreme Court, and as the need to get parliamentary authority through primary legislation before it could trigger Article 50, the pressure to set out its opening position became stronger. And in mid-January Theresa May did precisely that with her Lancaster House speech. This speech, far from demonstrating a more flexible and open-minded approach than her party conference speech the preceding October, painted the red lines ever more clearly and was a lot fuller of negatives than positives - no to the Single Market and the Customs Union, no to any jurisdiction of the ECJ and a first outing for the "no deal is better than a bad deal" mantra. Conciliatory it was not; it was a further prescription for a hard Brexit. If anything, its main effect on the EU 27 was to firm up their own negotiating position in an unhelpful way. My reaction was set out in an InFacts article on 23rd January, 2017:

May's Lancaster House speech no better on second look.

It is usually wise to take a second look at any important policy statement and that is certainly true of the Prime Minister's Lancaster House speech which is being hailed by the advocates of leaving as little short of the Sermon on the Mount in its significance. That second look reveals plenty of ambiguities and even internal contradictions; and some hard questions over the choice of priorities.

Was it really wise to give absolute priority to the introduction of immigration controls, as yet undefined, and to rule out from the outset remaining in the Single Market or the EU's Customs Union? By so doing the Prime Minister appears to have discarded the two options which most economic analysts agree would do least damage to the UK's manufacturing and service exports.

And then there is the continued flirtation with the slippery concept contained in the words "access to the EU's single market", the one which takes 44% of our exports. But this is not a single concept at all. There is access under WTO rules which is what the US currently enjoys. Your goods pay tariffs, have to be subjected to EU regulatory controls and go through costly and bureaucratic customs clearance checks. It is precisely to avoid all that that the US has been negotiating with the EU a transatlantic trade and investment deal and that American and other foreign financial institutions are so well represented in London.

Then there is privileged or preferential access to the Single Market which is what the Norwegians, the Swiss and the Canadians (the latter two without much access for services) enjoy; which exempts them from tariffs and regulatory controls but not all the customs clearance

117

checks. And thirdly there is being in the Single Market which is where we presently are. To treat these three widely different options as if they were one is either to misunderstand or to mislead.

Amidst all the sound and fury about escaping from the tutelage of the European Court of Justice it seems to be being totally overlooked that any new relationship of the scope and complexity of what is being envisaged with the EU will inevitably require international arbitration procedures to handle disputes. Not a word about that in the speech.

For those, like myself, who were trying to follow the evolution of the government's thinking on the handling of the forthcoming Article 50 negotiations and, if at all possible to influence it, this was an intensely frustrating period. Parliament was effectively ignored as the Supreme Court case played out; and the tiny circle of those around the Prime Minister, who one assumed were shaping policy, gave nothing away; as to the Prime Minister herself there was an increasing suspicion that she was, as Disraeli was once accused of being, "a sphynx without a secret". A lunch group of former European officials, civil servants and diplomats, to which I belonged, did have a useful lunch and discussion with Ollie Robbins; this left us impressed by his knowledge and grasp of the subject but none the wiser as to the government's direction of travel.

One member of the government's door always remained open to us and that was George Bridges', the DexEu minister in the House of Lords who had the thankless task of fending off questions and making bricks without straw. John Kerr and I met him and his officials on several occasions and were able to discuss the realities which lay behind the mantras. Prominent amongst these realities was a typically nitty-gritty Brussels tactical trap which was beginning to emerge from the EU 27's shaping of their opening position (of which, typically, much more was known than about ours). This trap was whether the negotiations to be opened in the late spring of 2017 should, as the EU 27 were planning to insist, be sequential, with the whole withdrawal agreement package being settled up front before any consideration was given to the future UK/EU relationship or to any transitional arrangements which might be needed, or whether the two sets of negotiations should be run concurrently. The text of Article 50 could be, and was, construed in either way. But the hard political facts behind the legal squabbling were that sequencing was advantageous to the EU 27 since the short-term objectives they minded most about - the UK's budget contributions, the status of their citizens in the UK, and the problems raised by the border in Ireland - would be settled before the negotiations moved onto the transition and more potentially divisive topics covered by the future relationship. For the UK the calculation was the opposite, although the citizens' status issue could and should have been taken out of the equation by a unilateral British offer. John Kerr and I were of the view that the sequencing issue was a crucially important choice, and Bridges and his officials were broadly in agreement. But, when we suggested that the government's main (perhaps only), leverage lay in threatening to delay the end-March triggering date until the EU 27 agreed that the two sets of negotiations should be concurrent, we hit a brick wall. Clearly the date was sacrosanct, being the thing the

119

government's Brexiter supporters minded about most, since it also set a date two years later for the UK actually to leave the EU. We would no doubt have been less encouraged by the common ground over sequencing v. concurrence had we known what was revealed at the time of Bridges' resignation following the 2017 general election that he had only seen the Prime Minister once, very briefly, during his year in office at DexEu.

The arguments over sequencing v. concurrence were set out in two InFacts articles, the first on 21st November, 2016 and the second on 23rd January, 2017. Here they are:

Fog in the Channel.

Meanwhile the preparations in Brussels and other European capitals for the two major Brexit negotiations which lie ahead - one on the terms of withdrawal, the other on the terms of the EU's new relationship with the UK - are not moving in a direction which is likely to produce the sort of positive and constructive outcome which all concerned with limiting the damage from this geopolitical upheaval would like to see. Quite the contrary.

The situation in Brussels may be less chaotic than in London - it could hardly be more so - but it is tending towards a lowest common denominator of the defence of national interests. Moreover the election of Donald Trump has now shifted Brexit down another notch in the ordering of priorities for our EU negotiating partners.

Brussels being Brussels the emphasis there is as much on process as on substance. But, as always, process has a habit of shaping substance. So the suggestion that

120

the two major Brexit negotiations should be rigidly sequential and not concurrent, with the time-limited withdrawal negotiations being completed before those on the new relationship begin, needs careful and urgent scrutiny. This idea, which has considerable support, looks a bad idea for all concerned.

For one thing it is hard to reconcile such an approach with the actual wording of Article 50 which says that the terms of withdrawal need to take account of the future relationship with the EU of the withdrawing member state. How on earth can a deal on withdrawal take account of a future relationship which has not yet begun to be discussed, let alone settled?

Moreover a sequential approach will greatly complicate the construction of any kind of interim or transitional regime, which is all too likely to be needed to bridge the gap between the two years provided for the divorce proceedings and the longer time needed to settle all the details of Britain's new relationship with the EU. Any transitional arrangement needs two questions to be answered: "From what?" and "To what?" If the second question cannot be answered, then you are trying to build a bridge without firm ground at one end. That does not usually work well. And since the withdrawal negotiation is certain to be an adversarial and zero-sum affair, to insist that it should be completed ahead of the new relationship negotiations is a recipe for a bad outcome for both.

So the sooner this bad idea is taken out and interred the better for everyone who wants to see Britain playing an effective and constructive role in the future of Europe. That objective would be a good deal easier to achieve if our government were to demonstrate in specifics as well as generalities that such a role is indeed what it aspires to.

And the second article read as follows:

> *In Brussels-based negotiations procedural choices are often as important as substantive ones. The issue of whether the two sets of negotiations - one over divorce, the other over the new, external relationship between the UK and the EU - are to be concurrent or consecutive (as the Commission wishes) is one such. Explaining quietly and without fanfare in other EU capitals why concurrent negotiations would be in our mutual interest and why consecutive negotiations would sharply reduce the chances of a successful outcome should be a high priority. It is hardly rocket science to calculate that the divorce negotiations will be adversarial and will cause a lot of anger in the UK, with no counter-balancing benefits, while the new relationship negotiations present a real opportunity to strike mutually beneficial deals.*

* * *

As soon as the Supreme Court had ruled that parliamentary authority was required before triggering Article 50 the government tabled a minimalist Bill providing that authority. The Bill passed the Commons with a huge majority, far bigger than the government's overall superiority, since the Labour Party supported it, leaving only the SNP, the Liberal Democrats, a few smaller parties and one solitary Conservative, Ken Clarke, voting against it. Passage through the Lords was a great deal slower (because the legislative timetable there cannot be guillotined) and more complicated. There was, however, never any question of the Lords either seeking to block the

Bill or to put at risk the government's proclaimed objective of triggering Article 50 by the end of March.

There were two main amendments moved (and carried) in the Lords. The first sought to lay down a proper parliamentary process for approving any deal struck with the EU The Prime Minister had provided something in her Lancaster House speech (speaking rather oddly of approval in both Houses, a formulation which took no account of the primacy of the Commons) but since then there had been silence from the government and nothing was provided in the Bill. So the case for setting out the parliamentary process to be followed if and when a deal was struck with the EU 27 was strong, all the more so when George Bridges, replying to a question about what would happen in the event of no deal being struck by the time of the two-year cut-off date in Article 50, said that in those circumstances the government would make a statement to Parliament. The second amendment required the government, within three months, to put forward a full, detailed offer for dealing with the status of EU citizens in the UK.

It was during the passage of this Bill that, for the first time, an informal, cross-party group to plan tactics and agree draft amendments was constituted. The group was broadly composed as follows: Angela Smith, Labour and Opposition Leader, Dianne Hayter, Labour Brexit spokesperson, Denis Tunnicliffe, Labour Whip. Dick Newby, Leader of the Liberal Democrats, Ben Stoneham, Liberal Democrat Chief Whip, Sarah Ludford, Liberal Democrat Brexit spokesperson, Peter Bowness, Douglas Hailsham and Ros Altmann, Conservatives opposing their

123

party's three-line whip, and John Kerr, David Pannick, David Anderson and myself from the Cross-Benches. For the next two and a half years this group met regularly whenever there was Brexit-related business before the House and worked harmoniously together to present a united front. Were there tensions within the group? Of course there were. For one thing the Liberal Democrats were already publicly supporting the holding of a further referendum on any deal the government struck, while the Labour Party only came to that view very late in the day, in 2019, and then quite ambiguously. Several of the Conservatives and Cross-Benchers shared the Liberal Democrat view. But we worked successfully to play down such tensions in debates and to avoid the sniping which so often handicaps cross-party alliances over legislation. We also did our best to keep in step with developments in the Commons, working closely in particular with Keir Starmer, the Labour front bench Brexit spokesperson and with Dominic Grieve, the former Attorney-General who gradually emerged as the leading figure among the Conservative rebels.

The Lords, after lengthy and pretty tempestuous debate, passed the two amendments by large majorities, and they duly went back to the Commons. I wrote three articles for InFacts commending them - on 10th February, and on 3rd and 9th March. Here they are:

Keep calm, Commons.

Now that the government's Article 50 Bill has passed in the Commons without amendment, it goes along the corridor to the House of Lords which will give it a

124

second reading on 20/21 February. A number of Brexiters have shifted from heavy breathing to frothing at the mouth at the prospect that the Lords might reject or amend the Bill. An unnamed government source is quoted in The Times as saying "if the Lords think they can play God, then the public will call for them to be abolished".

A bit over the top you might think; but no doubt it has been a stressful week in the Commons. The best advice to them is to calm down.

There has never, since June 23rd, been the slightest chance that the Lords would throw out a Bill authorising the government to trigger Article 50. If the government had not taken us all on a long and fruitless meander through the thickets of the royal prerogative and the Supreme Court, it could have had the green light from Parliament long ago.

In any case the Lords do not, as a general rule, reject government bills; they scrutinise them and, if there is a majority for that, they ask the Commons to think again on specific and limited amendments. Since every government bill that reaches the Lords from the Commons has, by definition, been approved by the elected house, to deny the possibility of amendment in the Lords would amount to abolishing the Lords here and now.

So what sort of amendments will be discussed when the Committee and Report stages are taken at the end of this month? There may be attempts to call for a second referendum or to tie the government's hands in the negotiations which are about to begin. It is doubtful whether this sort of amendment will get very far.

There will also be more important amendments dealing with process: to require the government to report regularly to Parliament ; to ensure that, if and when a deal is struck with the EU on either the divorce

125

settlement or the new partnership, or when a decision is taken to break off negotiations, it is submitted to both Houses for approval in a timely and meaningful fashion and at least as soon as it is submitted to the European Parliament; and to insist that the government re-assure EU citizens already living and working here that their right to do so will not be revoked.

Would any of these amendments be unreasonable? Surely not. Nor would any of them be justifiably described as wrecking amendments. Would any of them prevent the triggering of Article 50 by the end of March as the government wishes. Certainly not.

If we are to get through the next two years or more without inflicting even more damage on ourselves than is already being done by the original decision to leave the EU, there really is a need for calm and civility in the national discourse around the whole Brexit issue. Otherwise bad decisions will be taken and we will use up more energy negotiating with ourselves than in negotiating with our 27 EU partners.

And then this one on citizens' rights:

Why MPs should not overturn Lords' amendment on EU citizens.

On Wednesday the House of Lords, in the biggest vote since it was debating its own future composition in 1999 and by an unusually large three figure majority, asked the government to think again about how best to safeguard the rights of nationals from other EU member states living and working here after Brexit. The government was asked to guarantee those rights of its own free will as it opens negotiations for Britain's withdrawal from the EU.

126

You might have thought the case being advanced would be given some sober consideration. But you would be wrong. The government instantly announced that it would seek to reverse the amendment in the Commons. And the Eurosceptic press proceeded as usual to play the man (or woman) and not the ball. Articles about which members of the House of Lords receive EU pensions; expressions of contempt for former ministers; criticism of an unelected House by unelected journalists. Hardly a word about the rights and wrongs of relieving from uncertainty several million EU citizens who boost our economy, contribute to our well-being and are at risk of being deprived of rights which they had every reason to believe would be theirs in perpetuity when they first came here.

What does the amendment passed by the Lords not do? Well, it does not delay the triggering of Article 50 beyond the government's deadline of the end of this month. Nor does it attempt to define how the rights of those citizens are to be safeguarded; it merely requires the government to bring forward proposals to that effect within three months.

Does it mean that the cause of our own citizens living in other EU countries has been abandoned or given a lower priority? It does not. If it did, how can one explain why all the civil society groups standing up for our citizens in countries across Europe urged the Lords to pass the amendment, regarding it as the best possible way to ensure that the governments of other member states match our approach, and the best way to avoid those rights becoming bargaining chips in the negotiations about to begin? For what it is worth, speaking as one who has had a certain amount to do with European negotiations over the years, I believe that judgement is right. The transactional approach favoured by the government seems to me fraught with the risk that citizens on both sides will indeed, possibly inadvertently, become bargaining chips. And it will likely mean a much longer delay, perhaps two years before the uncertainty hanging over their daily lives will be lifted.

Meanwhile those uncertainties are already depriving us of doctors, carers, academics and those working in sectors of the economy where no home grown labour is available, as they slip away back to their own countries or elsewhere in the EU where they know they will be treated with more generosity.

The issues at stake here are therefore not simply moral ones, although those considerations are quite compelling. They relate too to the way in which these extremely complex and difficult negotiations get under way. Do we emphasise from the outset that the overall objective is mutual benefit or do we head off down a path that is all too likely to lead to mutually assured damage to all concerned?

And here is the third in the series:

This is about Parliament's sovereignty not about thwarting Brexit.

It might seem odd that the government is so determined to reject the amendment which sets out in the Article 50 Bill the necessary steps for parliament to approve any divorce settlement with the EU or any new partnership agreement, given that the Prime Minister promised in her Lancaster House speech that the government would put the final Brexit deal to a vote in both Houses of Parliament - a position repeated in its White Paper.

Yet, within minutes of the vote, it had vowed to reject the amendment. And it appears to be allocating just one hour next Monday to debating and voting on each of the Lords' two amendments - which involve the well-being of three million European citizens living and working here and the proper functioning of that parliamentary sovereignty for which the Brexiters campaigned to take back control.

What is there not to like about the latest amendment? Well, it certainly does not slow down the triggering of Article 50. Indeed the Bill could become law instantly on Monday if the government accepted the amendment.

Is it because promising votes in both Houses risks ending in deadlock, with one House approving the deal and the other rejecting it? Well, if that is a risk, it is one entirely of the Prime Minister's own making since she originally set out the formula in her Lancaster House speech. But it is not a real risk because the government is free to seek approval for a deal through primary legislation, which ensures the primacy of the House of Commons.

Is it then because the amendment requires the government to seek parliamentary approval before walking away from any attempt to negotiate a deal at all and thus crashing out of the EU without one? The Prime Minister has referred to that as a possibility, so it cannot be discounted. But, if such action can be carried through without parliamentary authority, where then is the recovery of parliamentary sovereignty?

The government has said that the amendment would drastically weaken the Prime Minister's negotiating hand and result in our EU partners offering us a really bad deal with the aim of getting the referendum decision and the triggering of Article 50 reversed. The people using that argument are the same ones who, a few weeks ago, were confidently asserting that we had an incomparably strong negotiating hand because our EU partners were so keen on selling us BMWs, Prosecco and Camemberts.

129

In any case it is a perfectly sustainable argument that provisions for parliamentary approval like those in the amendment would in fact strengthen the Prime Minister's negotiating hand. After all, Article 50 itself lays down the provision for parliamentary approval of any deal on the EU side and nobody seems to think that that is weakening its hand. It really would make sense for the Brexiters to get over their paranoia about EU intentions and accept that the amendments will strengthen our negotiating hand, not weaken it.

None of this was of any avail at the time since the government's majority held firm in the Commons and the Lords did not insist on their amendments. But the seeds of two crucial future debates were sown, one that of what came to be called a "meaningful" parliamentary process of approval for any deal and the other that of the parliamentary handling of a "no deal" eventuality. We were to hear plenty about both of those over the next two and a half years. In the meanwhile, the Article 50 process was triggered in Brussels on 29th March.

*   *   *

As a post-script to all this I also wrote an article on 22nd March 2017 about the extremely precarious situation of Gibraltar as a result of the Leave campaign's success in overriding Gibraltar's 97% majority in favour of Remain:

Brexiters casually threw Gibraltar under their battle bus.

Last night's debate in the House of Lords on the implications of Brexit for Gibraltar brought no surprises; and not the slightest indication of how the government plans to mitigate the potentially pretty damaging consequences for Gibraltar flowing from the UK's exit and its decision to walk away too from the Single Market, which underpins Gibraltar's successful economy. Just a lot of wishful thinking and the usual "It will be alright on the night" talk.

Gibraltar's status within the EU for the last 40 years has been as near to a "Goldilocks" situation as you could get - outside the Customs Union, spared the need to introduce VAT, inside the world's biggest single market and with its disputed border with Spain kept open by EU law. No wonder 97% of Gibraltarians voted to Remain in last June's referendum.

More surprisingly, perhaps, was the fact that many of Gibraltar's most vociferous supporters in Parliament were out there campaigning for Leave. Either they did not know what they were doing when they threw Gibraltar under the wheels of that infamous battle bus; or they did know, in which case their disloyalty is truly shameful.

Because the risks for Gibraltar from the Brexit negotiations are real. It cannot remain within the EU because it is umbilically (and democratically) linked to the UK. Its border with Spain will become an external frontier of the EU which means that EU law will not apply to those crossing it in the same way as before. If Britain leaves without a deal, then so too will Gibraltar. And every detail of any deal that is negotiated will have to be agreed by Spain.

As the unintended consequences of Brexit unfold, the fate of Gibraltar's economy will probably not trouble the sleep of many British voters. But it should do. They broke it; and now we, all of us, own it.

Chapter 8

Trench warfare: the divorce settlement (2017)

On a fine, sunny morning in April 2017, I was sitting in the Café des Voyageurs et des Touristes in St. Céré (a small market town in the south-west French *départment* of the Lot) sipping an espresso and scrolling through the BBC news items (my own house, up in the nearby hills around the village of Frayssinhes, not then having an internet connection). Out of the blue, the BBC switched to a familiar sight, the pavement outside N° 10 Downing Street and a small podium, unusually without the royal coat of arms on it. That could mean only one thing; we were going to have a snap general election just two years after the last one. Sure enough, a minute or two later and Theresa May emerged to reveal that, on an Easter walking holiday in Snowdonia, she had decided that an early election was needed to give her a decisive majority for the Brexit negotiations which were due to start within weeks and to ensure that Britain had, in the mantra of the moment to be repeated *ad nauseam*, a strong and stable government.

My own immediate reaction was downbeat. All the opinion polls were forecasting a substantially increased Conservative overall majority; and the government's plans for the Brexit negotiations, most recently spelled out in the

Article 50 triggering letter to Donald Tusk, the President of the European Council, on 29th March, seemed to me both defective and likely to lead to a bad outcome. My InFacts editor, Hugo Dixon, reacted more cheerfully, saying that this would provide a great opportunity to have the real debate about Brexit which had not occurred either during the referendum campaign more recently. I said I did not believe for one moment that that was what would actually happen. The Conservatives would simply camp on the approach set out in the Lancaster House speech, declining to develop it further on the grounds of not revealing our negotiating hand; and Labour would campaign on everything but Brexit, partly because they were themselves divided on the subject but also because of the calculation - correct as it turned out - that the electorate was more interested in other subjects like austerity, health and social care, and education. Unfortunately I was proved right on this occasion; and there was no serious debate about the Brexit negotiating options at any point during the campaign. InFacts continued publishing its two or three daily articles throughout, but not getting drawn into blatant party-political combat. My own contributions included a pre-election stock take on Brexit on 2nd May 2017:

Brexit talks so far: a catalogue of errors.

Well, now we know the positions of the two sides when the negotiations start. But we have no idea of the basis on which a deal will be struck - or even whether one will be reached at all given Theresa May's insistence that no deal would be better for Britain than a bad deal. And the chances of no deal have certainly not diminished as a result of last week's fraught Downing Street dinner (a reference to a May/Juncker dinner discussion, subsequently leaked to the press by Juncker's chief of staff, Martin Selmayr).

What's clear is that there is little in the guidelines adopted by the European Council on April 29 to gladden the hearts of those in the UK who really do want to establish a new, close, mutually beneficial partnership.

That it took only four minutes for the EU27 leaders to reach agreement last Saturday is trivial. That is always what happens at Council meetings when the conclusions have been negotiated in advance. It is also futile to muse about which galaxy the Prime Minister and the President of the Commission live in (another reference to that dinner table fracas).

What is more useful is to ask how a normally pretty fractious group such as the EU27, each with different national interests, managed to settle on an approach best described as a programme for a hard Brexit. The answer is glaringly obvious: because we made it so easy for them to do so.

Take trade, for example, on which so many businesses and livelihoods across Europe depend. Was it wise to discard, even before talks had begun, the possibility of Britain remaining in the Single Market or the Customs Union? Would it not have been more sensible to keep those two options on the table and compel the EU to respond? After all they both offer a way of avoiding the re-establishment of border controls between the two parts of Ireland which is an objective we share.

Was it wise, too, to give absolute priority over these trade issues to setting up new immigration controls which we have not yet defined and will be unable to describe when the Brexit negotiations open?

134

Then there is the issue of the status of EU *citizens* living and working in the UK and of British *citizens* in other member states. The government was urged time and again, in parliament and outside it, to make a unilateral commitment guaranteeing the rights of EU citizens here. Ministers refused on the specious grounds that this would be to abandon our compatriots living in the EU. They persisted even when the organisations representing those Britons said a unilateral UK pledge would be the best way of supporting them. With its guidelines the EU has now shown that view to be correct and has cheerfully occupied the moral high ground, leaving the UK to be drawn into messy, transactional talks which could well prolong the uncertainty hanging over everyone concerned.

And is demonising the European Court of Justice (ECJ) a useful way to open the negotiations? If the bargaining is to forge a new partnership of the sort Theresa May sketched out in her March 29 letter to Donald Tusk, it will inevitably require dispute settlement arrangements in which the ECJ will play an important role.

This certainly does not mean that the EU27 have made no errors of their own. It was pretty crass to leak the figure of €60 billion for the divorce bill before the two sides had even discussed the component parts of a settlement, let alone put figures to each one. And a rigid insistence that the divorce settlement must precede discussion of the shape of the new partnership could not only be contrary to Article 50 itself, which speaks of the first taking account of the second, but could well doom the negotiations to failure. Fortunately, the EU27 have left themselves some wiggle room by requiring only "sufficient progress" on the three priority divorce issues - which neither side disputes - before broadening out the talks.

135

So, not a great start. But there is a long way to go. A lot of flexibility will be needed on both sides to avoid a train wreck. Unfortunately the predominantly pro - Brexit UK press and their supporters in Parliament are already making clear that flexibility is the last thing they want the Prime Minister to show.

This was followed by an article on the Anglo-French relationship on 10th May, 2017 immediately after Emmanuel Macron's election as France's new President (about the only one of the electoral results in the period between 2015 and 2019 which I guessed more or less right - helped by having met Macron twice at the CER when he was a junior economics minister in Francois Hollande's administration and having been immediately struck by his brilliance and potential):

Stop looking at Macron through Brexit blinkers.

With Emmanuel Macron taking office this weekend, it is high time that we stopped looking at the new French President through Brexit blinkers. We may be obsessed by that topic; but he certainly is not, as he faces up to what he rightly called the "immense" task of championing reform in France and in the EU. Indeed he probably won't feel the need to play a particularly prominent role in the Brexit negotiations. After all a Frenchman, Michel Barnier, is in charge of the process on behalf of the EU27 and the French line in preparing these negotiations has already been as tough as Macron could wish it to be.

More profitable would be to consider Macron's likely approach as the ultimate shaper of French foreign and defence policy - because, like all presidents of the Fifth

Republic, that is what he will be. And consider too how the UK - as a fellow NATO ally and permanent member of the UN Security Council as well as of the G7 and the G20 - could work together even if the UK is no longer a member of the EU.

The auguries are encouraging. Based on what Macron has said, the new French President is clearly a liberal internationalist, committed to sustaining, and where possible strengthening, the rules-based international order which overall has brought such benefits since the end of the Second World War. He is a globalist, who is prepared to fight against the populist forces which favour a closed, protectionist, sometimes isolationist, approach to international affairs - and he won that encounter handsomely.

Macron was the only candidate in the French election who did not favour an immediate, unconditional rapprochement with President Vladimir Putin's Russia and the easing or lifting of economic sanctions. He is committed, like every other European leader, to the battle against terrorism, without slipping over into Islamophobia; and he will soon know what an effective contribution Britain makes and can continue to make to that battle. There are many other areas - climate change and human rights for example - where our views and his are likely to be close if not identical.

On defence the structures for cooperation are already there in the bilateral Lancaster House agreements negotiated by the Coalition government. But they are so far skimpily clad. Much more could be done if the political will was there to achieve it.

Should Britain be deterred by the emphasis President Macron is certainly going to put on strengthening European, especially Franco-German cooperation on security issues? No. Firstly because, now we are on our way out of the EU, there is nothing we can do to stop it.

Secondly because, if that helps Germany - which is responsible for by far the largest shortfall in achieving NATO's target for defence spending - to increase its efforts in the security field, that will be in our interest too.

No doubt there will be moments of difficulty and tension during the Brexit negotiations. Eurosceptics will be only too ready to turn that into the sort of Anglo-French food fight from which they get such satisfaction, even if it damages our national interests. Better surely to set Anglo-French cooperation off on the right foot and to remember there is much more at stake in working closely with France. We are the two European countries which can give meaning to strengthening European security.

*   *   *

On election night (8th June) I was dining with a young Californian friend, Alex Turkeltaub, and John Thornhill of the Financial Times. Both John and I, despite all the obvious weaknesses of Theresa May's campaign - the upset over the dementia tax and the Prime Minister's robotic performances on the campaign trail - were still predicting an overall Conservative majority of 50/60 seats. Imagine our surprise when the exit poll at 10.00 p.m. predicted (correctly) that there was going to be a hung parliament. Here is my InFacts article the following day (9th June) drawing some very preliminary conclusions so far as Brexit was concerned:

A time for cool heads on Brexit.

On the last day of campaigning in the general election Theresa May for the first time made a sensible comment

138

on Brexit in place of the mindless mantras with which the electorate has been being fed. "Brexit" she said "is the basis for everything else". She cannot at that time have envisaged the circumstances in which this precept would have to be given effect. But it remains as valid today in the aftermath of the election and with a hung parliament as the day it was uttered.

No doubt the electoral setback to the Conservatives has many other complex causes, but the election was quite explicitly called, three years earlier than necessary, in order to get a popular mandate for the Brexit negotiations scheduled to start on 19 June. That is what the Prime Minister asked for; and that is what she failed to get. So there is no mandate for the sort of hard Brexit set out in the January Lancaster House speech and in the 29 March letter to Donald Tusk. That approach is unlikely to command a majority in the new parliament. So to try to move ahead on that basis would surely be a travesty of the democratic process.

In the confused and unpredictable parliamentary situation that now exists, with the distinct possibility of another general election taking place before the expiry of the two-year Article 50 deadline, it would seem sensible to avoid trying to answer too many of the fundamental Brexit -related questions at once. Those who believe that any outcome to the negotiations should be submitted to a second referendum will continue to take that view. But there is no sense and no need to settle that now. We are at the beginning of the negotiations not near to their end . And a period of silence about the zany idea that no deal would be better than a bad deal would also be welcome.

What is needed is a more flexible, positive and open-minded approach than was previously envisaged. Why on earth try to rule out from the outset continued membership of the Single Market and the Customs

Union, particularly when either of those two frameworks would provide the most straightforward and effective way of avoiding re-imposing border controls in Ireland? Why splatter red lines about the jurisdiction of the European Court of Justice and about the absolute primacy of restrictions on the free movement of people which have yet to be devised.

Better, surely, to move forward with a clear and generous offer to protect the status of EU citizens here and of our citizens in other member states; and to spell out in clear and non-transactional terms the new partnership we are seeking in the fields of security, of research and of foreign policy. Such an approach ought to be able to get cross-party support in the new parliament and thus to provide the government with the sort of opening mandate it needs if it is to be taken seriously by our negotiating partners.

Would it not be sensible too to submit such an approach for approval to parliament before negotiations begin in Brussels? If that means a short delay in the June 19/20 date for opening negotiations, that should not be a drama, given the fact that serious negotiations are unlikely to get under way until after the German elections in September. In any case to open negotiations on the day of the Queen's Speech and before either House of Parliament has had an opportunity to debate the new government's programme, let alone to approve it, would seem a dangerous short cut.

The outcome of the election certainly does not make the Brexit negotiations any easier, but nor does it necessarily make a successful outcome to those negotiations less likely. What are needed in the new circumstances are cool heads and a more consensual, less ideological step-by-step approach.

The implications of a hung parliament both for the Brexit

negotiations and for the process of parliamentary approval for any deal that might be struck, or for leaving without a deal if none was reached, were multiple; but many were not properly or quickly appreciated; and fewer still were acted upon. The government seemed rather to be guided by Theresa May's, by now deeply discredited, response when her social care tax ideas imploded in the middle of the election campaign "nothing has changed". So no change in the ministerial team overseeing the negotiations, most of them ardent Brexiters; no pause to re-consider Britain's opening position in the light of what had passed before the negotiations opened on 19th/20th June; no attempt to reach out to main opposition parties, thus making it more difficult to peel away from Labour in particular some of its Brexit supporters in Parliament; no appreciation of the government's vulnerability in Parliament, both to the small group of Conservative pro-Europeans and to the much larger emerging group of ultra-Brexiters who came to be known by the Orwellian title of the European Research Group - Orwellian because the group was certainly not "European" in any but a strictly negative, anti-European sense and because it did not carry out research, merely conspired to trip up the government. Two changes did take place, one negative and one slightly positive. The negative one was the arrangement reached with the Democratic Unionist Party of Northern Ireland (DUP) to win the support of its 10 votes in the Commons. Teaming up with the only party in Northern Ireland which had campaigned for Leave (and lost the popular vote there) greatly complicated the task of finding a solution to the Irish border conundrum which did not transgress the Good

141

Friday agreement that had ended the "Troubles" in the province. The mildly positive change was the departure of the Prime Minister's two "know nothing about Europe" gatekeepers; and their replacement as Chief of Staff by Gavin Barwell who was to show himself more open-minded.

When the negotiations in Brussels began, things rapidly went from bad to worse. David Davis, having publicly predicted "the row of the summer" over sequencing v. concurrence, promptly surrendered the position at the first meeting and accepted the EU's sequencing approach. My despairing reaction and attempt to save something from this defeat was set out in an InFacts article on 30th June, 2017:

Forever on the back foot.

It may be that the government was never going to be able to avoid some sequencing of the Article 50 talks once the EU27 had nailed their colours to that mast - although David Davis's bluster that this issue was going to provide the row of the summer before conceding the point on day one was hardly a masterclass in negotiating technique. But that should not have inhibited ministers from spelling out already a broader, more positive vision for our future partnership. And it is not too late to do so in the weeks ahead.

What then is holding them back? Clearly all these areas of cooperation will cost money, perhaps quite substantial sums of money. So they will involve the UK making payments into the EU budget on a continuing basis, not just as part of the divorce settlement. Clearly too they will give rise to the need for some internationally structured dispute settlement procedure in which the

142

*European Court of Justice will have a role to play,
directly or indirectly. This is also proving to be the case
in negotiations over the status of EU citizens.*

*Crossing self-imposed red lines of budget
contributions and ECJ oversight will inevitably embroil
the government in an argument with some of its
supporters. So long as the government flinches from such
an argument it will inevitably remain on the back foot
in Brussels. That is hardly a recipe for a successful
negotiation.*

*The irony is that all three of these areas (science and
research, law enforcement and the fight against serious
international crime, foreign and security policy) of future
cooperation enjoy strong cross-party backing in
Parliament. So why not draw on that support and
construct a negotiating approach which is genuinely in
the national interest?*

And "no deal", like Banquo's ghost, continued to be
deployed by the British side in the mistaken belief that it
strengthened our hand, of which there was never any
evidence that it did then or later. I marshalled the
arguments against it in an article on 9th August, 2017:

Drop the "no deal" delusion.

*As talks finally get under way in Brussels over the
terms of Britain's divorce from the European Union,
one extremely smelly red herring needs to be discarded
right at the outset. Whoever it was in N° 10 or in the
Department for Exiting the European Union who
invented the silly slogan "No deal is better than a bad
deal" is either ignorant or a bluffer, or both. And it is
unwise to try to bluff when the other party to the
negotiation knows you are bluffing, and that you will do*

143

more damage to yourself than to them if you walk away without a deal.

So, to aid in such red herring destruction, here are 12 reasons why no deal would be the worst possible outcome. There are probably plenty more.

1. Individual rights. If there is no deal, both the roughly 1 million Brits in other member states and the more than 3 million EU citizens here will lose their automatic rights under the EU's Residence Directive and their protection against discrimination on, for example, health care and employment. And automatic rights of free movement to study, work or retire across the EU would go too.

2. Trade in goods. British exports to the EU (44% of the total) would become subject to the EU's Common External Tariff rates which, while modest in many cases, are substantial in others (see below). Our imports from the EU would be subject to similar charges, raising prices to consumers and inflation. Trade would be subject to non-tariff barriers and customs controls to verify origin and accordance with phyto-sanitary rules. Currently 14,000 trucks enter and leave the UK without such controls every day.

3. Trade in services. This accounts for 80%of UK economic activity, with a large surplus on that trade with the EU. World Trade Organisation rules would be of little help in this sector. Mutual recognition of professional qualifications under EU law would disappear.

4. Financial services. Financial services would feel particularly strong effects. The loss of "passporting" for banks and insurance companies in the UK (£40 billion of the UK's £200 billion in financial service revenues comes from EU business). Regulatory equivalence would not be there as an (anyway inadequate) replacement.

144

5. Automotive industry. There would immediately be 10%duties on cars in both directions, with corresponding damage to supply chains.

6. Pharmaceuticals, chemicals and nuclear industries. There would be severe problems as all these industries are currently regulated at EU level (more than 30 EU regulatory agencies would need to be replaced overnight by national ones - but exports to the EU would still need to meet EU regulatory requirements). 60% of UK exports in pharmaceuticals and chemicals go to the EU.

7. Agriculture and food. On this sector 70% of our trade is with the EU. Some EU tariffs are very substantial (25% on confectionery, 35.5% on dairy products, 87% on frozen beef). There would be major supply-chain problems here too, particularly between the two parts of Ireland.

8. Civil Aviation. Loss of the European Common Aviation Area regulatory framework (which also covers flying between Europe and the US). Loss of rights for budget airlines to fly between EU destinations. Immediate travel disruption and more expensive holiday flights.

9. Security and Justice. Loss of membership of Europol and Eurojust (the agencies for law enforcement and judicial cooperation). Loss of access to Schengen Information Service and other EU data bases, including those covering DNA. Loss of rapid extradition in both directions under the European Arrest Warrant.

10. Budget payments. This would at last produce a saving but probably an illusory one as the EU would pursue the UK through international courts ensuring that our mutual relationship would not calm down quickly after a no deal exit.

11. Foreign and security policy. Major loss of influence in an area of EU policy which is likely to

145

become more significant and which will adversely affect British influence worldwide.

12. Reputation. The UK has hitherto stood by its treaty obligations and worked for a rules-based international order. The reputational damage from leaving the EU without an Article 50 Agreement would be considerable.

That is quite a list you might think. It is surely up to those who, like the Foreign Secretary, Boris Johnson, say that leaving without a deal would be "perfectly OK" to debate the issues set out here; and, if they cannot gainsay them, to drop that silly slogan. Of course it is not possible at this stage to guarantee that Britain will not leave in March 2019 without a deal. But we do need to recognise that, if we do so, March 29th, 2019 would be a Black Friday for the British economy.

*　　　　　　*　　　　　　*

There did, however, after the summer holiday break, seem to be some dawning realisation in the government's ranks and in the Prime Minister's mind that they were not getting the tone of their approach to the negotiations right. This realisation bore fruit in the rather bizarre expedition by a large part of the cabinet to a church hall in Florence to listen to Theresa May's first full-dress speech on Brexit since Lancaster House. Why to Florence no one quite understood, as the Italian government carefully kept their distance, not wishing to be accused of breaking EU27 ranks. In reality the shift was more one of tone than substance. But it did also put out onto the table the idea of a transitional period which would follow Britain's actual exit, thus postponing the cliff-edge of a no deal exit even if it did not remove it entirely. Typically the Prime Minister insisted on calling it an "implementation phase", which it certainly was not, since virtually nothing would be being implemented except Britain's departure from the EU's institutions. It was in fact a two-year standstill period during which the UK would remain in the Single Market and the Customs Union and subject in most respects to the jurisdiction of the European Court of Justice. This shift in the government's position led to some distinct restiveness among the Brexiters, with Boris Johnson leading the pack, but no actual resignations or parliamentary rebellions. My own "two cheers" response to the Florence speech was contained in an InFacts article on 23rd September, 2017:

May's speech: another curate's egg.

What a weird venue Theresa May chose for her big (but certainly not her last) Brexit speech. And what a curate's egg of a speech it was; some parts good, some parts not good, and some parts missing.

This speech would far better have been made at the Conservative party conference in Manchester in just over a week, because that is the audience to whom the need to compromise has to be brought home. If Theresa May now puts on a Jekyll and Hyde show in Manchester, then any benefit from the softer tone of the Florence speech will be lost and our negotiating partners will be reinforced in the view that they simply do not know where the government stands on the main issues at stake.

Clearly recognising that a standstill of two years will be needed if going over a pretty disastrous cliff-edge in

147

March 2019 is to be avoided, is a welcome concession to reality. And the commitment to continue funding our share of the 2013/2020 budget obligations will substantially reduce the overall amount of the divorce bill. But it will not make it disappear; and the Brexiters' not-a-penny-more demand will be sorely disappointed. Their idea that the UK should make no further contributions to the EU budget after 2020 is completely inconsistent with the Brexit negotiating papers the government has already tabled on research and innovation and on internal security cooperation.

It is good too that the Prime Minister has made it clear that the rights of EU citizens in the UK will be entrenched in domestic law, which sounds like a new commitment to give effect to any Withdrawal Agreement through primary legislation. How that is proof against the constitutional doctrine that one parliament cannot bind the hands of another is, however, a bit of a mystery.

What about the bad? Well anyone who voted Remain will be unlikely to be happy about the unqualified majoritarian view Theresa May took of Britain's whole period of membership. Is it really tolerable to treat the views expressed by 37% of the electorate on 23 June, 2016 as the tablets of Moses? The same does not seem to apply to the two thirds of those who voted to remain in the European Communities in 1975.

And then there are the missing parts, most notably the absence of any clarity about the government's desired end-state for our trading relationship with far and away the biggest market for our goods and services. The reiterated ruling out of both a customs union and a single market solution, and the smokescreen laid down over the alternatives, means that this is no more a transition phase than it is an implementation phase. It is simply the postponement of a cliff-edge.

148

The case for going into the negotiations for a new partnership with all options, including a customs union and a single market, on the table remains a compelling one. That the government continues to reject that approach speaks volumes about the dissension within its own ranks.

Will this speech make it more likely that the negotiations on a new partnership can begin after the European Council in October? Slightly, perhaps; but after the December meeting is still a better bet. Much will depend on whether David Davis is able to fill out the details of the shifts in the government's position set out in Florence in a clear and convincing manner. In particular it really is high time to settle the issues relating to the future status of the EU citizens living and working here and of our compatriots across the rest of Europe if we are not to see a continuing and damaging exodus of people who make a real contribution to our economy.

∗   ∗   ∗

In the meantime, through the autumn, as the negotiators in Brussels wrestled with the challenge of reaching what could be called "Heads of Agreement" on the divorce settlement (that is to say not the precise text of the actual Article 50 Withdrawal Agreement which would be a legally binding international treaty, properly ratified by both parties, but rather the main policy components of such an agreement), Parliament was wrestling with a 60 page European Union (Withdrawal) Bill.

This Bill, which had originally been trailed as the grandiloquently titled "Great Repeal Bill", but which was now being promoted as a purely technical measure designed to ensure that the UK's statute book was in proper working order on the day we actually left the EU (always by now assumed to be 29th March, 2019). In reality it was neither of those two extremes. Much of the Bill was indeed technical, rather oddly designed to turn into domestic British law what had, up to then, been legal obligations derived either from directly applicable or indirectly applicable EU laws - a splendid example of Giuseppe de Lampedusa's famous aphorism in *The Leopard* "everything must change so that everything may stay the same". But the Bill also contained some juicy morsels of red meat being fed to the Brexiters, such as the provision that the jurisdiction of the ECJ in the UK should end on exit day (a provision that was highly unlikely to be consistent with what was under negotiation in Brussels) and, following the Conservative party conference in October, the insertion into the Bill of the actual exit date in 2019 (thus making statutory provision for what had, in the original draft, been left to be filled in by the DexEu Secretary of State under secondary legislation, and thus also making it far more difficult for the exit date to be extended beyond March 2019 - an extension explicitly foreseen, if necessary and agreed to by both sides, in the text of Article 50). Most significant of all, however, the Bill provided a platform onto which the "meaningful process" for Parliament to approve any deal that was struck in Brussels could be grafted. My own initial assessment of the Bill was contained in an InFacts article of 16th August, 2017; and my commentary on the October addition of the actual exit date followed on 16th November, 2017:

A flawed Bill that must be amended.

The 62 pages of the European Union (Withdrawal) Bill - the Orwellian title of "The Great Repeal Bill" having now been withdrawn from circulation - together with 66 pages of explanatory notes have now landed with a sickening thud in Parliament's in - tray. You can expect it to remain there for several months, being scrutinised and perhaps amended by Commons and Lords. It needs both.

If you listen to the government, this is just a little tidying-up operation to ensure that, the day we leave the EU, the transition runs smoothly and there are no gaps in the statute book. Indeed at times they make it sound as if the bill's sub-title ought to be the Prince of Lampedusa's wonderfully cynical description of revolution in his novel "The Leopard" - "everything must change so that everything may stay the same". In reality it is not quite like that. It represents a fundamental step and it has plenty of defects.

Part of the problem is that the government has put the cart before several horses. The normal constitutional practice on a major issue like this is for the government to get parliamentary approval to negotiate (in the present case this was done in March of this year). The government then negotiates a deal and brings it back to parliament. And then the two chambers either approve or reject it and enact the changes to our domestic law to give effect to the terms of the deal. Here we are, only a few weeks into the negotiations, without any clue as to their outcome, and Parliament is being asked to give the government a blank cheque by completing the final stage.

The Bill, by definition, takes no account of the outcome of the negotiations. Moreover the government has compounded that problem by rejecting in March any

151

amendment which could have made statutory provision for a meaningful process of approval for a deal or for no deal by Parliament. The Withdrawal Bill makes no provision for that either. That is a large lacuna which will need to be addressed.

Then there are the sweeping powers the government has proposed it should be given to act, with minimal parliamentary oversight or control, of the process - popularly known as "Henry VIII clauses" after the way in which that Tudor monarch legislated by proclamation, without parliamentary approval. There will be changes needed to take account of the outcome of the negotiations, those needed for the transformation of the 34 or so regulatory agencies which currently operate at EU level, and major issues of environmental and labour market law. The procedure would also enable the government to vary the Bill's ban on the jurisdiction of the European Court of Justice if, as now seems inevitable, that body retains a role in any dispute settlement procedures which are required by the terms of the Withdrawal Agreement or by those of the new partnership with the EU.

Parliament could well consider it excessive to give its agreement to this massive range of powers, in which case there will need to be more primary legislation in addition to the seven other bills already envisaged. Or there will need to be some new process for handling statutory instruments which give both Houses the right to amend them, which currently they do not have.

Devolution will be another bone of contention. The Bill proposes that all powers repatriated from Brussels should return to Westminster even when those concern matters which fall within the responsibilities of the devolved parliament or assemblies. The government admits that it will need legislative assent from these devolved administrations. So it cannot be surprised if its *determination to decide itself which powers currently exercised by Brussels should be passed on to Scotland, Wales and Northern Ireland and which retained by Westminster has already provoked a furore.*

Clearly the UK needs to be ready for what happens in March 2019. But the government's choice of the means of doing so is deeply flawed. The parliamentary fracas which will now ensue may be confusing, but it is necessary. The Brexiters will allege that every amendment to the Bill is designed to sabotage the entire process of leaving. It will not be so. It will be designed to give Parliament, and not just the government, control over what is being repatriated.

And now the second article:

Government is making a mess of retreat on the EU Withdrawal Bill.

It is often said that a successful retreat is the most difficult manoeuvre in the military playbook. The same can probably be said of parliamentary retreats.

So, what are we to think of the two "concessions" already made by the government on the EU Withdrawal Bill - and they will certainly not be the last - which had the first two days of debate in the Commons this week?

The idea of inserting a precise exit date (and even time of day) is a distinctly unwise one, even if it is no more so than what is currently in the Bill, which leaves it to David Davis to decide, depending on which side of the bed he gets out of one fine morning in the spring of 2019. It is of course yet another piece of red meat to feed to the Ultra-Brexiters, but none the more sensible for that.

153

For one thing it discards the option in the text of Article 50 of prolonging the two-year cut-off period for a brief or longer time if that should prove desirable to achieve a relatively trouble-free course for our exit. So that option is now to follow the Single Market and the Customs Union out of the window long before anyone can be sure that it will not prove to be in the general interest on both sides of the Channel.

Then there is the second move by the government: to undertake to bring forward a new piece of primary legislation giving effect in our domestic law to whatever may be agreed in the Article 50 Withdrawal Agreement and with respect to an implementation, transition or standstill period. That is probably sensible because it may be a necessary condition for clinching a deal next month on the status of EU citizens. But it imposes some pretty arduous time constraints on the government because, if it is to play that role, its parliamentary course will need to be complete ahead of the exit date.

*   *   *

When the Bill reached the Lords there were a mass of amendments, some highly detailed and technical, some dealing with high politics. None of the amendments were wrecking ones in the sense that they would have frustrated the government's proclaimed objective for the Bill of having our statute book in good working order on exit day, but some were highly contentious. The main ones were shared out between the members of the cross-party group which had been in existence since the debates the previous winter over the Article 50 triggering Bill. I found myself teamed up with the Duke of Wellington, a Conservative peer whom I had known in the 1980s when he was an

154

MEP - under his courtesy title of the Marquess of Douro - and I was Britain's Permanent Representative in Brussels. Our task was to remove from the Bill the statutory provision for exit day to be on 29th March, 2019 and to revert to the government's original preference for exit day to be specified nearer the time by secondary legislation. The argument for keeping the degree of flexibility over a possible extension of the Article 50 cut-off date in the government's hands was compelling and we carried our amendment by a large majority (some idea of the astonishingly febrile public atmosphere at the time was apparent in the rabid onslaught on Charles Wellington which then ensued in the tabloid press). Our amendment, along with a number of others passed in the Lords, several of which I supported in debate and in the voting lobby, were reversed in the Commons. My only satisfaction was, when the Lords decided not to insist on our amendment, telling the minister (Martin Callanan) that I looked forward to giving him my support when he was compelled in due course to repeal the date provision the government was insisting on - and indeed I did so in March 2019 when that came to pass! However one absolutely vital amendment which did survive - if only by a hair's-breadth majority of one in the Commons - was a "meaningful vote" provision which required approval by the Commons of any deal that was struck both on the divorce settlement and on the future relationship. The battlefield for the next two years was thus delineated; and it was the law of the land.

*　　　　　　*　　　　　　*

Away from Westminster and Brussels, out there in the real world, in which any country aspiring to global influence, as post-Brexit Britain did, had to operate, things were not going well. With a Foreign Secretary who was regarded more as a laughing stock than a good joke, and with a government being distracted and devoured by its internal divisions over Brexit and by the task of managing a parliament in which it did not have a secure majority, influence was ebbing away. The Trump administration, headed up by a narcissistic, bullying leader, was beginning to cause more problems for the UK, which regarded itself as the US's closest ally, than to offer solutions to the main global challenges. And that crucial measure which I named "the trepidation index" - how much other countries minded or feared kicking you on the shins rather than backing you with their support - was dropping fast so far as the UK was concerned. Here are a trio of InFacts articles on those issues; one on 15th October, 2017 about the problems with Trump; one on 13th November, 2017 about the emptiness of the "Global Britain" slogan; and one on 22nd November, 2017 about that "trepidation index":

Trump's Iran policy shows folly of quitting the EU.

It has taken Donald Trump's aberrant handling of the nuclear deal with Iran to bring home to the government that our national interests coincide at least as often with those of our European partners as they do with those of an erratically led and ill-informed US administration. About time too. This realisation has been creeping up on us ever since the Prime Minister's unfortunate hand-holding episode with the new president last winter.

156

Now Trump has swatted aside the arguments against putting the Iran deal at risk of both his own professional advisers and of his closest allies. He has embarked on a course of action which could very possibly result in Iran, over time, acquiring nuclear weapons; and one which runs the risk of triggering yet another conflict in the Middle East, a region on which we continue to depend for imports of oil and gas, for a substantial portion of our exports and to which we are particularly vulnerable from large migratory flows.

But Trump's actions have much wider negative consequences for us than simply regional ones. Our government has, quite rightly, identified as a major national interest the preservation and, where possible, the strengthening of a rules-based international order.

But here is a country we call our closest ally systematically dismantling that order - dropping out of the Paris climate change accords and acting contrary to them, withdrawing from UNESCO, pulling out of the Trans-Pacific Partnership negotiations and seeking to renegotiate the North Atlantic Free Trade Area. And, in the case of Iran, simply ignoring the testimony of the International Atomic Energy Agency, whose job it is to police the Iran Agreement, that Iran remains in full conformity with its provisions. Hardly an encouragement to anybody trying to find a diplomatic solution to the tensions arising over North Korea's nuclear weapons programme.

And which countries are in the lead in resisting this bonfire of international rules? Our European partners.

All this surely ought to point up how sensible the Prime Minister was in her Florence speech to put so much emphasis on her pitch for a strong and unconditional new security dimension to Britain's relations with its European partners; how feckless those who sought to leave the EU in the first place were in

157

failing to see how damaging that could be to our influence in an uncertain and rapidly changing world; and how utterly irresponsible are those who advocate ending our negotiations in acrimony and without a deal.

And here is the second of the trio:

Global Britain: a phrase in search of a meaning.

One by one Leave campaigners' promises are being revealed as the untruths they actually were. No £350 million sent each week to Brussels, no chance of Turkey becoming an EU member by 2020, no continued membership of the Single Market.

But one, less tangible, claim is still hovering out there, encapsulated in the phrase "Global Britain". It has no more substance than the others.

The Brexiter claim is that EU membership has prevented Britain from being a global power; and that leaving the EU will enable us to become one. Neither part of that proposition stands up to scrutiny.

For one thing Britain has been a global power since roughly the 16th century. Joining the European Communities in 1973 did not bring that to an end; it actually enhanced it, as our influence in Brussels helped to propel Europe into a succession of global trade liberalisation rounds, brought many of Britain's former colonies into a close trade and aid relationship with the EU, and made us a more interesting interlocutor for other global players such as the US, China and Japan. Ask any foreign ambassador in London whether the propositions in the preceding sentence are true and they will tell you they are.

So, what is the Global Britain that we will be better able to become if and when we leave the EU? Where is the added value going to come from? Some talk in nostalgic terms about the Commonwealth, but that organisation, valuable as it is, is not about to become a major trade bloc or to coordinate its foreign and security policies, however much we might wish that it would. Just ask the Indian government if you doubt that. Nothing that the Commonwealth can realistically be expected to do is prevented or hindered by EU membership.

How about trade, the environment, human rights, the fight against terrorism and the other great challenges we all, Britain and the EU, face? Will we be better able to handle them on our own? The EU is already negotiating or about to negotiate free trade arrangements with the most promising countries - Japan, India, Mercosur (the South American trade bloc that includes Brazil), Australia and New Zealand.

It is with our fellow Europeans that the Foreign Secretary is lobbying in Washington to head off Donald Trump's misguided aspiration to destroy the Iran nuclear deal. If the Paris environmental agreements are to be saved in the face of US withdrawal from them, it is going to be by the joint efforts of the EU and China - not by the UK, a relatively minor player so far as pollution is concerned.

So, next time you hear someone banging on about Global Britain or read, as a somewhat discredited Priti Patel put it in her resignation letter, about "a great future for Britain as a free, independent and sovereign country", reach for your critical faculties.

And here is the third one:

More global influence outside the EU? Just look at ICJ decision.

From the beginning of 2018 Britain will no longer have a judge on the International Court of Justice (ICJ), the senior international tribunal on which it has had a place ever since the UN was set up after the Second World War. An unwritten convention that the Permanent Members of the Security Council should have a Judge has been challenged and overturned, to our detriment.

Well, you might say, this is a development which falls into the "small earthquake in Chile, few casualties" category. And, up to a point, that is correct. The ICJ will continue to function perfectly well. The UK will also continue to accept its compulsory jurisdiction, the only one of the five permanent members to do so. That does mean of course that we will be subject to the rulings of an international court with foreign judges. Sound familiar?

But, in the world of international diplomacy, where perceptions and symbolic shifts often matter as much as hard facts, it is not as simple and untroubling as that.

Winning elections at the UN are a fraught business. Those elections are an odd mixture of a global beauty contest, a reflection of the international trepidation index (that is to say how much countries fear offending the country they are voting against), and of sheer diplomatic elbow grease put into lobbying in New York and in capitals around the world.

Clearly Britain fell short on this occasion. I doubt if we skimped on the hard work of our diplomats. But there is scant evidence that a Prime Minister distracted by the shenanigans in her cabinet and her party over Brexit, or a Foreign Secretary who is widely considered to be a laughing stock without being very funny, played a useful role.

We have clearly come a long way since the ICJ election in 1995 when Rosalyn Higgins won a seat by one of the largest majorities recorded and went on to become President of the ICJ. The direction of travel has been downward.

160

Nor is this the first straw in the wind at the UN to suggest our international influence and standing is in retreat. Earlier this year the UN General Assembly decided, over the UK's strenuous objections, to refer to the ICJ the case of the Chagos Islanders, who were displaced from Britain's Indian Ocean territory of Diego Garcia when it was turned into a massive US military base.

To what extent are these developments Brexit-related, unintended consequences of last year's referendum result? Hard to say. But one thing is clear beyond doubt. Brexiters' claims that ridding ourselves of the incubus of EU membership would open the way to increased international influence are proving to be completely unfounded.

The government never stops reminding us that we remain a Permanent Member of the UN Security Council, a member of the Commonwealth, of NATO and of countless other international organisations. But these are not silver trophies on the mantelpiece to be admired by visitors. Their importance depends on whether we can put them to good use to enhance our future influence on world events. And, so far, we do not seem to be doing very well at that.

*　　　　　　　*　　　　　　　*

In December agreement was reached in Brussels on the broad lines of the divorce settlement, but not without the Prime Minister having to abort a meeting with the President of the Commission due to the objections of the DUP to the text under discussion, followed a week later by a May/Juncker agreement to a slightly tweaked version. In the event the negotiations over the divorce payments and the status of EU citizens in the UK were less dramatic than

I had feared and predicted, mainly because the UK negotiators accepted pretty well everything on which the Commission insisted, including the continuance of ECJ jurisdiction in the UK for dealing with issues relating to EU citizens' rights for a period of eight years after exit day. On Ireland nothing really was settled definitively, but the salience and the intractability of the issues at stake, principally those with respect to trade both over the border between the two parts of the island and across the Irish Sea between Great Britain and Northern Ireland were there for all to see. Here are two InFacts articles, one on the Irish imbroglio, written on 9th August, 2017, but still as relevant as ever at the end of the year - and indeed at the end of the next year too; and the second one a short look at the December outline for a divorce settlement deal written on 8th December, 2017:

Ireland's Brexit border: a masterclass in fecklessness.

When the British government's archives on Brexit are opened to the public it is a fair bet that one of the most startling revelations will be the sheer fecklessness with which the Cameron and May governments drifted towards putting at serious risk the Good Friday Agreement which ended eighty years of tension over the division of the island of Ireland.

At that time we will finally get some idea whether that drift was the consequence of mere ignorance and inattention, or whether, worse still, it was a deliberate gamble, a Panglossian punt, that all would be for the best in the best of all possible worlds.

When you think of the blood and treasure that successive British governments devoted to maintaining the

162

unity of the United Kingdom of Great Britain and Northern Ireland, and of the massive efforts that the governments of John Major and Tony Blair put into finding a peaceful solution to the period of troubles, it is hard to credit that attention deficit disorder took over so quickly. But it did.

The Irish dimension was barely mentioned by the leading lights of the Leave campaign - indeed one of them was the then Secretary of State for Northern Ireland, Theresa Villiers, whose duty it was to uphold the Good Friday Agreement. And when John Major and Tony Blair spoke out in warning they were treated as mere blasts from the past.

Well, now the chickens are coming home to roost; and the government seems at a loss to know what to do. It is all very well saying how important it is to maintain the Common Travel Area between the UK and Ireland, and to express a desire to avoid the return of hard border controls on trade in goods and services between the two parts of the island.

But, in practical terms that does not take matters very far, particularly when Theresa May has ruled out, even before the Brexit negotiations had begun, the two most obvious ways of squaring the circle: remaining in the EU's Single Market or its Customs Union - or both.

And what about the de-politicisation of law enforcement on the island of Ireland and the strengthening of the fight against terrorism which flowed from the network of EU Justice and Home Affairs legislation and which could all lapse in March 2019?

So far these are all unanswered questions, and they will not be easy to answer.

It is indeed the case that the Common Travel Area has existed for far longer than the EU's freedom of movement. But it has never had to be applied by two

163

states, one of which remains legally bound by that freedom of movement obligation and one of which seems hell bent on rejecting it.

It is true too that free trade existed between the UK and Ireland in the past; but that was when they were both outside what has now become the European Union.

As for cooperation over law enforcement, there was little enough of that at a time when any extradition could become a major political issue and when there was no European framework to wrap around it.

It really is high time that the government put on the negotiating table some practical solutions to these complex and sensitive issues which, however much goodwill there is in Brussels - and there is plenty on the Irish dimension of Brexit - cannot just be resolved by warm words and vague generalities.

It would be a tragedy if the recent remarkable improvement in the relations between the UK and Ireland were to become just another piece of collateral damage in the wake of last year's referendum vote.

And here is the article on the December deal:

The events of the past week have shown that the wheels on the government's Brexit strategy are shaking loose, and that the risk of a car crash further down the road is increasing.

The fiasco on Monday in Brussels over the border arrangements on the island of Ireland has stolen most of the headlines. The resolution of the problem, for the meantime, is welcome. It opens the way to moving on to the second phase of the negotiations and, in particular, to reducing the uncertainties hanging over the status of a million of our citizens elsewhere in Europe and three million of those from other EU member states living and working here.

But the process has revealed just how precarious the government's negotiating position is. The Democratic Unionist Party's ten precious votes have demonstrated their capacity to stop the government in its tracks. There will be other instalments of Danegeld to be paid to the DUP, as Arlene Foster hinted in her statement on the Agreement.

That other fiasco, over David Davis's vanishing 58 sectoral analyses, has been overshadowed by events in Brussels. It looks as if he has escaped, by the skin of his teeth, from being found in contempt of parliament.

But it is pretty shameful to discover that, 17 months after the referendum, the government has still made no impact assessments on the various possible outcomes to the Brexit negotiations - while claiming they were doing so. Instead they have spent large amounts of scarce resources on amassing 850 pages of information, which can politely be described as underwhelming or, less politely, as worthless.

One major positive development was that the issue of sequencing was more or less laid to rest, with the EU 27 agreeing to move on in the New Year of 2018 to discussing a possible transitional period and the shape and content of the new, external UK /EU relationship. It was the end of the beginning but far from being the beginning of the end.

Chapter 9

Trench warfare: transition period (January/March 2018)

The idea of a substantial post-Brexit transition period (not simply a fix to deal with a technical overrun of the withdrawal and new partnership negotiations) had been on the table since Theresa May's Florence speech in September 2017. But the EU, while at no stage hostile to the idea (which was quite different from the option of lengthening the Article 50 two year cut-off period, which would delay the actual date of Brexit altogether) had not been prepared to engage in serious discussion of it until broad agreement was reached on the outline of the Withdrawal Agreement. The December deal having met that condition, the first three months of 2018 were spent in negotiating about little more than the details of such a transition period. This was partly because neither side was yet ready to talk about the new partnership, the British side in particular having no ideas - other than negative red lines - to put forward on the heart of that negotiation, the post-Brexit trading and economic relationship between the UK and the EU. It was hard to believe, but the UK, despite being nearly a year into the negotiation was unable to say at the conference table what it wanted, and thus to test what might be negotiable.

My own view of what lay ahead in negotiating a transitional period (still, with vanishing credibility, being called by ministers and government spokesmen an "implementation" phase) was contained in an InFacts article on 8th January, 2018:

Next, tricky talks over transition.

Quite obviously 2018 represents decision year for the Brexit negotiations. The government's impetuous and ill-prepared decision in March of last year to trigger the Article 50 process for withdrawal has locked us in, and Theresa May seems determined that any key which might offer an escape must be thrown out of the window.

The first few months of the year are likely to be devoted to negotiating a standstill arrangement - what everyone else considers a transition period but which is still oddly and misleadingly called by the government an implementation phase - on which there appears to be broad agreement in principle between the UK and the 27 other EU countries.

The government's determination to get that nailed down as quickly as possible demonstrates its concern at the haemorrhaging of investment, of a dwindling of the supply of EU workers already here, and at the increasing indications of plans for businesses to move away from the UK that have been fed by uncertainty over Brexit, all of which are feeding into the predictions of sluggish growth in 2018 from every economic forecaster.

Will the negotiations for a standstill arrangement be plain sailing? Not likely. For one thing, the detailed conditions for any such standstill, on which the EU27 are likely to insist, are going to be hugely unpalatable to the government's Ultra-Brexiter supporters: continued inclusion in the Single Market and the Customs Union, continued free movement of people, continued jurisdiction of the European Court of Justice, acceptance of all new EU legislation and regulatory decisions introduced during the standstill period even though we will have had no say over their adoption.

So we can expect much wriggling by the government, and much tension within its ranks, before they accept the inevitability of agreeing to most, if not all, the EU conditions; and that could well delay the conclusion of this part of the withdrawal deal.

Then there is the question of the duration of any standstill. On the face of it that might appear simple enough, since the EU27 wants it to end on the last day of 2020 and Theresa May's "about two years" is generally assumed to mean the end of March 2021. But the problem is that neither of those two dates looks like a realistic deadline for the completion of the new partnership negotiations and their entry into force, which almost every commentator believes will take a good deal longer than that.

If so, the cliff-edge will merely have been postponed, not avoided; and businesses will have to face two wrenching sets of changes, one at the end of the standstill and the other when the new partnership, assuming it can be agreed, comes into effect.

The obvious response to that quandary is either to agree a longer standstill period than the 24 or 21 months currently envisaged; or, perhaps more wisely, to provide for the period's subsequent extension by common accord beyond the period originally agreed. But such a safety valve is likely to be highly contentious on both sides of the Channel, Ultra-Brexiters seeing it as a back door to remaining in the EU indefinitely, and the EU being deprived of the neat cut-off date ahead of their next seven-year budgetary cycle. Nevertheless, a standstill without a degree of flexibility as to its duration is all too likely to be a flawed concept.

So the standstill negotiations of the next three months are not going to be a brief, technical interlude between the divorce negotiations and those for a new partnership. Rather they have the potential to add to the already long list of drawbacks to Brexit which will need to be weighed up by Parliament when it has to decide whether or not to approve any overall package deal.

And in an InFacts article on 15th January, 2018 I set out why the post-Brexit transition period would do nothing to fill the vacuum over foreign policy cooperation with the EU and its member states which was now only 15 months away:

In radically changing world, we need our EU ties.

It is all too easy, when a national debate is in full flow, as is the case in Britain with the debate over Brexit, to assume that the world is just standing still while we conduct that debate and some time at the end of this year bring it to some sort of conclusion. Easy too to assume that we can then just hop back onto the global bus and continue as if not much had happened. And, if those on both sides of the Brexit debate, as many of them are doing, simply double down on the main arguments they deployed in the referendum campaign in 2016 without taking much account of changes taking place in the world around us, that too is human nature.

But the real world is not like that, and it is changing, quite radically in some instances, before our eyes. The most consequential change since June 2016 has been the installation of Donald Trump in the White

169

House, with the likelihood that he will be there for at least three more years, perhaps longer. Many of the decisions he has taken are proving to be contrary to our national interest - withdrawal from the Paris accords on climate change, attempts to wreck the nuclear agreement with Iran (JCPOA), knocking a hole in the potential two state solution for the Israel/Palestine dispute by moving the US embassy to Jerusalem and recognising the city as the capital of Israel, egging on the Saudis in their destabilising actions in Yemen and the Gulf. And on not one of them does he seem to have found it necessary or desirable to consult a British government which prides itself on being his closest ally.

In every one of these instances the government, to its credit, but also, one suspects, to its dismay, has found itself working in close concert with the other main European powers - France and Germany - to push back against those decisions or at least to limit the damage they are causing. The Foreign Secretary has joined his European colleagues in an intense lobbying campaign in Washington to sustain the JCPOA and has then met the Iranian foreign minister in Brussels. In an odd way, the UK is discovering the strengths and benefits to us of European foreign policy cooperation just when we are negotiating to leave the organisation; and, in that wonderfully British illogical manner, we are drawing no wider, systemic conclusions from the experience.

How will we cooperate post-Brexit? We surely should be thinking this through a good deal more carefully. Because in less than 15 months' time we are going to drop out of all the European machinery for foreign policy coordination and concerted action. We will then become a third country, outside the meeting rooms where European decisions are taken, compelled to lobby about, rather than contribute to, the decisions being taken. And anyone who believes that the cooperation

170

between us and the other Europeans will then continue to work as smoothly and effectively as before is guilty of terminal complacency.

Over the next few months the government and the EU27 will be considering how best to ensure that such close cooperation can continue to take place after we leave and what institutional arrangements are made to underpin it. That will not be easy. But it will be important, and if the arrangements agreed prove to be less operationally effective than the existing ones then both sides will be the losers.

They will be the losers not just in their capacity to resist moves by others, as has been the case with the US in recent months, but also in their capacity to work together positively to promote their collective interests and values which coincide across a broad sweep of foreign and security policy: working out ways to remedy the JCPOA's chief defect, its relatively short duration, keeping a two state solution for the Israel/Palestine dispute on the table, strengthening the actions on climate change, working up a package of policies across Europe, the Middle East and Africa to reduce the pressure from economic migration.

Of course there is a simpler way to achieve a good outcome in this policy area and that is for Britain not to leave the EU in the first place. But that is a story for another day.

That first quarter of 2018 was a period of relative calm, both at home in Parliament and in Brussels, deceptively so since it turned out to be the calm before a whole series of storms on both fronts. For reasons not entirely easy to understand the Brexiters reacted reasonably calmly to the provisions for the transitional period as they began to leak out, even though one might have expected them to be intensely upset by them, involving as they did remaining in the EU's Single Market and Customs Union, under the oversight of the Commission and the jurisdiction of the European Court of Justice even when there was no British say over the contents of the rules being enacted in Brussels and no British representation in any of the EU institutions enacting them. Presumably the fact that a transition period did not put at risk the Holy Grail of actually leaving the EU on 29th March, 2019 provided the necessary sedation. And there was plenty of parliamentary activity finishing off the work on the EU Withdrawal Bill on which, as described in the previous chapter, the Brexiters won most of the battles, although not the one over the statutory requirement for a meaningful parliamentary process to approve any deal that was struck.

And, since the lull while a transition period was being negotiated did not remove the threat of a cliff-edge, no deal Brexit but merely postponed it, the drumbeat of "no deal is better than a bad deal" was sustained, as was the sort of riposte set out in my InFacts article of 24th January, 2018:

No deal slogan is Rasputin of Brexit talks.

It is premature to assume that we have heard the last of the slogan "no deal is better than a bad deal". It is the battle cry of the Brexit true believers, and there are plenty of them on the government benches in both Houses. The no deal slogan is the Rasputin of the Brexit negotiations: you can feed it with cyanide cakes, pump it full of bullets, and hold it under the ice and still it will emerge gibbering from the ordeal.

172

Why does this matter? Because the phase of the negotiations on the framework for a new UK/EU partnership, which will start in March, is going to be quite different from the divorce proceedings which were negotiated before Christmas. The latter were necessarily acrimonious and confrontational - divorce proceedings usually are. But the post-March negotiations on a new partnership need to establish a wide measure of mutual benefit if they are to succeed.

It is simply not the case that, if the UK is not prepared to walk away, it will be worsted in that negotiation. Was that the sort of basis on which we negotiated the establishment of the UN and of the Atlantic Alliance? Or that we successfully participated in three global rounds of trade negotiations (Kennedy, Tokyo and Uruguay) for freer and fairer world trade? And remember too that walking away from this negotiation will not leave us with the status quo ante but rather with us tipping over the cliff-edge in March 2019.

The government has made quite a good job of spelling out the scope for mutual benefit in a new partnership for foreign and security policy cooperation, for dealing with the challenges of international crime and terrorism, and for continued cooperation over scientific research and innovation. But on the most important area, that of trade in goods and services, it has done nothing but draw red lines, list models it does not like and hint at approaches which can all too easily be characterised as "cherry-picking" or, in the Foreign Secretary's demotic "having your cake and eating it".

The government is right to be seeking a new overall relationship which is unique - though it would be nice to get away from that appalling misnomer "bespoke". But it is no good expecting the trade dimension of our future partnership to drive a coach and horses through the single market structures so laboriously constructed over

173

the last 30 years - which, by the way, was one of the UK's proudest achievements.

The UK surely needs to be more open-minded when it moves into the post-March phase of the negotiations and to move beyond the straitjacket of the Lancaster House speech. If we cannot move beyond David Davis's "Canada plus, plus, plus" we are only too likely to end up with "EU membership minus, minus, minus".

Of the two main issues the negotiations over a transitional period needed to settle, first the substantive content of Britain's position after it had left the EU but while the transitional period was still running, and, second, the duration of the period and whether that should be flexible or not, the first was more straightforward but was highly sensitive, the second seemed largely procedural, but was not - and came later to prove seriously consequential.

The first issue really boiled down to recognising the validity of the old adage that it is not possible to be a little bit pregnant. The four freedoms and their application and adjudication could not be sliced and diced and could not be taken out of the hands of the EU institutions - principally the Commission and the European Court of Justice; and nor could the legislative functions of the EU be put on hold during the transitional period. So, if the UK wanted to avoid going over a cliff-edge in March 2019, at which point the new partnership negotiations proper would only just be beginning, then it would have to accept that there would need to be taxation, and a lot more besides, without representation. This bitter pill was swallowed by the government. Just about the only concession they won was for the UK to be exempted during the transitional period from the EU Treaty's prohibition on member states conducting their own trade negotiations with third countries. But the concession still prevented the UK from actually bringing into effect any such agreements until the transitional period was up. And for the reasons set out in an InFacts article of 5th March, 2018, the scope for such negotiations was more symbolic than real:

Government's trade policy is holed beneath the water line.

Last week saw two major developments affecting the government's trade policy. Both were negative.

In her Mansion House speech the Prime Minister for the first time admitted that the government's decision to reject remaining in the Single Market or in a customs union with the EU meant that the extraordinarily complex solution the UK has proposed would mean less good access to Britain's largest export market than it currently enjoys.

On the same day Donald Trump dashed any hopes the government might have had that a free trade agreement with the US would compensate for that loss. The president announced his intention to unilaterally impose swingeing import duties on steel and aluminium, including on the US's partners in free trade areas such as Canada.

The full significance of the Trump policy, coupled with his grossly irresponsible and misguided assertion that trade wars are a good thing and easy to win, has yet to sink in on this side of the Atlantic. If the president follows through on his intention, there will surely be retaliatory measures against US exports by some of that

175

*country's main trading partners and allies. There will
also be recourse to the dispute settlement procedures of
the WTO, which could well mean collateral damage to
that organisation's capacity to sustain international
trade rules should the US reject its rulings.*

*Britain, as a member of the EU at least until
March 2019 and as a member of the EU's customs
union for at least another two years of transition, will be
on the opposing side of that trade war from the US, with
whom constructing a new trade relationship has been
such a key part of Theresa May's post-Brexit narrative.*

*As if that was not bad enough, it seems likely that
the Prime Minister is still understating the amount of
damage that could result from the government's preferred
solution for a trade agreement with the EU - even if
that solution managed to survive intact the test of
negotiation with the other 27 EU members. It is not
just that that preferred solution is at odds with the
position likely to be endorsed within a few days by the
EU27, although it certainly is. It is also the fact that
the new customs arrangements it proposes are fiendishly
complex and will impose considerable bureaucratic
burdens on businesses and delays to the smooth
functioning of highly integrated industries; and that
virtually nothing will survive of the, admittedly imperfect,
but valuable, Single Market in services which make up
80% of our economy.*

*So, not a great week for Britain's trade policy. One
wonders how many more setbacks have to occur before
the government realises that it has put all our eggs in the
wrong basket.*

The issue of the duration of the transitional period was
tricky and both sides misjudged it as a result of allowing
domestic considerations to override objective reality. So far

as the EU was concerned it was infinitely more convenient if the transitional period were to finish at the end of the current seven-year Multi-annual Financial Framework (MFF), that is to say at the end of 2020. This would avoid any need to work out how the new seven-year MFF, not yet agreed, was to apply to a third country (the UK) which was not a party to it (as the UK was to the present one). So, end 2020 was what they proposed, whatever doubts they may have had about whether that date was likely to be sufficient to accommodate the new partnership negotiations. For the UK which, at Florence, had mentioned a period of "about two years" there were major tensions within the cabinet and the parliamentary party, with the Foreign Secretary having staked out a "not a minute more than two years" position in public. So, the gap between the two was small (three months); and, as usual, appeasement of the Brexiters was uppermost in the Prime Minister's mind. The outcome was that the UK accepted the EU date; and, while there was some provision for extension, this required both sides to agree, thus giving the UK government of the day a veto over any extension. And, since the date of the transitional period (March 2019 - December 2020) was actually specified in calendar terms, no account was taken of the possibility of that great unmentionable at the time, an agreed extension of the Article 50 cut off period (of which, in the end, there were three) eating up part of the already inadequate transitional period. The agreement on the transition period was thus a flawed one, however necessary it was to have such a deal in order to protect the interests of the UK and the EU. My assessment of it was set out in an InFacts article of 19th March:

> *As the government closes in on reaching agreement with the EU 27 this Friday on the terms of the standstill period for the first 21 months after we leave the EU, the full enormity of what they have conceded hardly seems to have sunk in to the minds of their usually extremely vocal Brexit supporters.*
>
> *During 2019/20 the UK will remain in the Customs Union and the Single Market, free movement of people, jurisdiction of the European Court of Justice, oversight of the Commission will continue just as now. No new fisheries policy. No new agricultural policy. Only we will have no say in the EU's decision-making processes, neither in the Council nor the European Parliament; and no representation in the Commission nor the ECJ. And all that for a standstill period of clearly inadequate duration which will merely postpone the cliff-edge to New Year's Day 2021. Quite a bonfire of the vanities.*
>
> *When we are asked next weekend to celebrate this second, remarkably Pyrrhic, Brexit negotiating victory following the first one last December, will there be no concessions to chalk up? Well we are to be permitted to begin negotiating new trade deals with third countries, although not to benefit from them. Unfortunately most of the third countries we will want to negotiate with will either already have free trade or customs union agreements with the EU (South Korea, Turkey, Norway, Switzerland) or will be giving top priority to negotiating such agreements (Japan, Australia, New Zealand, the Mercosur countries of Latin America) or will want to know the detailed terms of the UK's future*

trade relationship with the EU which we will be unable to predict for a considerable time to come (US, China).

So, why are the Ultra-Brexiters taking all this apparently so calmly? Why does Jacob Rees-Mogg describe criticism of it as "nit picking"? Presumably because the post-Brexit nirvana which they sold to the electorate in 2016 has now been reduced to one single objective, leaving the EU on 29 March, 2019 at any cost. To achieve that any sacrifice in the negotiations about to begin over the new framework for our post-Brexit relationship with the EU is likely to be accepted in order to avoid jeopardising that one objective. Inadequate specificity in the terms of this framework, blurring of red lines, substantial financial contributions to ensure continuing access to EU programmes for scientific research and law enforcement additional to those already accepted in the December divorce agreement; all these are likely to be accepted by the time a deal is struck later this year.

This time last year we were being told by the government that no deal was better than a bad deal. Anyone who questioned that dubious proposition was accused of unpatriotically weakening the UK 's negotiating hand. Since then we have seen the no deal scenario tested to destruction as the government's own calculations of the economic consequences, which have seeped into the public domain, point towards a substantial loss of economic growth which could not possibly be compensated by new trade deals with third countries. The logical conclusion to be drawn is that any deal, even quite a bad deal, is better than no deal. And that is only too likely to be what Parliament will be told is the choice whenever a deal is struck towards the end of the year.

As the government zig-zags and lurches towards the finishing line it becomes ever clearer that some

179

fundamental decisions will need to be taken by Parliament when the outcome of the negotiations is brought before them.

And reaching this deal was the occasion for a brief but worrying Anglo-Spanish spat over Gibraltar, which also contained the seeds of future difficulties as set out in an InFacts article of 13th March, 2018:

Brexiters heading for the Rock(s) on Gibraltar.

Nothing much has been heard about Gibraltar and Brexit since the initial shock last spring when it emerged that the EU27 had explicitly included in their Brexit negotiating guidelines a provision that any post-Brexit arrangements for the Rock would need to be agreed between Britain and Spain. That is understandable since the first phase of the negotiations, which ended in broad agreement just before Christmas, contained no elements which involved Gibraltar.

That state of grace is about to end. Both the standstill transitional period about to be negotiated and the end-state UK/EU partnership to be negotiated thereafter will need to address the issue of Gibraltar head on, or else the territory will be left in a far worse situation than it is in now.

The key point to remember is that Gibraltar's current status within the EU is solely due to the fact that it is a European territory of a member state, the UK. Once that member state ceases to be such the whole underpinning of Gibraltar's status disappears into thin air - and the Prime Minister is determined that this should happen in less than 15 months.

Gone will be the highly beneficial legal status which has Gibraltar within the Single Market but outside the customs union. This exempts it from the need to introduce a VAT. It also makes the border between Gibraltar and Spain an internal EU one, subject to Commission oversight and to the ultimate jurisdiction of the European Court of Justice.

Instead Gibraltar will become a third country (or territory) and its border with Spain will become an external border of the EU, with Spain responsible for controlling the movement of people in both directions across that border. Thus the whole basis of Gibraltar's current prosperity will be at risk. No wonder more than 90% of Gibraltarians voted to remain in the EU.

Did the Brexiters show any awareness of the predicament into which their referendum success would thrust Gibraltar? Absolutely not. Did they say a word about it at the time or since? None. If they did know about it, they acted with the greatest cynicism and fecklessness as they threw Gibraltar under the wheels of that infamous battle bus. Now all they do is beat the drums of hostility towards Spain, which is hardly likely to bring about a good outcome for the Rock.

What can and should the government do about all this? So far, as in other parts of the Brexit negotiations, they have done nothing except draw red lines - on the need for Gibraltarians to be directly involved in any negotiations, and on the unacceptability of any discussion of the sovereignty dispute with Spain. Since ministers seem to have no idea of what end-state they want for the UK itself, it is difficult, if not impossible, to address the main issues relating to Gibraltar after we leave. This cannot continue much longer; the risk of a car crash in March 2019 is there, one smaller in size but not dissimilar in nature to that in Ireland. And, in the case of Gibraltar, the standstill transitional period is not so easily available to buy time.

Is the government talking quietly to the Spanish government about how to manage the process? Not much sign of that. Rather oddly Gibraltar's Brexit-related issues are being handled by the Foreign and Commonwealth Office and not by the Department for Exiting the European Union. Does the idea of Boris Johnson being in charge instil confidence in the outcome? Not a lot.

*   *   *

It was about this time that the tone of the public debate about Brexit, both in Parliament and the press, began to change. Up till then it had been broadly accepted, pretty well across the board, that there was little or no alternative to implementing the outcome of the 2016 referendum and leaving the EU in March 2019. So that public debate had been focused on a soft Brexit v. hard Brexit outcome, without much of a no Brexit option. That had been the approach in my own commentaries, as anyone who has read this far will have noticed. Of course there had been those like the Liberal Democrats and the Scottish National Party who had promoted the idea of holding a further referendum on the outcome of the Brexit negotiations, with a Remain option as one alternative; but there were few open supporters in the Labour Party and fewer still among those Conservatives out of sympathy with their own government's policy. And the hard fact was that, without solid Labour Party backing in Parliament there was no chance either of rejecting any deal struck by the government or, even more daunting a challenge, of passing the legislation which would be required before a further referendum could be held.

As time went by, however, and it became ever clearer just how damaging and undesirable any deal which a government, continually appeasing its Brexiter supporters and dependent on the DUP for survival, was likely to strike, the mood shifted, not yet directly to full-blooded advocacy of another referendum but to pointing out, as forensically as possible, just how much worse for Britain, for its future prosperity, its security, and its influence in the world, the sort of Brexit which was beginning to emerge from the fog of battle in Brussels and around the cabinet table in London, was going to be. The debate thus shifted from hard Brexit v. soft Brexit to contrasting the government's emerging Brexit terms with Britain's position as an EU member, with its exceptionalism - over the budget, over the Euro, over Schengen, over the JHA opt-outs - all firmly entrenched in the treaties and subsequent legislation. That shift was expressed in my own writing and contributions to parliamentary debates throughout 2018.

Nothing has mystified me more during the nearly twenty years I have been a working member of the House of Lords than the ignorance, and, in the case of the Commons, disdain, at each end of the corridor that links the two Houses, for the views and procedures of the other House. This despite the fact that it is only through the joint action of the two that the government can effectively be held to account and legislation be passed. This fundamental reality applied in spades to Brexit. So, from an early stage following the referendum, pro-Europeans like myself and John Kerr in the Lords tried to keep in touch with the Labour Party in the Commons and with rebel Conservatives there too. This meant talking above all to

Labour's front bench spokesmen such as shadow ministers for Europe, Wayne David and Pat McFadden, and then, once he became shadow Secretary of State for DexEu, Keir Starmer. I had first come across Starmer when he was head of the Crown Prosecution Service and gave evidence to our Lords enquiry on Protocol 36 of the Lisbon Treaty and Britain's JHA opt-outs and opt-ins (described in Chapter 6), and explained cogently just how important the two EU agencies - Europol and Eurojust (the latter helping our prosecutors to navigate their way through the thickets of different jurisdictions across the EU) – were for our law enforcement endeavours. By now an MP and a key member of the shadow cabinet, Starmer was impressive; and, unlike so many of his colleagues in Jeremy Corbyn's shadow cabinet, the master of his brief with all its technicalities and twists and turns. I still remember an early discussion we had when I bemoaned the ambiguity of Labour's Brexit positions; and asked him whether he accepted that, at some point, they would need to come off the fence - "yes, of course" was the reply, which left no doubt either on which side of it he wanted to come down.

It was at that time, too, that I wrote a "compare and contrast" article juxtaposing Britain's accession negotiations in 1970/72, in which I had myself participated at the Brussels end in a junior capacity, and the current Brexit negotiations. It was a damning comparison. Here it is in an InFacts article of 1ˢᵗ March, 2018:

Compare joining Europe (1970/72) to Brexit chaos (2016/?)

Ahead of another major Brexit speech tomorrow Theresa May finds herself embroiled in a battle with Brussels over Northern Ireland and fighting to keep a fractious party together. It's a far cry from how another Tory government negotiated our entry into Europe in the 1970s.

The ink was barely dry on the UK's Accession Treaty to the European Communities in January 1972 when the UK's principal official level negotiator, Con O'Neill, sat down to write the history of the negotiations and to draw lessons from them. The final chapter was entitled "Did we make mistakes?"

His brilliant and unsparing analysis languished for several decades in the oubliettes of Whitehall, too sensitive to publish. It did finally see the light of day in 2000. Has anyone involved in the current Brexit negotiations even read this account, let alone sought to apply the lessons learned? Not much sign of that. An exercise in compare and contrast might not come amiss as the government fumbles its way towards the first anniversary of the triggering of Article 50.

Exhibit A: Government Unity

The Heath government in 1970 went into the negotiations united and emerged from them in similar condition. It was led by a Prime Minister whose experience in the earlier negotiations, vetoed by Charles de Gaulle, meant he was a master of the subject matter. The team at ministerial and official level was coherent and tightly knit, bringing in all government departments involved in the negotiations and in their subsequent implementation.

185

What do we have today? A Prime Minister who would make the Oracle of Delphi appear loquacious; a cabinet split from top to bottom; negotiations in the hands of a department without experience and without responsibility for implementing the most wrenching set of changes in recent British bureaucratic history. And, incidentally, why do we have two separate, entirely new departments each handling one half of the UK's international trade?

Exhibit B: Playing a weak hand.
How best do you negotiate if you are dealt a relatively weak hand? Because that was the case in 1970, as it was in 2016. Not, I would suggest, by a combination of denial and of bombast and bluster as the present government has been doing. Nor by flirting publicly with the concept that no deal would be better than a bad deal, when everyone can calculate that the UK will be worse affected than the EU by such an outcome. Nor by drawing a multiplicity of red lines around a non-existent preferred solution.

The Heath government did none of those things, but concentrated on negotiating well-prepared, pragmatic solutions to a limited number of key issues - trade, agriculture, fisheries, budget, Commonwealth sugar, New Zealand butter. And on only one of these, fisheries, did it fall seriously short, even as seen through the lens of subsequent developments.

Exhibit C: Divide and Rule.
Do you pursue the fantasy of a "divide and rule" approach, seeking to play on the differences between your negotiating partners? In 1970 those differences were much greater than they are between the 27 other EU countries today, with five of the six member states solidly

in favour of British accession and one, France, having vetoed us twice.

But the hard fact is that you need unanimity in Brussels to achieve the outcome you want and so you have to deal with the European institutions as you find them, not try to undermine them or split them up. That lesson does not seem to have been fully absorbed by the present negotiators.

Exhibit D: Time management.

You do not waste time. In 1970 the UK's main negotiating objectives were carefully prepared before the negotiations even began. The negotiations were admittedly less complex than the current ones, but no less unprecedented, since this was the first occasion on which the European Communities had been enlarged. They were completed in 18 months, from initiation to signature.

This is hardly what we are seeing now, with nearly a year gone by and still no clarity and no engagement on the main issue, the nature and content of our future partnership with the EU.

Of course historical parallels and analogies are never exact, and never provide all the answers. But those who ignore them do so at their, and also, alas, at our, risk.

Chapter 10

Trench warfare: the road to Chequers (April/July 2018)

Settling the outline terms of the UK's divorce agreement (in December 2017) and of a post-Brexit transitional period (in March 2018) in theory opened the way to negotiating with the EU on by far the most consequential aspect of Brexit, the form and substance of the UK's future relationship with the EU. The outcome of this negotiation, which was to be set out in a Political Declaration that would not in itself be legally binding although it would be an international agreement and it would need to be approved by the House of Commons alongside the legally binding Withdrawal Agreement, from now on became the focus of attention in Westminster and Whitehall, and also in Brussels. So, turning whatever was included in the Political Declaration into the legally binding structure of the future UK/EU relationship would be a task for the parties once Britain had actually left the EU - hence in part the need for a transitional period. This awkward and vulnerable sequencing had been imposed from the outset by the EU on the legalistic grounds that the EU could not even begin to negotiate the specifics of the future relationship until after the UK had actually left and become a third country, at which point the provisions of Article 50 would cease to apply and those relating to relationships with third countries would come into play. At the time not much attention was paid to the potential pitfalls in this approach; and the UK simply accepted it as a given. But the Ultra-Brexiters were already calculating that, since the Political Declaration was not legally binding, they would be able to junk it after we left the EU. In addition, the fact that the Political Declaration was not legally binding was also a temptation to fudge its terms so that they meant all things to all men - a temptation which was not to be resisted by the May government; and the general assumption that putting flesh on the bones of the Political Declaration would be carried out by the May government became more precarious as the year wore on and a series of resignations by Brexiter ministers cast increasing doubt on that. In retrospect this piece of sequencing was clearly an error. Whether, given the EU's attachment to the letter of its laws, it could have been avoided is another matter.

In any case, for a number of different reasons, the words "in theory" applied throughout the next few months to any real engagement over the future relationship. For one thing there were some loose ends from the December outline divorce agreement which needed to be settled. One of these, the Irish dimension, and how to give practical effect to the commitment to avoid in all circumstances any new controls on the border between Ireland and Northern Ireland, had a massive explosive potential (which remains to this day, after we have left and the Withdrawal Agreement has to be implemented). Some of these loose ends were examined in an InFacts article I wrote on 4th April, 2018:

4 Brexit loose ends government yet to tie.

We are in a lull. Parliament has risen for its Easter recess and the negotiations over the UK's post-Brexit end-state are yet to really get under way. It therefore makes sense to look at the loose ends left untied, now that the broad basis of the divorce settlement and the 21-month standstill transition have been agreed. And there are plenty of those loose ends; indeed there is little but loose ends, and few indications from the government on how and when they think they should be tied up.

The most obvious loose end is the patent inadequacy of the duration of the standstill period. From one end of Europe to the other there are vanishingly few people who consider that it will be feasible to negotiate the details of the new relationship and have them in force by New Year's Day 2021. Even the government knows the period is inadequate, since it asked for longer.

And then, what? Transition to where? Do we go over the cliff-edge only to scramble back a few years later when a full deal is concluded - precisely that double shock which business fears the most and which will be the most damaging to our economy and to inward investment?

It was remarkably irresponsible of the government to agree to 21 months without making any provision for the possible future extension of the standstill, which could be needed to avoid a cliff-edge. But then the Brexiters would not have stood for that. As usual, they got their way.

Then there are the complexities of Ireland and Gibraltar. The government still seems to hope that some technological magic carpet will materialise and waft us all over a control-free border between Ireland and Northern Ireland. But their resistance to the backstop arrangement which was reached last December leaves one in doubt that they have much confidence that the magic carpet, the design of which they are remarkably coy about, will actually turn up in time.

As to Gibraltar, the government does nothing but breathe defiance towards Spain, irrespective of the fact that the whole underpinning of Gibraltar's relationship with the EU will vanish when we leave and need to be replaced. Sooner or later the government will need to engage in a serious discussion with Spain about our mutual interest in avoiding a last-minute crisis.

And a more detailed look at the Irish conundrum is contained in another InFacts article on 8th June, 2018:

Five things we've learnt from the Irish backstop saga.

The latest round in the Brexit negotiations saga really is enough to make you weep. What conclusions can one draw from the "agreement" reached between Theresa May and David Davis on the Irish backstop paper which will now apparently be fed into the hopper in Brussels?

- first that the government is still negotiating with itself rather than with the EU27 who have to agree to any solution;

- second that the government has not yet faced up to the inbuilt contradictions between the backstop text it agreed to last December and its determination to leave the customs union and the single market;

- third that, yet again , all they have done is to kick the can down the road, this time only a very little way down the road, since it is highly unlikely that this proposal will survive beyond the European Council meeting on 29 June;

- fourth that yet more precious time has been wasted failing to get to grips with the big issues of UK/EU trade, security, foreign policy cooperation, research and innovation, regulatory management and whole raft of other issues crucial to the future well-being of our economy;

- fifth that the government, and thus the country, is having to pay dearly for that initial error in triggering Article 50 without a coherent post-Brexit game plan and without having first agreed with the EU 27 a sensible approach to the sequencing of the negotiations.

So, what will happen next? Presumably the EU 27 will say politely but firmly that adding an extra year onto the already inadequate transitional period will not guarantee a smooth transition to whatever end-state arrangements are then to be put in place; that it does not therefore constitute the fail-safe backstop that the Irish government and anyone who minds seriously about the possible consequences of Brexit for the Good Friday Agreement is seeking; and that an end 2021 limit on the backstop will have to be dropped if there is to be an agreement.

What will the UK government do then? Face up to the prospect of losing some Brexiter ministers if they agree? Or simply soldier on in deadlock, with time and negotiating goodwill being frittered away? The choice will be the one they faced and funked this week.

*　　　　　　　*　　　　　　　*

But of more immediate interest to all on both sides of the Channel were the rising tensions within the Cabinet and the Conservative parliamentary party over the nature of the UK's post-Brexit trade relationship with the EU, which was at the heart of any future partnership, but which could not even be properly addressed in Brussels so long as the UK did not have an agreed position on it. And there was also an awareness of the whole raft of additional, complex Brexit-related primary legislation which needed to be got through a parliament where the government did not have a secure majority but which would necessarily affect that post-Brexit relationship. Of those bills the one dealing with immigration once free movement of people within the EU ceased to apply was likely to be one of the most contentious; it was assessed in an InFacts article of 23rd April, 2018:

Silence on post-Brexit immigration will become deafening.

The government and its Brexit supporters continue to claim divine democratic legitimacy from the referendum result. They use it to make policy choices which were either barely mentioned in the referendum campaign or on which precisely contrary indications were given, leaving the single market and the customs union are the most notable examples.

But what about immigration, a policy area which actually did figure prominently in the campaign - albeit in the form of false innuendoes, plain lies and a promise to take back control over a policy we already controlled, namely immigration from countries outside the EU? Remember the claims that Turkish accession was imminent - with 80 million Turks free to come to Britain? Or the posters showing an endless queue of asylum seekers - whose access to the UK we in fact controlled ourselves?

So, why the silence about Britain's new post-Brexit immigration regime? The government has said precisely nothing so far in all the floods of prime ministerial speeches and UK position papers for the Brexit negotiations.

The answers are a bit different between the government and the Brexiters. The government is genuinely conflicted about what to do and paralysed by divided counsels. Too liberal regime and they will be assailed by many of their own supporters in Parliament and by many millions of voters who opted for Leave. Too tough a regime and they will inflict serious damage on the economy and will prejudice the chances of negotiating a good trade deal with the other 27 EU countries. For the Brexiters this is just another awkward issue which is better left until after the door slams shut behind us in March 2019.

Hence the government's absurdly dilatory timetable which involves losing the immigration ball in the long grass of the Migration Advisory Committee until the autumn, and then promising a White Paper and legislation at unspecified points beyond that.

Does this matter? It most certainly does. For one thing it means that, in all likelihood Parliament will be asked to take its decision on the outcome of the Brexit negotiations without knowing what the government intends to do on the critically important issue of immigration. For another there is not the slightest chance of getting any specificity about the future trade relationship between the UK and the EU until we can say how we are going to treat EU citizens coming to work or study in this country after January 2021. Britain's negotiators in Brussels, where negotiations on trade are now getting under way, will simply have to say they don't know the answer to that question, and are not likely to do so any time soon. Hardly a comfortable position for negotiators to find themselves in.

Meanwhile in the real world in which we actually live, the parameters of the problem are changing all the time. Immigration from the other EU countries is dropping steadily, driven by the lethargic economy here and the more rapidly growing one in the rest of the EU and by the lower value of sterling following the Brexit vote adjustment. And important sectors of our economy - the NHS, seasonal agricultural labour, the hospitality sector, universities - are already beginning to feel the pinch from the lower availability of EU labour, a *harbinger of things to come if the government goes for a tough new regime.*

Oddly too, the government has just opted to retain full free movement for the 21 month transitional period after exit, provoking no serious protest at all. And, as we have seen over the Windrush saga in recent days, the doubts over our capacity to actually implement and operate in a humane manner a complex restrictive immigration regime remain unanswered.

So it is high time for the government to come clean on its future plans for immigration and subject them to public and parliamentary scrutiny. Otherwise both they and we are storing up some unpleasant surprises for the future; and Parliament risks being asked to buy a pig in a poke in the autumn when the promise of a "meaningful" Brexit process is put to the test.

*   *   *

Nor was the background against which the Brexit negotiations were being played out in any way a benign one. In May there was a completely unnecessary row between the UK and the EU over the former's continuing role in the EU's Galileo project for a satellite positioning system matching the US's GPS. Just in case the reader may feel by now that I was invariably critical of our own government's handling of Brexit-related issues an InFacts article of 8th May, 2018 on Galileo shows this was not always so; and I took the same line when the matter was debated in the House of Lords:

EU satellite spat prime example of Brexit unintelligence.

The angry debate over Britain's future involvement in the EU's Galileo space project, into which the UK has already sunk more than £1 billion, is a perfect example of how the Brexit process is creating more problems than it resolves - and of how it scrambles the brains of otherwise intelligent actors on both sides.

On one side you have European Commission officials insisting that the UK, as a non-member state, must be deprived of access to sensitive parts of the Galileo project, including participating in their construction.

On the other side you have the government apparently doing its best to delay Galileo and to proceed with a British-only competitor, egged on by the usual Brexit claque. Defence Secretary Gavin Williamson has revealed "Defence scientists and military experts" are already scoping out the possibility for a new British system, which the Telegraph reports could cost more than £3 billion.

On the face of it both sides seem to be sliding towards what can only be described as Mutually Assured Damage, a variant on the acronym familiar to participants in the Cold War's nuclear confrontation.

Is this avoidable? In a sensible world you would have thought so. Does it really make sense to cut the UK out of the full participation in Galileo it currently enjoys? This is on pretty spurious security grounds, given that we are a NATO ally of many of the EU participants in the project.

There are no doubt stacks of legal advisers and institutional ayatollahs in Brussels busy marshalling arguments as to why continued full UK participation is unthinkable after Brexit. But political leaders are there to test such arguments against scientific and political realities and not simply to succumb to them.

As to the "Britain only" idea, it may (just about) pass muster as a negotiating ploy - even if its credibility, like so many other "no deal" outcomes is not great. Where precisely is the money to come from when the government is strapped for cash? And will the market bear and reward another competitor with the US's GPS, the Russian scheme and Galileo?

In any case, the basis for avoiding a completely unnecessary row is already at hand. The Prime Minister's proposal, in both her Florence and Munich speeches, for a new security treaty between the UK and the other 27 EU members, surely provides the framework needed to avoid the security problems which have surfaced over Galileo? But what has happened to that proposal? Where have the negotiations got to, if anywhere? On that the silence is deafening.

Before allowing the dispute over Galileo to further poison an already pretty fraught atmosphere, would it not be wiser to put that proposed framework to proper use? Failure to do so will only add one more item to the already long list of the unnecessary costs of Brexit.

And the international scene was far from tranquil, with President Trump's lack of support for NATO, his bizarre and not very helpful foray to the UK and his even more bizarre meeting with President Putin in Helsinki, causing plenty of waves and underlining, yet again, how inconsistent with our interests Trump's policies were and how much closer on many foreign policy issues we now were to our main EU partners. This aspect was covered in an InFacts article of 18th June, 2018:

Trump's NATO bluster risks all our security.

The fallout from last weekend's G7 meeting in Quebec focused largely on Donald Trump's bad-tempered outburst against Justin Trudeau, calling his Canadian counterpart "dishonest and weak". More attention should probably have been given to another Trump tweet from Air Force One on his way to Singapore, raging against the amount EU countries pay into NATO and their trade arrangements with the US.

By now most observers have long since stopped expecting factual accuracy from Trump. It's to be expected that he ignored the fact that the EU's level of tariff protection and that of the US is similar, and generally low. As was the fact that those levels were established by common accord in the 1990s and have since been applied by both Republican and Democrat administrations. So too was the fact that the? EU was quite recently negotiating away those tariffs in a transatlantic free trade partnership deal, which the Trump administration has now blocked.

But the President linking NATO members' levels of military spending to trade policy reaches a new degree of irresponsibility and risk. NATO's outstanding success over its 70 year existence in providing security to its members without a shot being fired has depended crucially on the effectiveness of its deterrent capacity - specifically the commitment in Article 5 of the NATO Treaty for each member to defend all others against aggressive action. By subjecting this to the transactional calculations of trade flows, Trump risks fatally undermining that deterrence. This point will not have escaped NATO's adversaries.

The security with which Trump is playing fast and loose is the UK's too, not just that of those NATO members who are failing so far to hit the 2% of GDP target to support the alliance. NATO's leaders will be meeting at a summit in Brussels in three weeks' time. If the potential damage from that tweet is not repaired then - by making it clear that the Article 5 commitment is an unconditional one and, most crucially, by ensuring the trade linkage is not repeated - then the security of all of us will have been jeopardised.

Our own government will, quite rightly, be pressing our partners to move more rapidly towards the 2% target. But it must not lend itself to any such linkage, which will be as damaging to us as to those to whom it is directed.

As we move into the closing stage of the Brexit negotiations, it is becoming clearer by the day that the Trump policy prescription of disrupting his allies is going to catch us at a peculiarly vulnerable moment. We are

200

already at odds with US policies on climate change, trade, Palestine, and their reneging on the Iran nuclear deal. Seeing our own security put into play by our closest ally is surely something we need to do all we can to resist.

*   *   *

There was one piece of good news for the government that June; its EU (Withdrawal) Bill finally made it onto the statute book and became an act of parliament after a marathon passage through both Houses (for the earlier stages, see Chapter 10). The government had, however, been forced to concede a number of changes and been compelled to accept the "meaningful process" provision for getting Commons approval for any Brexit deal before it could be ratified and enter into force. That provision had, incidentally, excluded the House of Lords from any decision-making role in the "meaningful process", an acceptance of the primacy of the Commons which no one I knew in the Lords, certainly not me, contested. This exclusion from the decision-making process was to have consequences for the Lords' handling of Theresa May's deal once it was put before Parliament for approval in the early months of 2019. My own assessment of the new Act was contained in an InFacts article on 23rd June, 2018:

May has her Withdrawal Act… but road ahead is no easier.

No doubt many people would have greatly preferred it if what is now the EU Withdrawal Act had contained clear and detailed provisions for the parliamentary handling of a "no deal" outcome to the Brexit negotiations, as proposed by the House of Lords last Monday. Instead we have got a lot of fudge.

But, if the government thinks that they can turn up on January 21 next year (as they are now required to do by the Act), and report to Parliament that there will be no deal and that we are going to crash out of the EU in less than three months' time, and that Parliament will just acquiesce and let them tickle its tummy, they are likely to be in for a rude shock. Far more likely that would trigger a full-blown governmental crisis.

In any case, in the two more likely eventualities than a "no deal" - a really bad deal (usually called "hard Brexit") or a slightly less bad outcome (usually called "soft Brexit") - the parliamentary procedures are indeed now clear and detailed. And they require the Commons to approve any deal before it can be ratified and for the Lords to have their say too. So we have got a bit more than two thirds of a meaningful process, thanks to the exertions of cross-party alliances in both Lords and Commons.

More than that the bill which originally contained no reference at all to the border between the two parts of Ireland now has a clear and binding provision preventing new border controls. So the contradictions between the government's determination to leave the customs union and the single market and the need to avoid new border controls is now hard-wired into our domestic law.

Add to that further important amendments which make those 11 months hard slog in Parliament seem almost worthwhile:

- the government's new environmental watchdog will now have teeth, enabling it to prosecute infringements;

- parliamentary input into post-Brexit primary and secondary legislation has been considerably strengthened;

- better provisions for re-uniting families of asylum seekers;

- a potential opening towards the UK remaining in a customs union with the EU.

The adoption of this Act does not make the road ahead in the Brexit negotiations any easier or less strewn with elephant traps, into which the government's hapless negotiating team are all too likely to fall. Next week's European Council will demonstrate that the government has wasted another three months of precious negotiating time since the Council last met getting absolutely nowhere - and that Brexit is even further down the EU's list of "must do" issues its 27 members are willing to devote the limited amount of political will at their disposal.

Then there is the White Paper promised for July, which is all too likely to contain more helpings of fudge and unachievable aspirations. The government's Customs and Trade Bills are due to come back to Parliament, offering a clear opportunity to press for abandonment of the red line on a customs union. And producing that other White Paper on immigration is hardly going to be a walk in the park.

One could almost feel sorry for the government if they were not the principal architects of their own predicament. The amount of road down which cans are able to be kicked is running out. And running out of road usually precedes a car crash.

*   *   *

By this time even Theresa May had accepted that the robotic repetition of Brexit mantras and speeches festooned with red lines were not going to advance the negotiations in Brussels. The boast of the Brexiters that the EU 27 would come to us on their knees, ready to accept our terms, in order to protect their exports of BMWs, Prosecco and Camembert, had been shown up for the empty bombast it had always been. So, she began a cautious, extremely secretive process of fashioning a new position on post-Brexit UK/EU trade relations. In this search she relied almost exclusively on her Sherpa and chief negotiator at the official level, Ollie Robbins; and she completely cut out the DexEu department and its Secretary of State, David Davis, as well as ministers from other departments responsible for aspects of Brexit. When this new approach finally emerged at Chequers it did represent a crab-like move closer to some EU requirements, including the need to avoid undermining the customs union and the single market, while preserving as frictionless as possible trade, between the UK and the EU. But it was incredibly complex; and it had elements that were never going to pass muster with the EU 27. My ahead of time analyses were contained in InFacts articles of 2nd and 6th

July, 2018, the latter of which also treats the perennial problem of British leaders when they say one thing in Brussels and another to their domestic audience:

We must nail down future partnership before Brexit.

As attention turns to the Cabinet's away day on Friday at Chequers, ministers would do well to listen carefully to what George Bridges told the Today programme last week. The former Brexit minister had four main messages: stop lobbing hand grenades at each other from pre-conceived trenches; go for a customs union and full regulatory alignment for goods, but not services; nail down the agreement on a new partnership this autumn rather than leave it until after Brexit; and prepare seriously for a "no deal" outcome as a negotiating ploy.

My own take on those pieces of advice is: first is quixotic; second is conceivable if the red line on dispute settlement is thrown in; third is spot on; and fourth is plain wrong.

Lobbing grenades is all the Brexiters in and outside the Cabinet know how to do. They have not produced a single idea since the referendum campaign began which has a snowball's chance in hell of being agreed by the EU 27. They are probably not going to stop their grenade lobbing now, so the journey might have a better chance of success if they left the train at this point. But, do not hold your breath.

The second prescription might conceivably be acceptable to the EU 27 if a robust dispute settlement procedure involving a role for the European Court of

Justice were part of it. The only way to find out is to try it on. It could, in addition, solve the Ireland/Northern Ireland border problem. It would leave little space for the UK to negotiate about trade with third countries.

The third piece of advice, to get all this nailed down in the autumn and not left over to be negotiated after the UK has left must be right. Anyone who seriously believes we will be better placed to negotiate with the EU from outside must either be deluded or is a closet supporter of "no deal".

What about the fourth piece of advice - that we set in hand preparations for a "no deal" outcome, not as an objective (Bridges was admirably clear about just how damaging such an outcome would be for the UK), but as a negotiating ploy to get a better deal? Rather an expensive ploy one might have thought.

But in any case Bridges' advocacy is seriously awry. He said "Without that the EU will always have the upper hand". Unfortunately that is the case with or without those preparations, because they too know that we would be more severely damaged by a "no deal" outcome. Better surely to be a little realistic about the real balance of forces?

And now the second:

May's doublespeak could waste yet more precious time.

Negotiating within and with the EU has presented successive British governments with almost insurmountable difficulties. And none more so than how

206

to reconcile the way they present the desired outcome of the negotiations to the Cabinet, Parliament and the people on the one hand, and to their negotiating partners in Brussels on the other; and how, in due course, to get the first group to accept the outcome of the negotiations when a deal is struck.

Up to now no British government has quite done the splits, although some have come perilously close to doing so. But the Brexit negotiations look likely to be the occasion when they do so, if not at Chequers then not far down the road.

The problems at both ends of the negotiations - in Westminster and in Brussels - are that the participants at one end can see and hear what is being said by the British government at the other end, and that in real time. That hardly contributes to the creation of trust, that precious commodity without which negotiations are hard to conclude; all the more so when what is being said by the government at each end is inherently contradictory.

So this week you have Theresa May saying to Parliament that we shall be leaving the Single Market, the Customs Union and the jurisdiction of the European Court of Justice; and that we will be able to strike our own deals with third countries. All that in blithe disregard of the fact that, applied literally, that would mean new border controls between the two parts of the island of Ireland and would mean kissing goodbye to frictionless trade with the rest of the EU.

And this same week the Cabinet is contemplating putting forward in Brussels - when they have finished speed-reading the 120 pages of the draft White Paper -

an approach which involves accepting many elements of remaining in the Single Market and the Customs Union and accepting the jurisdiction of the ECJ; and which will inhibit our ability to negotiate with third countries like the US.

No doubt semantic wonders will in due course be performed by government spokespeople - not "direct" jurisdiction of the ECJ, you know; only covers trade in goods, not services, you realise; and so on and so forth.

And all that is before the new approach has even reached the negotiating table in Brussels, where it is all too likely, if it survives at all, to be metamorphosed into something a bit different. This week we have been treated to the somewhat humiliating spectacle of the Prime Minister travelling to The Hague and Berlin to plead, not for the acceptance of this new approach which she was in no position to put forward to her interlocutors, but that it not be dismissed summarily and in short order. That plea could succeed. But to what benefit other than wasting another three months of precious time?

What can be said with some degree of certainty is that none of these complexities and contradictions were even contemplated when the electorate cast their votes in the referendum two years ago. After all Boris Johnson was saying that we could remain in the Single Market and that Turkey, as an EU member state, would shortly have free movement rights. So the case for testing whatever outcome emerges becomes daily less easy and less credible to resist.

The Chequers meeting in itself will surely merit a mention in any history of British cabinet practice, preceded as it was by the rather humiliating dash by the Prime Minister to The Hague and Berlin, not apparently designed to present her new thinking to Rutte and Merkel, since the risk of leaks was too great, but merely to plead for the EU to give it careful consideration and not to dismiss it out of hand. At Chequers the members of the Cabinet, having had their mobile phones impounded and having been told that, if they could not accept the outcome of the meeting they would not be able to use their official cars to get back to London but would have to call a taxi, were sat down to peruse a 120 page White Paper, which none of them had seen before, in advance of discussion. The Prime Minister appeared to have got her way; the Cabinet approved the document; and it was so announced. But, within days first David Davis and then Boris Johnson had resigned; and the response of the ERG was thunderous, although there was no parliamentary approval required before the new position was put forward in Brussels. From then on the Conservative Parliamentary Party moved from a stage of high tension to open warfare.

My own assessment of the Chequers proposals is contained in an InFacts article of 16th July, 2018:

A White Paper that is full of holes.

Amidst all the vicious squabbling in Conservative ranks over the government's White Paper, it is all too easy to lose sight of the substance of the position the government has, at last, put on the table. Two years after the referendum, sixteen months after the withdrawal negotiations began and a mere three months before they are scheduled to conclude, probably the kindest thing that can be said about it is "too little and too late".

In reality the White Paper is as full of holes as a piece of Swiss cheese. It is as notable for what it does not say as for what it does. Here are seven gaps or missteps which will need to be sorted out if progress is to be made over the next three months.

1. The proposed Customs Facilitation Arrangement to replace the existing Customs Union is incredibly complex, completely untried and far more likely to collapse like a house of cards than ever to be operational. It provides for us to hand over customs duties on goods destined for the EU 27, while putting no matching obligations on them to hand over duties on goods coming to the UK, for example via Rotterdam. Moreover the arrangement may not even be compatible with WTO rules: exporting countries and companies are entitled to know which tariff rate they face, not to be faced with a choice of two.

2. The Irish backstop is blithely dismissed in a single reference as something "which will not have to be used". The form in which last December's deal on this point is to be put in the Withdrawal Treaty remains contested, with Theresa May saying that the Commission's proposed text could not be accepted by any

British Prime Minister. So, what could the government accept? "Don't know" or "It won't happen" are scarcely acceptable answers.

3. Simply hanging the service industries out to dry, as the White Paper does, is an astonishingly irresponsible way to treat what amounts to 80% of the UK economy. Exports are rising steadily as progress is made in freeing up EU trade in services. It is the one area where the UK already boasts a trade surplus with the EU. This is not just about banks and financial services, but includes culture and the creative industries, architecture, accountancy, legal and many other professional services at which we excel.

4. The dispute settlement procedures proposed are also incredibly complex and are not suited at all to the handling of cases of individuals, such as would arise in respect of the European Arrest Warrant. A much more straightforward solution would be to use an instrument like the EFTA Court, which makes clear provision for the European Court of Justice's role.

5. The government has at last tiptoed up to the sensitive issue of the free movement of people. There is talk of negotiating a mobility framework. But nothing useful for the negotiators is said about the specifics of such a framework; and there is no hope of the

211

negotiations being concluded without those specifics being filled in.

6. *The promise that Parliament will be able to reject any change in the common rulebook for goods is a sham. Any such rejection would be likely to bring the whole partnership tumbling down, as the Swiss found out when they tried unilaterally to change the rules on free movement. Moreover such an arrangement would be a continuing temptation to Brexiters in Parliament to re-open the partnership agreement.*

7. *Saying what is set out in the White Paper would not inhibit our capacity to negotiate trade agreements with third countries has already been given the lie by President Trump. The hard fact is that Liam Fox, as minister responsible for such international trade deals, is likely to find time hanging heavy on his hands.*

Suggesting that the White Paper is the final word on what the government should accept, as the Brexiters are demanding, is simply another way of working for a "no deal" outcome. The Cabinet now knows, although Parliament has not been told, just how damaging that would be.

* * *

One footnote to these events, specific to the Foreign Secretary, Boris Johnson, is worth recording. It shines a harsh light on the relative priority he attached to advancing his future political career and to performing his public duties. The Monday after the Chequers weekend meeting and the day at the end of which Johnson resigned, he was due to preside over a West Balkan EU Summit in London's Dockland. This meeting had been designed to begin to re-build British influence in a region where, during the twentieth century, three major wars, each of which had involved the UK in considerable cost in blood and treasure, had been waged. That influence had gone into free fall after the referendum vote in 2016, as all the evidence taken by the House of Lords' International Relations Committee on which I served and which earlier in 2018 conducted an extensive enquiry into our relations with the West Balkans, testified. The countries of the West Balkans (Albania, Bosnia and Herzegovina, Kosovo, Montenegro, North Macedonia, Serbia) saw Britain's departure from the EU as the loss of one of the strongest advocates of further enlargement to include their countries and of a prominent participant in EU programmes to strengthen democracy, the rule of law and respect for human rights and to combat international crime. The London conference seemed to our Committee and to the FCO as an ideal opportunity to counter that impression and to show that the UK was not losing interest in the region. But Johnson never turned up at the meeting, over which he was meant to be presiding; instead he retreated to his official residence in Carlton Gardens to compose the long, rambling and not very convincing resignation letter he subsequently sent, and to prepare for a television presentation of his decision. It was not a good example of the public service ethos in which I and many others had been trained and had tried to practice in our professional careers.

Chapter 11

Trench warfare: May's best shot (July/December 2018)

Theresa May's plea that the Chequers proposals should not be dismissed by the EU in short order met with some, very short term, success. There was no official reaction before Europeans departed on their summer holidays. British ministers criss-crossed continental Europe during the holiday period with no obvious success in attracting support for the proposals nor in stimulating divisions among the EU 27. And, when the Heads of State and Government met informally in September in Salzburg, there was a trivial but disagreeable incident when Donald Tusk, the President of the European Council, was pictured handing Theresa May a cake crowned with cherries, an all too blatant signal of the main EU criticism that the UK indulged in "cherry picking". This rather ill considered incident was of course not lost on the press; it was a bad augury for the intensive period of negotiation which was about to start. My own analysis of the challenges facing the government after Chequers was contained in an InFacts article of 1ˢᵗ August, 2018:

PM's hard choices for the autumn.

Theresa May is to interrupt her Alpine walking holiday this week to visit Emmanuel Macron in an attempt to get the French President to soften his Brexit position. This follows her recent announcement that she is assuming personal charge of the Brexit negotiations.

The Prime Minister's more active role not only downgrades the position of her new Brexit secretary, ensuring that none of Dominic Raab's EU interlocutors will take what he says very seriously, but it also raises the stakes for herself. Of course she has always had overall responsibility for the negotiations, but this step ensures she will be held directly responsible for every future policy move and decision. Here are some of the main issues at stake.

Timing

Anyone who expects that we will have negotiated a deal, or even see a conclusive failure to reach one, by the October target date, really is demonstrating the triumph of hope over experience.

The Conservative Party conference in early October leaves little time for negotiation before the European Council meeting later that month. And the efforts of ministers to travel around Europe during August stirring up apathy aren't likely to get very far. Much more likely is an outcome of some sort by November or December.

Substance v. waffle.

Will any document on the new relationship, which the government has insisted will be available for

Parliament to approve, contain real substance or just consist of waffle and warm words? The UK's negotiating position after Brexit is likely to be even weaker: we will have lost the leverage of having to reach a Withdrawal Agreement and be constrained by the ridiculously inadequate 21 -month transitional period, with the prospect of a cliff-edge in January 2021. We therefore need substance rather than waffle. But that will require more compromises.

No deal.

Even if the government has finally realised that no deal is not better than a bad deal, the Brexiters propping May up have yet to reach that common-sense conclusion. So the weeks ahead are going to be filled with self-generated scare stories about the perils for trade flows and the inadequacies of stockpiling - Project Fear orchestrated by the Brexiters themselves. All of which will only weaken the government's negotiating hand in Brussels, not strengthen it, as is being claimed.

UK/EU trade after Brexit.

The government's much-touted Facilitated Customs Arrangement is clearly not going to fly in anything like its original form. Will the government have the courage to recognise that a customs union of some sort will be needed, together with a substantial degree of regulatory alignment? Don't count on it.

The role of the European Court of Justice.

The government's elaborate contortions to avoid an acceptable role for the ECJ in dispute settlement is now preventing progress on a whole range of issues. Most important is the government's proposals on internal security and the European Arrest Warrant. Will this Gordian knot be cut?

Loose ends from the divorce agreement.
Obviously the most important of these is what has come to be known as the Irish "backstop". So far the government has only said what it will not accept. But without a solution there will not be a deal. Meanwhile there is still the matter of Gibraltar to be resolved.

As to the treatment of EU citizens the government has probably complicated matters by revealing in its most recent White Paper that it would rely on powers under the 1971 Immigration Act to implement the agreement reached last December, arguing that this would provide more flexibility and certainty. Flexibility perhaps, but certainty is less sure. So, why not take the whole matter out of this negotiation by announcing unilaterally that, deal or no deal, we would honour our obligations to those citizens? That really would provide certainty.

It is really hard to look at this list without a sinking feeling. So much to resolve in such a short time. It is surely time to rethink the whole enterprise or at least to commit to a People's Vote on the outcome.

And a further piece looking at the geo-strategic backdrop against which the Brexit negotiations were being played out was in an InFacts article of 21st August, 2018:

No deal would be a huge geo-strategic mistake.

Reasonably enough much of the public debate about the consequences of a no deal outcome to the Brexit negotiations has so far concentrated on important day-to-day issues like accessibility of fresh food and medicines, the effect on prices and on the near half of our trade which is with the rest of the EU.

But the Foreign Secretary (Jeremy Hunt) has put his finger on a quite different, less tangible bit still serious aspect of such an outcome when he last week described no deal as a "mistake we would regret for generations" and as a "huge geo-strategic mistake" - a message he is expected to repeat in Washington today. Since then desperate efforts have been made to clarify these statements as being directed at the EU 27, demonstrating the knots the government is tying itself in as it tries to placate its own no deal advocates, to put the wind up the other EU countries and to avoid actually having a no deal outcome, all at the same time.

The most profound geo-strategic consequences would be on our own relationship with the rest of Europe which would inevitably be plunged into deep and enduring acrimony. Brexiters like to think that we would be laughing all the way to the bank as we made off with the £39 billion divorce settlement. Dream on! These are debts accrued from our membership, which we agreed last December were owed as part of our leaving. We can be quite sure that the EU would pursue us over non-payment through every kind of

219

international court and arbitration machinery available to them. It is, after all, not in their own interest that any other member should believe that it can leave scot free. So any hope of a strong and enduring security relationship with the EU and of free trade with them would founder in a welter of name-calling and bad blood. Only our adversaries, like Vladimir Putin, would derive any satisfaction from that.

Then, how about the relationship with our principal ally, the United States? President Trump is nothing if he is not transactional; and a Britain locked in endless rows with its former European partners might not look like much of a transaction. In those circumstances any future US president would re-orient their foreign policy activity away from London and towards Paris and Berlin, calculating, no doubt correctly, that any line of policy they could agree with those two and the rest of the EU would inevitably be accepted by London too. So much for our vaunted influence in Washington.

Would the Commonwealth provide a substitute for these negative consequences? Not a hope. The Commonwealth is not, and is not going to become, a trade bloc or a foreign policy actor. India is already a major regional power in its own right, very possibly on its way to becoming a global one. The members of the Commonwealth will be a lot more interested in their trade and investment links with the remaining 27 EU countries than with us, particularly if our economy remains in the doldrums, as it is now. And they will not forget that we did not appear to have much time for them before we voted to leave the EU.

220

And then, closer to home, there is that other union, rightly described by Theresa May as "precious", uniting the four nations of the United Kingdom. That will be deeply and adversely affected by a no deal outcome. Not many Scots will blame the EU for that. So, while there is no immediate pressure for an early, second independence vote, it would be foolhardy to assume that that state of grace would long survive leaving without a deal and would not be strengthened by its damaging consequences.

In Ireland the geo-strategic consequences would be far more immediate and more serious. No chance, in those circumstances, of avoiding border controls to levy tariffs and carry out regulatory checks. And Ireland would suffer the most collateral damage of any EU member state from a no deal outcome. So do not expect sweetness and light to characterise a relationship which has, until we voted to leave in 2016, been in an unprecedented period of harmony.

So, quite a litany of geo-strategic damage to our interests awaits if we crash out without a deal. Enough, surely, to show just how reckless and irresponsible are those who advocate such a course. And enough too to buttress the case for the electorate having the final say in those circumstances.

*　　　　　　　*　　　　　　　*

That September the government's Trade Bill, one of its Brexit-related pieces of primary legislation, reached the Lords, having passed through the Commons without significant amendment. As so often the government tried to pass the Bill off as a minor piece of largely technical law-making designed to ensure that our statute book was in good shape for Brexit. In truth it was anything but minor, particularly since, if, as the government kept insisting, leaving without any deal at all in March 2019 was a possible outcome, it could become the sole basis for conducting the UK's newly independent trade policy in six months' time. No British government had undertaken trade policy negotiations since 1973 when the UK's accession handed that task over to the Commission on the EU's behalf. In addition the international framework for conducting trade policy had been completely different then, so this was breaking new ground; and, that in a policy area to which the Leave campaign, and now the government, attached great, perhaps disproportionate, political and economic significance. Moreover the Bill provided a platform for pursuing the issue of the UK remaining in a customs union with the EU after Brexit, for which there was much cross-party support. So, no wonder a long and troubled passage through the Lords was in the offing.

I had myself, in the 1960s, been a junior member of the UK team negotiating the multilateral trade liberalisation round (known as the Kennedy Round); and in the 1970s my professional life in the Commission, immediately after we joined, had involved working for the Commissioner responsible for trade policy. So I was reasonable familiar with the, often rather arcane, subject matter of the Trade Bill; and I was one of the few British officials still around, who had had practical experience of what it had been like to negotiate on our own, and also how things worked when the Commission worked on our behalf. I therefore played a moderately prominent role in the Lords' handling of the Bill as a member of the cross-party alliance which moved amendments to it in the months that lay ahead.

There were two principal bones of contention in the Bill. The first was whether or not remaining in a customs union with the EU should be set out as an objective of our post-Brexit trade policy. This was a highly political issue since it cut right across the government's intention of leaving the customs union; and it was all the more so because an independent trade policy was the Brexiters' jewel in the crown, and giving it up would have meant losing another member of the cabinet, Liam Fox. On the plus side, though not seen as such by the government, it provided a way of partially resolving the Irish conundrum (since, if we remained in a customs union with the EU there would be no need for, and no question of, levying tariffs either on the border between the two parts of Ireland or between Northern Ireland and Great Britain). The amendment providing for this approach passed by a large majority.

The second issue was about what role parliament would play in future in mandating, scrutinising and approving any trade agreements, whether bilateral or multilateral, the government wished to negotiate. The government wanted no mandating, minimum scrutiny and a one shot, up or down, nuclear option for approval or rejection once the agreement had been negotiated. Unfortunately for them this involved giving our own Parliament, which was meant to be taking back control as a result of Brexit, a less influential role over our trade policy than the European Parliament, with British MEPs in it, already had. This was not a discrepancy which was easy to defend. Our amendment remedied the lacunas on these points in a fairly comprehensive way; but, despite offers from our side to negotiate somewhat less ambitious provisions, the government, as was often the case, gave its ministers in the Lords no leeway at all. And the result was that the opposition amendments passed with a large majority. The Trade Bill then languished in the Commons' in-tray for many long months, the government fearing that they would not be able to muster a majority there to reject the customs union amendment; and it then died when Parliament was dissolved in November 2019. Here is a view of the Trade Bill and the international background to it, when it first appeared, in an article for InFacts on 13th September, 2018:

Brexit dream of independent trade is no prize at all.

The institute for Economic Affairs, a pro-Brexit think tank, recently described an independent trade policy for the UK as "the only prize remaining from Brexit". But is it a prize? And is the game really worth the candle? No one listening to the House of Lords debate on the government's Trade Bill earlier this week could be encouraged to think that the answer to either of those questions is positive.

First, nearly half of our overseas trade is with the other 27 EU countries. The Prime Minister herself admitted some time ago that, even under the Chequers proposal, trade would not be as frictionless and free of barriers and bureaucracy as it is now, or even as it would have been if she had not ruled out staying in a customs union and the single market. And that Chequers proposal is probably not going to fly anyway.

So you start off straight away with an unquantifiable minus on the ledger which would need to be compensated by an increase in our trade outside the EU before any talk of a prize would be in order.

Then there is our trade with a large range of countries around the world, which already have trade liberalisation agreements of one kind or another with the EU, and are thus available to us if we are in a customs union or stay in the EU. Such countries include Japan, South Korea, Turkey, Mexico, Canada, Colombia, Chile, several nations in Africa, the Caribbean and the Pacific, as well as countries around the Mediterranean and in the Caucasus. Additional free trade agreements with the countries of the Mercosur block in Latin America and with Australia and New Zealand are under negotiation. Our government is currently scrambling to negotiate roll-over arrangements with all these countries so that we do not lose out on our access to their markets in March 2019. So we find ourselves running just to stand still; no prize there either.

The US, China and India fall under none of those categories, it is true. But does anyone seriously believe that a trade agreement with the US will be a free lunch? With a narrowly transactional US President at the helm, far more likely that we would be asked to pay dearly in concessions - on food standards, on access to health care - to get a deal. Ask the Mexicans or the

Canadians about that as they are forced to re-negotiate NAFTA.

And while China does do free trade deals, the one with Switzerland phases out Swiss tariffs immediately and Chinese tariffs rather slowly. India and Brazil are both likely to ask for concessions on our visa policy for their students, researchers and businessmen. And Australia and New Zealand will seek concessions on beef and lamb which will hurt our farmers, already at risk of losing their valuable continental European markets.

With the multilateral world trade system, embodied in the WTO, under daily assault from US unilateral protectionist measures, this is, in any case, hardly a brilliant moment to be launching our fragile barque of an independent trade policy committed to liberalising world trade. Even if the WTO survives, as we must hope it will and do our best to ensure that it does, we will hardly be a heavy hitter in its councils. When last we were going it alone, in the 1960s, we were not. Then deals were cut between the US, Japan and the European Communities. In future it will be between the US, China, Japan, the EU and India.

So the case for putting our eggs in the basket of an independent trade policy does not stack up. Staying in a customs union looks like a far better bet. But the real prize is staying in the EU full stop.

*   *   *

It was around about this time that a number of organisations and pressure groups campaigning for another referendum on the outcome of the Brexit negotiations before the UK left the EU - foremost amongst them People's Vote and involving many others such as Best for Britain, Our Future Our Choice and the European Movement - began to pick up steam and to get wider public support right across the UK; and began too to concert their efforts at weekly coordination meetings. The People's Vote campaign was a cross-party grouping with prominent MPs from all parties - Anna Soubry, Sarah Wollaston and Heidi Allen from the Conservatives, Chuka Umunna, David Lammy and Mike Gapes from Labour and virtually total support from the Liberal Democrats, the Scottish National Party and Plaid Cymru. Its very effective staff, who briefed daily on upcoming parliamentary business as well as organising events up and down the country and setting up organisations to widen local support, was composed mainly but not exclusively of veterans from Labour and Liberal Democrat campaigns, the Labour contingent being drawn largely from enemies of Jeremy Corbyn, which was not a great help on that side of the parliamentary equation. The weekly coordination meetings were chaired originally by Chuka Umunna and then, after he had left the Labour Party in January 2019 and was no longer able to play that role, by John Kerr. Hugo Dixon, editor of InFacts, was a member of that committee, so I had no lack of information about its activities, the tensions within its ranks and the direction of the campaign.

It was in that period too that the first of four large public demonstrations took place - in London in mid-

October as the Brexit negotiations moved towards a crescendo in Brussels (the others were in March, July and October of 2019). That first demonstration was a resounding success far exceeding advance expectations (and subsequent ones were even larger, the March and October ones in 2019 reaching estimates of a million). Hundreds of thousands marched through central London, from Park Lane to Parliament Square, waving European flags and holding delightfully original placards, not the normal, formulaic print-outs seen at such events. To someone like me who had become inured, but not reconciled, to the mixture of apathy, misconceptions and mild hostility which had characterised public attitudes towards Europe, except very briefly during the 1975 referendum campaign, these were astonishing events - good humoured, not a pane of glass broken, and notably family occasions. The majority of marchers were, of course, from the London area but hundreds of buses brought marchers in from all over the country; and the efforts of Nigel Farage and other Brexiters to depict them as purely metropolitan events were not all that convincing, especially when Farage's own attempt to organise a march flopped completely, with only a handful of participants. It was ironic that no such occasion, no million strong crowds with European flags, had been seen in any other European capital; but then no other European capital had been brought face to face with the prospect of leaving the EU. I overcame a lifetime of not joining in such marches (not for Suez, nor Aldermaston, nor Iraq) and took part in all the first three, along with many members of the family, ranging from me at the aged end to Theodore, the youngest grandchild, at the other (I missed the last one in October 2019 as I was shut inside Parliament seeing off an attempted filibuster on the legislation designed to prevent us leaving the EU at the end of that month without a deal). Did these massive demonstrations have any political effect? Not directly. Political events in Britain take place in Parliament, not on the streets. But, indirectly, they helped to encourage parliamentarians rebelling against party discipline and facing the prospect of losing their seats and their careers at the next election by showing that they were not just voices crying in the wilderness but part of a genuinely popular movement.

My own progress towards full-blooded support for another referendum was slow and painful. I have recounted earlier in this book my visceral dislike of plebiscitary democracy as a means of taking fundamental but complex decisions such as whether or not to leave the EU. Plebiscitary democracy might work in Switzerland, but the study of history told me that our predecessors in this country had fought long and hard to establish representative parliamentary democracy as the way in which Britain took such decisions. The farce of the May 2011 referendum on the voting system had merely confirmed me in that view. But, as the months wore on and as the chances of the Brexit negotiations yielding anything but a hard Brexit outcome or a no deal one, and as opinion polls showed a modest shift in attitudes towards remaining in the EU, I came to recognise that there was no politically viable way of reversing the 2016 vote other than through another referendum - put simply you could only nix one referendum by another. And, while the possibility of

229

getting the legislation necessary to hold a referendum through Parliament started as a long shot, it was steadily picking up support, particularly as the log jam in a hung parliament blocked other outcomes. The chances of ever mustering a majority in Parliament simply to reverse the 2016 vote and to withdraw Britain's Article 50 notification without a referendum were vanishingly small. What I was clear about was that, unlike in 2016, when the referendum had notionally been advisory and not mandatory (although the Cameron and May governments chose to treat it as if it was the latter), this one, if it ever took place, needed to be explicitly mandatory, thus bringing the whole process to a definitive conclusion and thus too answering critics who spoke about a "neverendum" or "the best of three". On this point my view prevailed once I had won over an initially hesitant John Kerr. Did I think another referendum was certain to produce a Remain victory? Certainly not. It was clear that many voters were averse to recognising that they had made a mistake in 2016; and the campaigning prowess of the Leave campaigners was evident, even if their methods were dubious in the extreme. But it seemed to me that a Remain outcome was so much more in the national interest than any other outcome on offer that it was worth the risk. Did I recognise that another referendum campaign would be deeply divisive? Of course I did. But I sincerely believed it was the best and quickest way to cutting the Gordian knot which Brexit had become.

October and the first half of November were short on any significant developments in the Brexit negotiations themselves. The October meeting of the European Council came and went without any sign of progress in the negotiations. At the end of October, however, the negotiators in Brussels went into what was called in the jargon a "tunnel", when negotiations were continuous and the government was even more economical with what they told Parliament, or indeed anyone else, about what was going on. What was clear to everyone on both sides of the Channel was that for any deal to have a chance of getting parliamentary approval and thus of ratification by the British side, a deal would have to be struck before Christmas, if the March 2019 deadline for Brexit was to be met without a no deal outcome. In truth a lot more attention was being paid by both sides to the obscure procedures of the parliamentary Conservative party for triggering a challenge to Theresa May and a leadership election. As the necessary number of letters to the Chair of the 1922 Committee (48 required to trigger a challenge) crept up, it looked more and more likely that this was a question of when and not whether. The denouement, when it came, came quickly. The threshold was crossed, the vote was held on 12th December, and Theresa May emerged still leader of her party and still Prime Minister, but with 117 of her parliamentary colleagues having voted to remove her. This was very much a Pyrrhic victory since, if that number of Conservative MPs expressed no confidence in their leader, it was probable that a sizeable proportion of them would vote against the deal she had by then struck in Brussels a few days before, whatever wiles the party whips exercised and whatever thumb screws they applied. One thing was already clear and that was that the detailed , legal provisions on the Irish backstop, agreed in principle in December 2017 would be a crucial battle ground. I had written about that in an article for InFacts on 24th September, 2018:

PM takes another step deeper into the Irish quagmire.

Boris Johnson is fond of drawing parallels with Churchill. Perhaps he is therefore familiar with the letter Lord Randolph Churchill, father of Winston, wrote at the height of the Irish Home Rule crisis in the 1880s, revealing his intention to mobilise and agitate Ulster unionist feeling in a bid to defeat Gladstone's Home Rule Bill. "The Orange card will be the one to play. Please God it may be the ace of trumps and not the two".

That deeply cynical gamble paid off at the time in Westminster parliamentary terms but at the cost of dreadful suffering of all the peoples of Ireland thereafter. It is a pity that Johnson and his colleagues in government, including the Prime Minister, showed no awareness of the risks they were running when, following the fiasco of the 2017 general election, they handed the keys of the Brexit negotiation to the Democratic Unionist Party (DUP).

Now those risks are becoming all too evident as the Irish dimension of the Brexit negotiations becomes the touchstone of success or failure in the autumn. So far there is no sign of an agreed way of reconciling the red line of avoiding any new border controls between the two parts of Ireland, now enshrined in our domestic law in the EU Withdrawal Act, with the government's determination to quit both the EU's Single Market and its Customs Union. Nor any breakthrough in finding any formulation for a legally binding backstop in the Withdrawal Treaty being negotiated in Brussels.

It is not even entirely clear that Theresa May herself fully understands the implications for the Irish border of a no deal outcome. In her plaintively defiant statement last Friday after the Salzburg meeting she offered reassurance that even crashing out would not imperil the commitment to avoid any new border controls. But WTO rules, under which the UK would be operating in those circumstances would require us to charge the same tariffs from Ireland into Northern Ireland as we would on all other imports into the UK worldwide. So the only way of avoiding applying tariffs on those imports from Ireland as part of the EU and thus of the need for controls, would be if we removed all tariff protection on all our global imports. This was confirmed by the trade minister, Rona Fairhead, in the Lords debate on the Trade Bill on 11 September.

A zero tariff on all the UK's imports is the solution proposed by hard-Brexit economist Patrick Minford, which all commentators agree would lay waste to Britain's industry and agriculture. Was the Prime Minister contemplating that as a possibility? Presumably not.

So, if the Irish knot is to be untied, it is going to require some further blurring or erasing of red lines. This will have to be done in the legally binding text of a backstop which will have to be given effect in domestic law if the Withdrawal Treaty is to be ratified before March 29, 2019. Will this be acceptable to the DUP and the ultra-Brexiters? If not, and if there is a no deal outcome, then that will be another step deeper into the Irish quagmire.

∗   ∗   ∗

In that early November lull I wrote two historical articles for InFacts. The first on 5th November, 2018 looked back at the whole period of the Brexit negotiations to date and tabulated the list of mistakes which had, in my view, been made, and which made it close to certain that any deal now struck in Brussels would fall a very long way short of the status and advantages we currently enjoyed as an EU member:

> *Six biggest steps in the wrong direction on Brexit.*

> *With Brexit negotiations entering a secretive phase known as the "tunnel" this week, speculation of an imminent deal - or total breakdown of talks - is everywhere. It therefore seems fitting, at this important juncture, to look back and tot up the list of mistakes the government has made in these negotiations. There is no lack of them and every one was an unforced error.*

> 1. *Setting a date for triggering Article 50 without having a plan. That is precisely what the Prime Minister did when she told the Conservative Party Conference in October 2016 that Article 50, with its two year cut-off date, would be triggered, willy-nilly, by the end of March*

234

2017. And instead of working up a plan and a negotiating strategy over the next five months, the government devoted all its time and energy to a failed attempt to deny Parliament the right to authorise the move.

2. *Drawing red lines which ruled out a soft Brexit - making the avoidance of new border control in Ireland almost impossible.*

    The Prime Minister's Lancaster House speech in January 2017 - now regarded by Brexiters as the tablets of Moses - ruled out staying in the single market and the customs union, and insisted that the jurisdiction of the European Court of Justice would end on exit day. In this way a number of potentially promising avenues were ruled out before the negotiations had even begun. Ever since the Prime Minister has been forced to smudge those red lines - most obviously with the provisions for a transitional period and in the Chequers plan of July 2018 - while insisting that "nothing has changed".

3. *Accepting a sequencing of negotiations that disadvantaged the UK.*

    The government triggered Article 50 on 29 March 2017 without making any attempt to challenge the guideline on sequencing the negotiations in a way that disadvantaged the UK. This fundamental error, which has bedevilled the negotiations ever since and which David Davis made no attempt to contest when the negotiations began, has ensured that absolute priority was given to the terms of withdrawal and almost no serious effort has been put into laying the foundations for a new, post-Brexit relationship with the EU. It makes it almost certain that, in any deal struck in the next few weeks, the new relationship will be more of a fudge than a secure basis for the future.

4. *Agreeing to an Irish backstop in December 2017 without having the slightest idea as to how it was to be implemented.*

    Ever since that agreement in principle was reached on the backstop the government has turned down every effort to convert it into a legally binding text, which it has to be in the Withdrawal Treaty. The latest twist in the tale is to propose a short lengthening of the transitional period as a substitute for an insurance policy. That will not fly.

5. *Accepting a grossly inadequate 21-month transitional period back in March 2018.*

    No one involved in negotiating with the EU believes that this is sufficient to avoid a cliff-edge in December 2020. At the very least the government should have insisted on a provision enabling the transitional period to be extended by common accord. Now there is talk of extension by a few months. Again, inadequate.

6. *Wasting all of March to July 2018 in internal Tory wrangling over the government's plan for a new relationship.*

The Chequers plan, now it has finally emerged, has few friends, and a substantial part of it - the proposed customs arrangement for trade in goods - is simply unnegotiable in the form it was put forward. Meanwhile trade in services, which make up 80% of today's UK economy has been left on the beach. Is there nothing on the positive side of the ledger? Not really. We are asked to admire the Prime Minister's resilience in the face of adversity in Brussels and dissension in her own party. Her resilience is indeed remarkable. But is that a virtue when it is taking the country in the wrong direction?

The second article in this historical group situated Brexit in a much longer time frame and came out on 11th November, 2018 to mark the centenary of the armistice which ended the First World War. As someone who had lived their early childhood through the Second World War and who, as a student of history, had always regarded the two great wars of the first half of the twentieth century as pivotal to the case for the European project and for Britain's participation in it, I had regretted the gradual fading of that compelling rationale in the minds of succeeding generations (at least in Britain, although not elsewhere in Europe) and deplored the failure of today's political leaders to build those appalling experiences and the peace, stability and rising prosperity which followed them, into their own narratives when addressing the electorate:

Lest we forget, the EU has helped bring peace to Europe.

All across Europe this week commemorative events are taking place to mark the centenary of the guns falling silent on the Western Front in November 1918, after a disastrously destructive and catastrophic war between Europe's leading nation states.

It was called a "world war" but its origins and causes lay in Europe, what happened outside Europe consisted largely of a series of colonial wars between parts of European powers' empires. Twenty one years later, another even more terrible global war broke out and, although it was more truly a world war, its roots too lay in Europe - as did much of the death and destruction which flowed from it.

In those two wars Britain played a crucial and, for the most part, an honourable role. But we did not emerge unscathed any more than any other of the main participants. Unlike them, however, we were slow to draw the conclusion that, as a key part of ensuring that such disasters never happened again and as a way of binding up the wounds from those conflicts, a new structure for economic and political cooperation between Europe's different states was needed. So we helped to found NATO, but we stood aside from the European Communities.

Now, seventy years later, we are preparing to leave the European Union. Does that decision make any sort of sense, either in geo-political or economic terms? It's not *easy to find any. And our timing could hardly be worse, as the rules based international order, which we and our European allies have done so much to build, is under greater threat than at any point in recent history. Shifting power relationships and Donald Trump's "America First" foreign policy are shaking the foundations on which our future prosperity and security depend. And the European states, of whom we are one, will either hang together or we will hang separately.*

That, of course, is the logic on which Theresa May has based her proposal for a new security treaty with the other 27 EU countries after we have left. But that proposal is very much a second-best option. It will leave us with our ear pressed to the keyhole of the meeting room in which the EU 27 will work out their policy responses to international events. This will not just weaken our influence in Brussels, but in Washington too.

Why should we settle for second best? We do not have to, after all. The choice is ours, and it should be made by the electorate. The question that we will need to answer is whether it is in the UK's national interest to distance ourselves from European policy making, in which we have played such a vital role in the past centuries, and from the consequences of which we have not the slightest chance of escaping.

*   *   *

When the deal was finally struck in Brussels, right at the end of November, it rapidly became clear that it was beset on both sides of the argument in London by determined opponents. For the Brexiters the way in which the Irish backstop was expressed in legal terms was the last straw, particularly as it gradually leaked out that the Attorney-General had warned the cabinet that the text left no scope for the UK unilaterally to leave the temporary customs union with the EU in which it was to remain until both sides agreed that any post-Brexit trade and regulatory arrangements rendered the backstop unnecessary. A first, frantic effort by the Prime Minister to clarify this at the December European Council meeting was rebuffed, which only made matters worse, as did the decision not to submit the deal to an up or down vote in the Commons straight away. Had she done so and lost reasonably narrowly she might have been able to go back to Brussels and to try to squeeze a bit more juice out of the lemon. For the other side at Westminster - the opposition parties and the Conservative rebels - the Political Declaration on the future partnership (25 pages in contrast to the Withdrawal Agreement's 550+) was indeed that confection of warm words and waffle about which I had warned earlier in the year. There were many alternative, and sometimes contradictory, options, many uses of the word "consider", and no firm choices on anything. And that was not as if the Political Declaration did not contain many things that the Brexiters did not like too. So, the deal looked doomed from the start and that was how I assessed the position in an InFacts article on 14th December, 2018:

This was a bad week for Britain.

Well, that was the week that was - and, in Brexit terms, a pretty awful one for the UK by anyone's analysis. First came the government's handbrake turn preventing Parliament pronouncing on Theresa May's deal. Then came the helter-skelter dash around Europe in an effort to persuade 27 other EU countries to re-open or, more realistically, to embellish the Brexit deal which the Prime Minister had signed up to with such fanfare a mere two weeks earlier.

Act Three was the Prime Minister's survival in a vote of confidence by her MPs, which left her with 117 angry, mutinous members of her crew, determined to vote against her deal whenever it is brought back to Parliament. And finally back to Brussels to be told by the EU 27 that, much though they would prefer the original deal to be ratified, the Withdrawal Agreement, including the Irish backstop, was untouchable.

So, what has changed as a result of all this frantic and, let's admit it, rather humiliating, activity? Nothing has changed, as May herself is wont to say.

In terms of the negotiations in Brussels, that handbrake turn was probably unhelpful. If the deal had been rejected in the Commons on Tuesday, May would have arrived in Brussels on Thursday with a stronger and more clear-cut case for seeking those re-assurances which she says she needs.

As it was our neighbours refused to give any assurances that we wouldn't be trapped in an unending Irish backstop. The language on the other side of the Channel noticeably hardened. Out went pledges that the backstop "does not represent a desirable outcome", that "it would only be in place for a short period", and that the EU "stands ready to examine whether any further assurance can be provided". In went commitments to the integrity of the single market first and foremost, and to ramp up preparations for a no deal Brexit.

Very little was forthcoming, in either substance or form, which will lead to the Attorney-General updating the advice he gave to the cabinet, before the original deal was concluded, that the UK could not unilaterally avoid or terminate the backstop. The chances of that are vanishingly small. And, without it, what are the chances of those 117 mutineers - and of the Democratic Unionist Party - changing their view on the deal?

There was one piece of good news this week and that was the ruling by the European Court of Justice that the UK could unilaterally withdraw its notification to leave the EU at any time before March 29 and, by so doing, stay in the bloc on the current basis of our membership. So it really is up to us to decide whether we want Brexit, and no one else gets a say.

Where do things go from here? Anyone who expects the Prime Minister to shed much light on that when she reports back to Parliament next Monday on the European Council meeting is likely to be disappointed. Prevarication and obfuscation are more probable. But time really is running down. Both business and the government are incurring heavy costs as a result of the uncertainty and of the need to plan for the eventuality of crashing out with no deal - even though that remains unlikely.

But, until the present deal is put to the test in Parliament, it is impossible to move on to considering a preferable Plan B. When that time comes, a clear front runner will be giving the electorate a say on the whole sorry mess.

Indeed it clearly looked pretty hopeless too from Theresa May's side of the fence as an outburst on the possibility of a further referendum demonstrated, described in an InFacts article on 16th December, 2018:

May's attack on Blair shows strain is taking its toll.

Theresa May's latest outburst against Tony Blair's support for a further referendum on Brexit shows that the strain is really beginning to take its toll. Not surprising after a terrible week both in Westminster and Brussels; but deeply alarming in that it shows not a hint of new thinking in the predicament she finds herself in, just opportunistic lashing out.

Is John Major also guilty of an "insult to the office he once held"? He has, after all, called for a new referendum too. And Gordon Brown? Next we will be being asked to criticise Barack Obama when he opposes some of Donald Trump's wilder policies. But of course Blair is a soft target because he is disliked by many Labour supporters who May is hoping will stem the shift towards that referendum.

What should the Prime Minister be doing at this stage? Well, first of all she needs to recognise that she is not going to get out of the EU 27 the sort of legally binding qualifications to the Irish backstop in the Withdrawal Treaty which she needs if she is to have any hope of getting the backing of the DUP and of those 117 mutineers in her own ranks. Non-binding clarifications in bucket loads may be available, but nothing likely to vary the judgement of her own Attorney-General that there will be no way for the UK to unilaterally exit from the backstop once it has been triggered by failure to reach new trade arrangements which remove any requirement for new controls on the border between Ireland and Northern Ireland.

So the present deal, however embellished with warm words, is not going to get through Parliament and be ratified. Further delay will not change that harsh reality; it will only increase the damage to British business and the economy as more resources are poured by the government and the private sector into no deal contingency planning. It really is, therefore, time to weigh up Plan B options; time for a calmer approach and less rigidity in outlook.

What are the options? Well, one is to switch horses and go for the so-called "Norway plus" approach. But this comes with an obligation to maintain free movement and with a heavy budgetary contribution and membership of the customs union; and with exclusion from shaping the EU policies we would find ourselves having to apply. It is rather hard to see why this should be preferable to remaining a member.

The other main option, if one regards a no deal exit as unacceptably damaging - as most members of both Houses do so regard it - is to have a People's Vote.

That is now the only way the Prime Minister's deal has any chance of being approved. It also offers the electorate a chance to express a view on Brexit now that they can actually see what it entails, rather than having it sold to them, as it was in 2016, by a bunch of fantasists who have been demonstrated as incapable of delivering what they promised.

An insult to democracy? Hardly.

Chapter 12

Trench warfare: death throes of a government (January/July 2019)

It did not take much prescience in the first days of 2019 to realise that we were getting close to the Brexit end-game and that every one of a range of eventualities was just around the corner. But opinions, both in Parliament and in the country, were, if anything, more polarised than ever; and this made finding a way out of the maze difficult, if not impossible. There has been some tendency, both at the time and since, to depict that polarisation and the resultant deadlock as in some way a failure of the UK's whole political system, as if there was somewhere an "open sesame" magic formula out there which, if only we looked harder, could be found and would resolve all problems. But it gradually became clear as several such formulas were tried, mostly by government back-benchers like Kit Malthouse trying to attract the support of Ultra-Brexiters, that no such magic formula was waiting to be found. My own view was that this did not in any sense represent a failure of our political system, merely that the body politic was now grappling, rather belatedly, with the most consequential set of decisions in recent British history and was finding it desperately difficult to find a way forward.

Of the three main routes ahead being so hotly debated at the New Year by far the least likely to succeed was the one pressed on Parliament repeatedly by the government, approval of Theresa May's deal struck at the end of 2018 and now embellished with any number of "clarifications" - sometimes presented by the Attorney-General as "codicils" - none of which altered the legal force of the text that had been agreed by the Prime Minister, in particular with respect to the Irish backstop. The chances of this deal being approved and ratified were close to zero because the Conservative Brexiters, otherwise known as the European Research Group, were determined to kill it on the spurious but incontrovertible ground that it would lock the UK into a customs union with the EU for an unlimited and perhaps open-ended period. And also because, for the Labour opposition, the Political Declaration was far too vague and contradictory and was missing the main elements they would want to see in it, to attract more than a tiny number of Labour Brexiters and none of the other principal opposition parties. So, only the scale of the government's three successive defeats was a surprise; and, while the size of the majority against the deal did diminish, it remained insurmountably large.

By this time, in any case, the ERG had set their hearts on a no deal exit, to be brought about by default on 29th March, as the Article 50 cut-off expired. They were undeterred by the mounting evidence that a no deal exit would cause massive economic dislocation and damage and by the chaotic attempts of the government to prepare for such an outcome (hiring non-existent ferries to use a port - Ramsgate - which could not accommodate them, preparing lorry parks far inland in Kent, doubts over the adequacy of medical supplies). A no deal exit was opposed by majorities in both Houses - in the Lords by huge majorities - expressed in clear votes opposing that outcome. And the government itself, while still remaining trapped in its mantra of "no deal is better than a bad deal" was actually operating under the unspoken version of it that "any deal is better than no deal". Hence its eventual acceptance of the fact that extending the Article 50 cut-off by agreement with the EU was a better option.

And then, thirdly, there was the campaign for a People's Vote - a further referendum with either Theresa May's deal or no deal being pitted against remaining in the EU. This campaign continued to pick up momentum and was close to winning a majority in the Commons by the middle of March. But it was handicapped by the ambivalence of Jeremy Corbyn and by violent and vocal opposition of some Labour MPs, even if Labour's Brexit front-bench spokesman, Keir Starmer and many others were strong supporters.

A complicating factor, which considerably muddied the waters, was the decision in January of a group of Conservative MPs (Anna Soubry, Heidi Allen, Sarah Wollaston prominent among them) and a group of Labour MPs (Chuka Umunna, Mike Gapes and others) to leave their parties and to form an independent group in Parliament campaigning for a People's Vote. My own view - and there I differed from Hugo Dixon who was a strong advocate of some kind of centre party in British politics - was that this development would prove to be a distraction and was unlikely to succeed in any durable way. I had lived, as an observer, through the experience in the 1980s of the break away from the Labour Party of the Gang of Four (Roy Jenkins, Shirley Williams, David Owen and Bill Rogers) to form the Social Democrat Party and had personally had a good deal of sympathy with their objectives - as I did now with the 2019 breakaways; but, despite their much greater political prominence and name recognition than the 2019 group I had watched that initiative fail when brought up against the harsh reality of our "first past the post" electoral system. The timing of the 2019 breakaway also seemed to me far from ideal as it set up unhelpful cross-currents in both the Labour and Conservative parties, hampering the efforts of those in both parties who did not break away but continued to work within their parties for a referendum. It did, however, deprive the May government of its theoretical working majority in the Commons; and it made its dependence on the votes of the DUP even greater, thus explaining the humiliating contortions the Prime Minister went through in Brussels as she tried, unsuccessfully, to make the Irish backstop look less objectionable to them and to the ERG. So far as the latter was concerned, not even Theresa May's announcement of her intention of resigning in the summer was enough to persuade them to vote for her deal; and she thus became the fourth leader of the Conservative Party to be brought down by the European issue.

During this extremely fraught period the House of Lords played a relatively minor and ancillary role. The Lords were not part of the decision-making process on whether or not to approve the Prime Minister's deal, since the "meaningful process" provisions of the EU Withdrawal

Act gave that role exclusively to the Commons, thus recognising their primacy; and we stuck firmly to that division of labour. We therefore concentrated our fire on trying to rule out a no deal Brexit and avoiding that occurring as a default option at the end of March by simply allowing the clock to run down; and following several lengthy and unusually ill-tempered debates, we expressed that view categorically, endorsed by very large cross-party majorities.

During those first three months of 2019 my frequent articles for InFacts covered much of the ground in the preceding paragraphs. I had written often enough already setting out why a no deal Brexit would be a very bad deal for the UK. But, as the picketing of Parliament by both Brexiters and supporters of another referendum became a daily feature of our lives, with flags flying, bullhorns blaring and placards of many sorts, I did notice a prevalence of Brexiter placards welcoming the idea of the UK falling back on WTO trade rules, the default setting for a no deal Brexit. I never did summon up the courage to ask one of the holders of WTO placards whether they knew what WTO trade rules were or perhaps even what the acronym WTO actually signified. I did, however, write an InFacts article on 2nd January, 2019, which was designed to set out the realities:

WTO is the problem not the answer to trade under "no deal".

When the European Commission surfaced its contingency plans for a no deal Brexit shortly before

Christmas, most of the media comment focused on provisions for citizens' rights, air travel, road haulage and financial transactions. All these demonstrated some potential flexibility and a desire to avoid the worst immediate disruption if the UK crashed out without a deal.

These are all policy areas where neither the EU nor the UK are bound by wider international rules. But that is not the case where trade in goods is concerned, where both the EU and the UK are bound by WTO rules.

In particular both must follow the WTO's "most favoured nation" rules. This means giving equal treatment to all countries with whom they do not have free trade or customs union agreements covering "substantially all their trade". The UK and the EU would end up levying the same tariffs on each other's exports as they do to those from countries such as the US or Brazil or India.

On this the Commission showed no flexibility at all: "If the Withdrawal Agreement is not ratified, all relevant EU legislation on imported goods and exported goods will apply as of the withdrawal date". Not surprising, really, since it cannot be in the EU's - nor the UK's - interest to flout WTO rules.

The Commission goes on to add: "Member states must be in a position as from the withdrawal date to apply the EU Customs Code and the relevant rules on indirect taxation to all imports from and exports to the United Kingdom." So bang also goes the current frictionless handling of VAT between the EU and the UK.

All this will apply to trade across the border between Ireland and Northern Ireland, since that will become an external border between the EU and a non-EU "third country" (the UK). This will not be imposed due to EU ill will and inflexibility, but by the application of WTO rules. And the UK will be bound by those rules too in respect of trade across that border.

In theory the UK could avoid the imposition of tariffs on trade with the EU and stay within WTO rules. But it would have to reduce to zero any levies on imports from all other countries on a worldwide basis. That would damage both our industry and our agriculture by removing all protection for our businesses and farmers from cheaper foreign imports. It would also lose us any leverage in the subsequent negotiation of free trade agreements with countries outside the EU. What's more the EU would not be compelled to slash its tariffs on our exports in the same way. Indeed EU countries are not going to remove their protection to the rest of the world just to retain duty free access to the UK market.

And don't forget that a no deal scenario will also mean that, as of March 29 this year, the UK would lose the benefit of all the EU's free trade agreements with other countries. These cover a substantial proportion of our exports on top of the 44% which go to the EU.

Not a pretty prospect. And that does not seem to concern the Brexiters, who continue to maintain that a no deal exit would be a walk in the park. And they prattle on about a "managed no deal" which could be easily achieved, even though the same WTO rules would apply in those ill-defined circumstances too.

All the more reason, therefore, for Parliament categorically to rule out a no deal Brexit, and for the government to accept that judgement and act accordingly - by proposing postponement of the Article 50 cut-off date and by giving the people a say in a new referendum.

And, immediately after the House of Lords held the first of its day long debates, which focussed principally on no deal, and voted overwhelmingly against that outcome, I wrote the following InFacts article on 15th January, 2019:

Meanwhile, in the Lords.

Last night the House of Lords voted by a stonking majority of 169 (321 votes to 152) for a motion stating that a no deal outcome to the Brexit negotiations must be emphatically rejected and regretting that the Prime Minister's deal would damage the future economic prosperity, internal security and global influence of the UK. That majority contained substantial numbers of Conservative peers and cross-benchers, as well as almost all Labour and Liberal Democrats. It was therefore a genuine cross-party expression of views.

How consequential will that vote be? It comes in good time for members of the House of Commons to be aware of it when they vote on the Prime Minister's deal later today. But of course it does not have the force of law, nor was it ever intended to do so, as the wording of the motion made clear that the decisive say rested with the Commons.

But it is also a clear indication of the rocky road that lies ahead for the government as it seeks to pass in the ever-shrinking period before March 29 a whole raft of legislation - on trade, immigration, agriculture and fisheries and above all a bill giving effect in domestic law to all the provisions in the Prime Minister's deal if it, or any variant of it, ever passed the Commons.

Already there is an amendment down for the Trade Bill, which could resume its passage through the Lords as soon as next Monday (January 21) after a hiatus of four months. This amendment would ensure that the act's provisions could not enter into force unless the Commons has either approved a deal or had approved exiting without a deal; that is to say it would not enter into force in the event of a default no deal exit.

There were plenty of references in the Lords debate to the possibility of another referendum on the outcome of the Brexit negotiations. That had its supporters, growing in number, and its detractors, many of them apocalyptic in their warnings. The issue was not referred to in the motion and there is no question of the Lords taking the lead on this. But it does show that, should a new referendum bill emerge from the Commons, it would not lack for support in the Lords.

One other, fairly astonishing, feature of the debate was the lukewarm support for the Prime Minister's deal even amongst those who voted against the motion. "Not perfect" and "lesser evil" could be said to characterise their contributions. With backing like that it is hardly surprising that the Prime Minister's deal seems to be heading for defeat in the Commons later today (it was defeated by a majority of 230 votes).

I did not, however, neglect the case for another referendum, nor the need to address the practicalities of going down that road if Parliament should, in the end, decide to do so. Hence the following article I wrote for InFacts on 3rd January, 2019:

6 things we must plan for ahead of a People's Vote.

It might seem a bit presumptuous to write about the detail of the referendum legislation that would be required if and when a People's Vote is secured. But, when that moment does come, events are likely to move pretty fast. It will be in no one's interest to see Brexit uncertainty prolonged unnecessarily. And it will be important that supporters of a new referendum do not get at cross purposes over its broad structure.

Here are six questions which will need to be examined:

1. Timing.
The date of a vote probably lies between June and October. Any earlier than June is likely to present insuperable problems over passing the necessary legislation and implementing it in an orderly way.

The timing will not be entirely in the UK's gift. There will need to be a prolongation of the two-year Article 50 period, and this requires the agreement of all

255

28 member states. But problems arising over clashes with the European Parliament elections, due in May, are likely to be surmountable, both politically and legally, if the purpose is to allow the people a say on Brexit.

2. Question(s).

This will be the most hotly debated issue of all. Should there be a binary choice, either between the Prime Minister's deal and not leaving or between no deal and not leaving? A binary choice which attempted to exclude the option of not leaving is unlikely to be acceptable to either House of Parliament.

There are partisans of a triple choice, or even of a referendum in two stages, but those options are unlikely to be chosen when the issue becomes a real and not a theoretical one. The lack of any experience in this country of a complex set of choices and the difficulty of implementing the result will weigh in the balance against them.

3. Franchise.

Those issues were sharply contested in 2015/16. The Lords backed a vote for 16- and 17-year olds (as in the Scottish referendum and as is now the law in Wales). But the Commons rejected the idea. That case remains compelling. Then there is the predicament of the UK citizens living elsewhere in the EU who have lost the vote if they have been absent from the country for 15 years or more.

Speed and simplicity, as well as the need to avoid any accusations that the new vote is rigged against Brexit, point away from re-opening these issues and keeping the franchise the same as 2016.

4. Thresholds.

There were no minimum thresholds required in 2016 for constituting a majority. This has since been much criticised in the light of the narrowness of the outcome - only 37.4% of the electorate voted to leave in 2016 even though this was 51.9% of those who voted. But introducing a threshold at this stage would be hard to justify.

5. Should the result be binding or advisory?

In 2016 the outcome was, formally, only advisory - although the government has since chosen to interpret it as if it was one of the Tablets of Moses. Should it be binding this time? There are arguments in favour. To do so would help to counter the specious "best of three" scare story (actually this one would in any case be the third - after 1975 and 2016). And it would strengthen the contention that a new referendum was the best way to achieve closure on the Brexit issue.

6. Fraud or manipulation.

Hardly a trivial issue after the activities of Arron Banks and Cambridge Analytica have had more light shone onto them. There is, surely, at least a case to increase massively the penalties for proven breaches of the electoral law.

The fact that all these questions are now hot topics is a major advance on where we were this time last year. Then the government seemed to be coasting towards the exit, following the preliminary divorce deal struck in December 2017. But for a People's Vote to become reality, all these questions will need to be answered quickly and surely.

And nor did I neglect the need to present the positive case for remaining in the EU, should another referendum become a reality, a case for which I coined the phrase, about that time, of Project Hope - a response to the Brexiters' labelling of any arguments against leaving as Project Fear. In an InFacts article of 20th February, 2019 I picked out the internal security sector and, responding to a peculiarly unwise remark of the then Home Secretary, Sajid Javid, about the disruption to the fight against international crime which a no deal exit would cause, I wrote a spoof letter of reply from one of his EU colleagues:

When it comes to security, UK is safer in the EU.

The Home Secretary, Sajid Javid, has written to EU counterparts urging them to ensure everything is ready for the disruption no deal Brexit might bring to security on March 29. Below InFacts imagines a reply to that letter from an unspecified, small European country - let's call it Ruritania.

Dear Home Secretary,

I received your letter asking me and our other EU colleagues to consider what steps we could take, in the event of the UK leaving the EU without a deal, to mitigate the damage to our mutual ability to combat the risks of terrorism, people trafficking, drug smuggling and other forms of serious international crime.

I am relieved that you seem to appreciate just how serious that damage would be. This is not surprising, perhaps, since your law enforcement agencies make more use of the EU's information sharing than most other member states.

Yet sometimes, reading the reports our Embassy in London sends us, I have the impression that many supporters of Brexit in the UK Parliament believe that ditching the European Arrest Warrant, leaving Europol and Eurojust, and ceasing to participate in the systems for exchanging information about criminals would be a blessed release.

Take the European Arrest Warrant, for example. I would deeply regret it if I could no longer seek the speedy extradition of criminals who have committed serious crimes in my country and who were in the UK; and instead had to fall back on the slower, more cumbersome and less effective procedures of the Council of Europe's Convention. Meanwhile, of course, the criminal in question would remain at large in your country.

I note that, in the 1990s, it took several years to extradite to France a terrorist who was subsequently convicted of bombing the Paris Metro. It is also worth mentioning that, Ireland, a member state with which, in the past, you had quite a few problems over extradition, pulled out of the Council of Europe Convention when it ratified the European Arrest Warrant.

I am particularly baffled because, as recently as 2014, your Prime Minister - then Home Secretary and my colleague in the EU's Justice and Home Affairs Council - told your Parliament that it was "in the national interest" for the UK to keep the EAW and all the other main instruments of security cooperation. At the time it was perfectly legal under the EU Treaty for you to opt out of all of them.

Since then the challenges from serious international crime we all face have got a great deal worse and the need to work closely together has increased.

Our Embassy in London frequently reports you and your colleagues saying that leaving without a deal on March 29, and causing us all the problems you are asking us to mitigate, is the "default" option for Downing Street. I am afraid my English, learned when I studied in your country, is a bit rusty. So I consulted the dictionary and found that "default" is a word most normally associated with bankruptcy. Does that mean you are likely to be bankrupt at the end of March?

In any case there are a number of possible solutions which are in your own hands. You could change some of those red lines your Prime Minister has imposed on your negotiators? Or you could make use of the option under Article 50 to extend the cut-off period of two years? I am sure you are familiar with that possibility, since it was drafted by one of your own civil servants. Would any of us be likely to refuse such a request for more time? You could always try asking.

260

Yours sincerely,
Minister of the Interior, Republic of Ruritania.

I addressed too the growing groundswell of Brexiter comment, directed towards Parliament in general, frequently described as "broken" simply because it did not do what the Brexiters wanted it to do, and towards the Commons Speaker, John Bercow, in particular because his rulings on procedure cut across the government's attempts to force Parliament to approve its deal. The argument was that it was the government, not Parliament, which was standing constitutional conventions on their head and driving a coach and horses through precedent and past practice. This argument I set out in an InFacts article on 13th February, 2019:

Pursuit of Brexit is turning parliamentary world upside down.

Back in January - yes, it does seem a long time ago as zig follows zag in the government's Brexit policy - there was a massive amount of righteous indignation amongst Brexiters against the Speaker of the House of Commons. John Bercow had used his powers to call certain amendments rather than others during the first effort to rule out in a legally binding form the UK leaving the EU without a deal at the end of March.

Parliamentary pundits were marshalled to argue that our (admittedly unwritten) constitution was being overturned and that civilisation as we knew it was about to come to an end.

But the real disrupter of British constitutional practice has been the government itself. Take January 15, for example, when the government lost the "meaningful vote" on its Brexit deal by 230 votes. Has any UK government been defeated in such a way and not either resigned or fundamentally changed its policy? No, because that is what is meant to happen in a parliamentary system of government.

But this government just sailed on towards another "meaningful vote" at an unknown date in the future as if nothing had happened. It is precisely this kind of practice, of not taking no for an answer, of which the EU is accused by ardent Brexiters.

And then there is the prospect of leaving by default without a deal at the end of March. Both Houses of Parliament have voted to reject that option. Has any government ignored such a united expression of parliamentary opinion in the past? No is the answer again.

The government takes refuge behind a palisade of excuses which are manifestly untrue and presses on towards the cliff edge, arguing that it is not within its power to avoid no deal and hoping that playing chicken in this way will squeeze out a majority for its approach. In truth the government has several alternative options to no deal. For example, it could either shift its red lines or propose to the EU postponement of the March deadline; or it could indicate its intention of giving the electorate the final say on its deal.

And ministers are not just flouting parliamentary authority. How about the precedent the government has created by going back on the outcome of an arduous and lengthy negotiation, concluded last November, by a Prime Minister who assured anyone willing to listen that it was the best deal available? Now she is back in Brussels trying to unpick the Irish backstop which she and the rest of the government accepted not once but twice, in December 2017 and in November 2018. What does that do for the credibility of a government which is about to embark on a whole series of international negotiations both with the EU and others?

This is, frankly, a pretty shameful record, and one which is likely to cost the UK dear in the years ahead. It is no good attempting to justify it with arcane interpretations of parliamentary procedure about what is or what is not legally binding. It is surely time to apply a bit of common sense, and to give priority to the national interest over party solidarity. And that requires a fundamental shift of policy.

Inevitably, as February turned to March and the 29th March deadline approached without any sign of the deadlock at Westminster being broken ahead of that date, the debate shifted towards the most obvious safety valve available, an extension of the two year cut-off period for Article 50, which was explicitly envisaged in that Lisbon Treaty provision. Quite apart from the difficulty for the government of eating quite so many of its words and asking for an extension, there was the additional complication of the regular five yearly elections to the

European Parliament, scheduled for the end of May and thus pretty well certain to fall within any even faintly realistic extension period. Should the UK be required to hold such elections even though it was, prospectively, on the way out, so that any MEPs elected from the UK might only serve for a few months? Or could some way be found around that obligation? I felt distinctly uneasy about the implications of compelling the UK to go ahead with an election which would seem to most voters pretty meaningless and to Brexiters as something of an insult, coming as it would at a date by which they believed we should have left the EU. The most obvious escape route would have been to leave the existing British MEPs in situ until the matter was resolved, either by Parliament approving Theresa May's deal or by another referendum. This sort of approach (appointing rather than electing MEPs) had been used in the past when a new member state's accession fell between European parliamentary elections. Why not use it now for a country that might be leaving? But, whatever misgivings I, and no doubt others, may have felt about the UK participating fully in the May elections, the weight of political and legal opinion on both sides of the Channel came down in favour of UK participation. Here in an InFacts article of 15th March, 2019 are the arguments for extension and non-participation:

Let's get the extension we need from EU to rethink Brexit.

Amidst the sea of uncertainty which surrounds Brexit, this week's votes in the Commons have given one small piece of certainty. The European Council summit in Brussels on Thursday and Friday next week will decide whether or not the UK will have an extension of the Article 50 cut-off for negotiating its withdrawal.

Which way will the decision go? All the signals coming out of the other 27 EU capitals point towards an extension being agreed next week by all 28. Remember, this is a decision which requires our agreement as well as that of the EU 27 - although postponement has now been mandated by Parliament.

This is not too surprising really. None of the other 27 EU countries have an interest in the sort of disruption and damage which would result from going over a cliff-edge on March 29. It means gaps in their budgets, a loss of rights for their citizens in the UK, trade dislocation. And do not forget that this is a decision for the 27 EU Heads of State and Government, not for the Commission and Council presidents, although their views will weigh in the balance.

So, irritated as they may be by the confusion in Westminster, the EU 27 are likely to agree to an extension which costs them nothing of substance. But will the complication of the European Parliament elections on May 23 deter them? Probably not. There are a number of different legal and procedural ways of handling that complication. And the advice coming from the legal services of all the institutions is that a failure by the UK to hold such elections would not invalidate the legitimacy of the new European Parliament that will be

265

elected in May, although it would certainly put us on the wrong side of the law.

A less predictable question is how long the extension will be for? For three months as Theresa May will propose in the event of her deal squeaking through the Commons next week? Or for a longer period, offering time and space to rethink some of those lamentable red lines and come up with a better deal? Or leave the extension open-ended?

None of the participants has an interest in merely postponing the cliff-edge until the end of June. And, even in the fairly unlikely event of the deal coming through its parliamentary ordeal next week, how confident can anyone be that the necessary changes to our domestic law - which have to be enacted in new primary legislation before we can finally ratify the deal - will emerge unscathed? All these considerations point away from a short, three month extension, although of course what has once been extended can always be extended again.

Concern over the government's ability to get further legislation needed to actually implement any Brexit deal through Parliament will certainly weigh on the minds of our 27 EU partners. After all, 188 of the Prime Minister's own party, including cabinet ministers, voted against an extension full stop - and only 112 in favour of it - even though that would have meant ineluctably going over the cliff-edge on March 29.

Down the line, will those Conservatives happily vote for the supply motion required if the £39 billion divorce settlement is to be paid? Will they happily repeal the provision in the EU Withdrawal Act that ends the

266

jurisdiction of the European Court of Justice on exit day? There are plenty of these stumbling blocks ahead.

Better, surely, to allow time to negotiate a different deal and time too for a public vote on any outcome which could, if it was mandatory, enable those implementation complications to be averted? Better still for the electorate to decide that, now that they know what Brexit involves, as they did not in 2016, staying in the EU might be the preferable solution.

In the end, after an incredibly messy and muddled decision-making process both in London and Brussels, the Article 50 cut-off period was extended twice; the first time only for a few days while the Prime Minister decided whether or not to accept the European Parliament election obligation; and then on the second occasion, until the end of October, to allow time, at least in the Prime Minister's mind, to have yet another go at getting parliamentary approval for her deal. The second extension was, in the view of many observers, like so many of the government's Brexit negotiation decisions, still unfit for any useful purpose. I set out the arguments for that point of view in an InFacts article of 7th April, 2019:

EU should pay no attention to Rees-Mogg.

Theresa May's bid for another short extension of the Article 50 deadline - until 30 June - should not really surprise anybody. No doubt its principal appeal to its author is that it merely repeats what she asked for last time and therefore does not break new and dangerous ground in party terms. It is par for the course from a Prime Minister whose policy making invariably runs on tram lines and who seems to find repetition a virtue. But it does not have anything else to commend it.

From the UK's own point of view it provides too little time for the thorough re-shaping of our approach to the new relationship with the EU which is so urgently required. It then needs, in due course, to be reflected in a new version of the Political Declaration negotiated with the EU 27 before Parliament should be asked to approve it, as it is required to do by law, in a meaningful vote. It also provides too little time to consult the electorate which is so essential now that the outcome will be so far removed from what was promised by the Brexiters in 2016 (which no doubt makes it attractive to those who oppose such a confirmatory referendum).

From the point of view of the EU 27, 30 June is not only something they have already rejected. It raises the nightmare of an unending series of cliff-edge crises; and the absorption of successive meetings of the European Council in Brexit business to the exclusion of everything else, including pressing issues over Eurozone governance, migration, the next budget framework and the appointment of a new leadership team for the EU's institutions.

It is these other entirely legitimate preoccupations which seem to be weighing on the minds of those among the EU 27 who hesitate over a longer extension. So far as the day to day running of the EU is concerned, a longer extension should raise no fears. After all it closely replicates for short term budgetary and trade matters

268

what is already provided for in the transitional arrangements contained in the Withdrawal Treaty. So, are those concerns well founded? With someone like Jacob Rees-Mogg urging the government, which he still goes through the motions of supporting, to be as awkward as possible as long as we remain a member, the EU 27 could be forgiven for being concerned.

But, if you look at these non-Brexit issues one by one, there does not seem to be much justified cause for concern. On appointments to the key EU institutions it was already demonstrated the last time round, when David Cameron's attempt to block Jean-Claude Juncker's appointment as President of the Commission, failed that no single member state has a veto. On migration the UK has as much interest as other member states in the EU's external border controls being made more effective and in illegal immigration from the Middle East and Africa being discouraged.

As to the new Multi-Annual Financial Framework (MFF) for the next seven year period beyond 2020, it is realistically unlikely that the key decisions will be taken until well into 2020, probably after the end of any new Article 50 extension. And how likely is it that a UK, about to embark on a very tricky post-Brexit negotiation with the EU 27, will infuriate its future negotiating partners by attempting to veto a new MFF? Far more likely it will share the views of many other member states in wanting to increase spending on research and innovation and on external policies designed to protect and promote European interests and values in a troubled world. What to worry about there?

269

Throughout these extension decision processes Parliament and the readers of the press were regaled with a deluge of arguments to the effect that the only way to succeed in international negotiations was to threaten credibly to walk away and, if necessary, to do so - what could be called the Donald Trump school of diplomacy. I set out in an InFacts article of 6th April, 2019 to demonstrate that, as a standard operating procedure for diplomacy, this simply did not stack up:

> *Art of the deal in diplomacy is not to walk from the table.*

> *Sitting through seven hours of shameless filibustering in the House of Lords last Thursday, as a gang of Ultra-Brexiter Conservatives did their best to wreck the Cooper-Letwin Bill designed to mandate the Prime Minister to extend the Article 50 negotiating period, was painful enough. But the endless assertions that passing the Bill through all its stages in one day - as was eventually agreed to be done on Monday- would bring British democracy to its knees, ruin the reputation of the House of Lords, and much else of that kind, was a mild soporific.*

> *And then I heard one of the gang, who shall remain nameless as he is one of the dimmer bulbs in the pro-Brexit firmament, beginning to lecture on how it was impossible to negotiate successfully unless you were prepared to, and actually did, walk away from the negotiating table. As a businessman he could tell us that*

refusal to do that had doomed the Prime Minister's Article 50 negotiations from the outset. Apart from hair colour and accent, it could have been Donald Trump lecturing on "The Art of the Deal".

Having myself spent much of the past fifty-five years in international negotiations, not all of which had been complete failures - the UK budget rebate, the establishment of the Single Market, designing Britain's euro opt-out, the UN authorisation of the use of force to expel Iraq from Kuwait in 1991 - I thought I would test the speaker's thesis against actual experience.

Take Cyprus, a problem to the solution of which I devoted seven, ultimately fruitless, years. Each side of the dispute, both Greek Cypriots and Turkish Cypriots, has frequently walked away from the negotiating table, indeed they spent more time doing that than they did in negotiation. But it produced no results, leaving the island divided, insecure and less prosperous than it would otherwise have been.

Take also the Israelis and the Palestinians. They too, particularly the Israelis, have walked away from the negotiating table on a number of occasions. That dispute also remains, if anything further from resolution than it has ever been.

And then take the negotiations to establish the UN, NATO and the European Communities. Would they have been successful at laying the foundations of international peace, security and prosperity if any of the participants had threatened to walk away if they did not get everything they wanted? Of course not.

The real lessons are that neither empty chairs nor the drawing of red lines and refusing to compromise on them has proved to be a recipe for success in international negotiations between states, however successful those tactics may have proved in reaching business deals. So the Prime Minister is surely right now, at last, to have turned her back on such foolish advice.

The trouble is that too many of her supporters remain wedded to that sort of thinking; and her own lack of imagination and flexibility are preventing her from successfully setting a new course in shaping our future relationship with the EU 27.

Rejecting leaving the EU without a deal is the wise thing to do. But it does not bring us closer to a viable solution, just a bit further away from a deeply damaging one.

*   *   *

Several weeks in April and May were also taken up in one of the most, if not the most, futile exercises in an overall Brexit saga with plenty of futility to spare - namely talks between the government and the Labour Party to see whether enough common ground could be found to persuade Labour to vote for Theresa May's deal or at least to abstain. The government side in the talks was mainly led by David Lidington, formerly David Cameron's Europe minister and generally regarded as Theresa May's deputy once Damian Green had been forced to resign. Lidington, whom I had known since he was Douglas Hurd's special political adviser in the 1990s, was as decent, knowledgeable and flexible a negotiator as you could find, but even he could not squeeze out enough concessions to persuade Labour to join what was, by then, quite clearly, a sinking ship. The Labour side was headed up by a mixture - Keir Starmer, a declared Remainer and Rebecca Long Bailey who was emerging as Jeremy Corbyn's preferred successor if he should throw in the towel. The fact that I did not write a single article about this exercise shows how low an opinion I had of its chances of success.

∗   ∗   ∗

The European Parliament elections held in May were, in the UK at least, largely an exercise in futility and in the nurturing of false expectations. The overall turnout was, as usual in Britain, rather pitiful - although a fraction higher than on previous such occasions (elsewhere in Europe participation was a good deal up on previous elections). Hardly surprising since it was not easy to explain what electors were being asked to vote for, particularly as one main party, the Conservatives, barely campaigned at all, and the other, Labour, campaigned on every issue under the sun except Brexit. The results were, as was to transpire, deeply misleading. Nigel Farage's newly formed Brexit Party came out ahead of the others in both seats and votes; but the seats were mainly those held previously by UKIP; and, while the size of the Brexit Party vote certainly put the wind up the Conservatives and strengthened the hand of those Ultra-Brexiters who argued that it was only by endorsing Farage's policies that they could fend off the threat from that quarter in a general election, it was not in fact a credible indicator for an election carried out under "first past the post" rules, rather than, as in European elections, on the basis of proportional representation. Labour did reasonably well, at least in comparison with the previous European election in 2014, but this concealed the fact that what would be called the "Corbyn factor" was not really relevant to this election. The Liberal Democrats won back a lot of the seats they had lost in 2014 (when they had been left with only one), rewarded for being the one national party with a clear policy on Brexit; but were tempted by that into thinking that could be interpreted as support for reversing Brexit at any price. The Conservatives had an appalling outcome, pushed into fourth place and losing many of their seats in Strasbourg; and this proved to be the final nail in the coffin of the May government. From then on the government was living on borrowed time and the election of a new leader of the Conservative party and thus of a new Prime Minister was only a matter of weeks away. The new Independent grouping, caught before they had any proper national organisation, won no seats and not many votes; and they embraced the policy of reversing Article 50 without another referendum, which provoked me (usually carefully keeping out of electoral politics) into an InFacts article on 20th May, 2019 putting the arguments against that:

Better to hold new Brexit vote than rush to revoke.

Both Chuka Umunna and Anna Soubry are now arguing in favour of revoking the UK's Article 50 notification without further ado. Their Change UK colleague Heidi Allen, interim leader of the new party, has applied for an emergency debate on the matter in Parliament. They argue that there is no chance of holding a referendum before October and that the 27 other EU countries will not agree to a further extension of the cut-off date beyond that deadline.

Whatever one may think of the legitimacy of cancelling the outcome of the 2016 referendum without another public vote, the assumption about the irrevocable nature of the October deadline seems to be extraordinarily premature at this point of time - and very possibly moot even when that date comes closer.

After all the to-ings and fro-ings that went on right down to the wire on March 29 and April 12, who can possibly predict six months in advance what decision will be taken at the end of October?

For one thing, we cannot at this stage know what the circumstances will be when those decisions come to be taken. Will the processes of appointing new leadership teams for the EU institutions have gone reasonably smoothly, without the UK trying to upset them? Probably yes. Will the UK have acted in the meantime as a wrecker in other EU decision-making? Probably not. Will the UK by then have moved, or be moving towards, either a general election or, more likely, another referendum? Who can say, with the near certainty of a Conservative leadership election in the offing and the unknown consequences in terms of parliamentary arithmetic?

Given the impossibility of answering any of these questions now, can anything be usefully said about whether the EU will have more appetite in October for the UK leaving without a deal than they did in March or April? It is hard to see that appetite growing irresistibly, however fed up everyone in Brussels and the other EU capitals may be with the whole Brexit imbroglio. It is opinion in those capitals which will matter in October. The EU's institutions will still be settling down after the European Parliament elections and will be in no shape to give a strong lead, in contrast to their role in Brexit negotiations up to now.

Is this just an argument in favour of more can kicking of the sort loved by Theresa May? Certainly not. It is an argument for pressing on with the case for giving the electorate the final say on Brexit so that, if more time is needed in October, the prospect of such a decision being made in the near future is clear.

As it worked out the preceding article turned out to be reasonably accurate in its prediction of what might happen at the end of October. What was clear at the time of its writing was that the UK was already in the process of squandering four out of the seven months Article 50 extension in internal squabbling and a leadership contest in the ruling party to replace the person who had up to then led the British side of the Brexit negotiations.

*   *   *

Two events in that period, one historical, one highly topical, seemed to me to underline the wider significance of Brexit, in particular for our most important overseas relationships - with the rest of Europe and with the United States. The first of these was the 75th anniversary of D-Day on which I wrote an InFacts article on 5th June, 2019:

We must not desert the values fought for on D-Day.

As we commemorate the 75th anniversary of D-Day, we should both look back at an event which liberated Europe from fascism and look forward to the lessons for today. This is especially so given that the controversy surrounding the state visit of Donald Trump risks overshadowing the real and continuing significance of D-Day.

First and foremost, we should salute the courage and sacrifice of those Americans and Canadians and others who joined our own armed forces in a truly unprecedented military operation which led, a year later, to the liberation of Europe. Let us face it, they saved our bacon; and helped to deliver a victory which we could not have secured without their aid.

Are we sufficiently grateful? I doubt it. Why have we not, as the French have done towards our own D-Day veterans, honoured all the surviving US veterans of D-Day? We should surely do so.

In the context of today we need to realise that the Anglo-American alliance remains as important to our continued security as it did then. This is easy to forget when the Trump administration takes a whole range of

277

decisions which are contrary to our own view of our national interest - on policy towards Iran, on the UN, on climate change, on trade policy - and does so without paying much attention to our government's views.

But we must not let our criticism of this administration metamorphose into that ugly brand of anti-Americanism which so disfigured our politics forty years or so ago. And we must do our best to ensure that the NATO summit to be held here in December strengthens the alliance and demonstrates its continuing validity.

And then there are the lessons of D-Day for our own place in Europe, of which we are an integral part, not just geographically, but culturally, economically and historically. Our failure to grasp the full implications of that in the 1920s and 1930s contributed to our having to fight our way ashore in Normandy 75 years ago. There are no direct analogies with the present day. But we need to realise that there is no EU-isolationist option available to us which would not damage our future prosperity and security.

And we do need to remember that D-Day was fought to uphold a range of values, eloquently set out in the Atlantic Charter drawn up by Franklin D. Roosevelt and Winston Churchill two years or so before, and which became those of the United Nations when it was founded in 1945 - of democracy, of freedom of thought and speech, of the rule of law and many others.

Amidst a lot of loose talk about the rebirth of nationalism, we need to remember that our compatriots died to uphold these values. We must not desert them now.

And the second was the truly disgraceful sequence of events following the leaking in London of the political reporting from our Embassy in Washington on the policies of the Trump administration which led to the resignation of the Ambassador, Kim Darroch, a good friend and one of the best of my successors as Permanent Representative to the EU in Brussels. This episode illustrated one of the better-hidden facts of Brexit, the way it was destroying the vital relationship of confidence between ministers and officials. My InFacts article of 9th July, 2019 sets out my view of that turn of events:

If we Brexit, will UK appoint its ambassadors... or Trump?

In classical Greek times it was said that those whom the gods wished to destroy they first made mad. This phenomenon seems to be recurring in the ranks of the Brexiters, both Nigel Farage and his sympathisers on the Tory backbenches, as they hack away at one of the essential underpinnings of British political life since the middle of the nineteenth century: the impartiality and loyalty of a non-political civil service.

Olly Robbins, the government's chief negotiator with the EU, has been subjected for months to sniping and innuendo, despite the fact that everything he was doing in Brussels was under the authority and on the explicit instruction of the Prime Minister.

279

When the Governor of the Bank of England dared to make some pretty cautious observations about the costs and implications of a Brexit without a deal, he was subjected to the same treatment.

Now we have the reaction to the unforgivable leaking of confidential diplomatic reporting by the UK's ambassador to the US, Kim Darroch, to ministers on the Trump administration - no doubt replicated, albeit in less clear and balanced terms, by any number of Washington-based diplomats. This has led to Farage criticising the ambassador for not sharing his own agenda of leaving the EU, despite the policy of the government which originally appointed Darroch being to remain in the EU.

Bill Cash, the Ultra-Brexiter chair of the Commons EU Scrutiny Committee, has lent support in Parliament to Trump's intemperate tweeting by echoing Farage's criticism. Those tweets were added to this lunch time by the President calling Darroch "a very stupid guy" and "pompous fool", ruling Theresa May's Brexit policy a "disaster" and observing that America's "economy and military" was "only getting bigger, better and stronger".

More insidiously Bernard Jenkin, another stalwart of the hard line European Research Group, has suggested that retired former diplomats and civil servants still active in public life were somehow betraying their impartiality if they speak out about the problems that Brexit poses.

Let us deal with that last claim first. In my own personal case, I served British governments from

Macmillan to Blair. Every one of them came to the settled conclusion that the country's best interests were served by being a member of the European Community or EU. There was therefore never any conflict during my service between my own personal views, based on my education studying modern history and on my experience in the 1960s of the UK being pushed around by the bigger players (the US, the EC and Japan) in the Kennedy Round of multilateral trade negotiations, and those of any UK governments.

Since I ceased to have any government employment, in 2003, Jenkin and many of his colleagues have changed their own minds about EU membership and campaigned successfully for the 2016 referendum. Why am I expected to change my mind? Or to shut up?

More widely, it really is time to stop this process of denigrating civil service loyalty and impartiality. The new prime minister needs to show by his first decisions that he will have none of it; and that the UK's ambassador in Washington is chosen by our government and not by Donald Trump - and that diplomats are expected to report without fear or favour.

But who can be sure of this when Johnson today responded to the president's insults by saying the US was "for the foreseeable future our number one political, military friend" and boasting about his good relationship with the White House. If a strong line is not taken, then the damage being done by Brexit to our body politic will be even greater than it has been up to now.

Chapter 13

Trench warfare: the end game
(July 2019/January 2020)

The Conservative leadership contest which filled the political scene in Britain through most of June and July was hardly a gripping spectacle. For one thing the result, victory for Boris Johnson, was easy to predict from the outset; he had stitched up the Brexiter vote, both in Parliament and in the wider party membership; and he offered his usual blend of jokes (quite good ones sometimes), unfulfillable promises and a narrative leading to the sunlit uplands, which was a welcome relief after Theresa May's gloomy determination and pointless resilience. For another there was no real debate about policy between the candidates. Each vied with the others to be more adamantine about Brexit. Only Rory Stewart even dared to mention words like flexibility and compromise; and that was one of the reasons he did not get very far. One could speculate that Jeremy Hunt, the Foreign Secretary, would provide some room for negotiation; but that too was one of the reasons why he fell short in the final round and in the country wide vote (and why he lost his job when the new government was formed). There was speculation too that Johnson, who had flip-flopped often enough in his political career and whose capacity to embellish the facts and to go back on his promises was well known, might somersault into some kind of a deal.

Any doubt that this was a hard Brexit victory disappeared with the formation of the government. Pragmatists like David Lidington, David Gauke, Philip Hammond, Rory Stewart and Jeremy Hunt either refused to serve or were booted out. Key posts went to ultra-Brexiters like Dominic Raab (Foreign Secretary), Priti Patel (Home Secretary), Michael Gove (coordinating Brexit preparations in the Cabinet Office) and Theresa Villiers (DEFRA); and, while there were a few former Remainers around the cabinet table - Amber Rudd (Work and Pensions) and Matt Hancock (Health) - they had all taken an oath in blood to follow the Johnson line on Brexit and were in any case placed in departments which had little or nothing to do with Brexit. Even more significantly the Svengali of the Leave campaign, Dominic Cummings, moved into Nº 10 and soon began a purge of special political advisers designed to ensure they all toed the line, either out of conviction or fear.

Policy decisions to match the hard Brexit line followed soon enough. The first of these, an attempt to prorogue Parliament at the end of July - with the new Prime Minister spared any questioning on his Brexit policy - until the middle of October, perilously close to the end-October Article 50 deadline, was a blatant and, as it turned out, illegal attempt to muzzle the only institution with the capacity to hold the government to account. In a bizarre move conducted in great secrecy the leaders of the Commons and the Lords (Jacob Rees-Mogg and Natalie Evans) flew up to Balmoral to get the Queen to sign off on prorogation. Neither had any mandate from the institution they represented to act in this way. In the end this shoddy manoeuvre failed. A case was brought before the Supreme Court, which ruled unanimously that the government had acted illegally - a conclusion easily reached when some of the inner workings at N° 10 leaked into the public domain - and the prorogation was declared null and void.

A second early decision by the new government was not illegal but it was ill-conceived. In August it was announced that, from now onwards, the UK would no longer participate in EU decision-making for all issues not of direct or vital interest to the UK, even though, as a full member it still had every right to do so, and even, some would argue, a duty to do so. The object, clearly, was to please the government's Brexit supporters and to send a message to Brussels of Johnson's determination to be out on 31st October. In truth the May government had been edging crab-wise towards a "half empty chair" policy, with the then Prime Minister's refusal to attend an anniversary meeting of Heads of State and Government to commemorate the founding of what had since become the EU, and her refusal also to go to two informal meetings in the same format in Bratislava (Slovakia) and Sibiu (Romania) during their countries' presidencies. I had written about the failure to go to the Sibiu meeting in an InFacts article on 9th May, 2019:

Skipping Sibiu summit is May's latest unforced error with EU.

Theresa May's decision not to attend this week's informal

284

meeting of EU leaders at Sibiu in Romania (and it was her decision, not theirs) was yet another in the long list of unforced errors in her handling of the UK's relations with the EU. It is just another occasion when the national interest has been subordinated to the need to avoid upsetting her own party supporters - a dwindling band, perhaps, but still capable of terrifying a prime minister whose hold on office is as tenuous as hers is.

Why is the decision to absent herself from the Sibiu meeting such a bad one? Well, the Prime Minister would have done well to heed the wisdom of an old French saying: "The absent are always in the wrong". Charles de Gaulle tried an empty chair policy in 1965/6 and it did not work then. It is certainly not going to work now.

Every one of the matters under discussion at Sibiu will be of importance to the UK, whether we eventually leave the EU and negotiate a new relationship with it or, alternatively, remain a member following another referendum. In those circumstances, does it really make sense for us to voluntarily surrender any role in shaping policy decisions while we are still a member - to have less influence than, say, Malta or Luxembourg?

It is not as if the matters under discussion are trivial ones. Take the issue of migration into the EU. The UK has a major interest in strengthening the external border controls of our closest neighbours and to developing policies which will stem the flow of economic migrants from Africa and the Middle East. Or take the need to further develop the Single Market so that it covers more widely and more effectively service industries and the digital economy in which the UK is a leader.

And consider the desirability of weighing into the burgeoning debate over whether the EU should weaken its competition policy in order to promote "European champions" or rather to strengthen it to deal more effectively with large multinational companies which risk dominating our markets and which pay few of our taxes. And there is surely also a need to get involved in the fraught issues caused by the rise of populism and by the challenges to the rule of law which are surfacing in some member states?

On the international stage the need for the Europeans (including the UK) to have a collective response to the daily increasing attacks on the rules-based international order from the Trump administration is now urgent. In a week which has seen the tightening of US sanctions against Iran and their attempted imposition on our companies, the politicisation of the Arctic Council in the name of denying the reality of climate change, and threats of an all-out trade war between the US and China in open defiance of WTO rules, what has hitherto been a nagging concern is now moving towards a full and far-reaching crisis between the US and its European allies.

It is little short of tragic that none of these considerations seems to count in the national debate over Brexit and in the bizarre confabulations over customs unions and Irish backstops. Should we not rather be focusing on all the compelling reasons why Britain is better off influencing EU policy formulation than abdicating any such role?

Now I wrote again on the same theme in an InFacts article of 23rd August, 2019, responding to the Johnson government's latest move towards an "empty chair" policy and explaining why it was both misguided and futile:

Johnson's empty seat policy is a futile gesture.

Britain's latest move in the Brexit negotiations - withdrawing from participating in EU decision-making for all issues not of direct and vital interest to the UK - seems to have been drawn from that skit in "Beyond the Fringe" which begins with the words "This is the time in the war when we need a really futile gesture". Perhaps that shouldn't be a surprise. After all Britain's new Prime Minister is obsessed with Second World War memorabilia.

Leave on one side for the moment the extraordinarily presumptuous approach of a government towards its sovereign parliament thus insisting that the UK will leave the EU on October 31 come what may. Leave on one side also that the government has no mandate to act in this way - the sole mandate which exists, established when we joined the European Communities in 1973, being that the UK should participate in all European decision-making at every level so long as it remains a member. This new decision bristles with technical complexities and pitfalls.

1. *Pretty well every decision taken by the EU will have direct implications for the UK whether or not we leave on October 31. Even if we leave,*

those decisions will affect any new relationship we manage eventually to negotiate with the EU.

2. *How will it be decided which EU decisions will have a direct impact on the UK, in which we will continue to participate, and which will not? Do not expect individual departments affected by such decisions to come to the same conclusions on that as the ideologically driven group around the Prime Minister. So there will be plenty of time and effort expended quite unnecessarily in Whitehall sorting that out.*

3. *What will the implications be for EU decision-making in Brussels of the absence of a member state from the whole process? These will be complex, particularly with regard to decisions requiring unanimity. The EU will want to ensure that the legality of all the decisions it takes is not compromised - and that will not be entirely straightforward.*

4. *How will British ministers manage attendance at Council meetings? There will be several in every week of September and October. Each one will have a lengthy agenda and, at the outset, a whole number of decisions - the "A" points - will be taken on the nod. Will British ministers duck in and out, making fools of themselves in the process?*

No doubt the government will assert that this latest move will concentrate the minds of the EU 27 on the prospect of the UK leaving without a deal on October 31. And that this prospect will persuade them to jettison

288

the Irish backstop. But is it likely to have that effect? Almost certainly not. Giving in to that sort of crude blackmail will not seem an appealing prospect, however much they may wish to avoid a no deal exit. And they will not thank the UK for raising yet another gratuitous complexity in a process of which they are all heartily sick.

The more likely, if unintended, consequence of the latest move will be to concentrate the minds of the majority in Parliament of all parties who are determined to avoid a no deal exit; and to remind them that a government which is prepared to play ducks and drakes with Britain's national interests needs to be stopped before it goes any further.

It was thus becoming clear, within weeks of the formation of the new government, that we really were heading, in October or soon after, into the end-game of the whole Brexit saga. An end-game in which the options of leaving without a deal, of a new, Johnson deal, and of another referendum would all be in play, as would be the sanctity of the end-October exit date. My own writing for InFacts was influenced by the imminence of that end-game, as was demonstrated by an article on 6th August, 2019 on the lessons to be learned (and applied) from the earlier European referendum in 1975:

We must learn lessons from the successful 1975 referendum.

The new government makes no secret of the fact that it is

in campaigning mode, whether for an early election or another referendum - although its face is firmly set against the latter, usually described as undemocratic, an affront to the will of the people etc. That is an odd way to characterise a narrow victory on the basis of a false prospectus. Never mind, we will get there.

But it is surely time to study and to apply some of the lessons from 1975 and 2016.

Collective leadership.

The 1975 "Yes" campaign had no single leader. The Prime Minister, Harold Wilson, supported its objective. So did his Foreign Secretary and eventual successor, James Callaghan, who had re-negotiated the terms of Britain's entry which provided the basis for the referendum. But they were not part of that campaign and would not share platforms with their cross-party allies. The Leader of the Opposition, Margaret Thatcher, was not a leader of it either.

From the outset there was a collective leadership drawn from across the three main parties. They shared platforms up and down the country and agreed policies on European issues, although they remained adversaries in Parliament. So it can be done. And it won a 2:1 victory.

Avoid gaming post-referendum options for government.

At no stage in 1975 did the "Yes" campaign flirt with ideas of a government of national unity after the referendum. The break-away from the Labour Party of

290

the Gang of Four (Roy Jenkins, Shirley Williams, David Owen, Bill Rogers) came later, when control of the party fell into the hands of the leaders of the "No" campaign (Michael Foot, Tony Benn and Peter Shore) and it headed for the manifesto commitment in the 1983 election to leave the European Communities.

Positive or negative campaign?

The "Yes" campaign in 1975 was determinedly positive. The same could not be said of the Remain campaign in 2016 and that was surely an error. Now the government has taken ownership of Project Fear and is going to spend millions on the communications campaign setting out the consequences of leaving the EU without a deal - and they will not be pretty. Leave them to it.

Supporters of Remain in a future referendum campaign should concentrate this time on Project Hope, not Project Fear - on setting out the positive policies which a UK still in the EU would champion: environmental policies to combat climate change, completing the Single Market in services (80% of our economy), a free and fair global trade policy, tough competition and tax avoidance rules to face the challenge of multinational companies, effective action against terrorism and cross-border crime, foreign and security policies to stand up for the values and interests we share with the rest of Europe and to avoid simply bobbing along in the wake of Donald Trump's erratic attempts to disrupt the rules-based international order. Quite a list - and more besides.

Try truth, not fiction.

No doubt some aspects of the 1975 campaign were not perfect and some untruths were told on both sides. But it was not the case that the "Yes" campaign advocated staying in a common market rather than a political body. If you do not believe that just read Thatcher's speeches at the time.

And in 2016 Leave told some real whoppers - about the sums of money sent to Brussels and which could easily be switched to the NHS, about the millions of Turks who would shortly benefit from free movement, about staying in the Single Market after we left. Next time they must not be allowed to get away with it. Not by fighting fire with fire; but by rigorous fact-checking and transparent advocacy.

Argument by historical analogy is never exact or perfect. But those who ignore the lessons of history are all too likely to repeat it. Talk of post-referendum options for government sets up tensions within the campaign leadership and risks alienating the electorate, and brings no compensating benefits.

It was evident too that any attempt to fashion a Johnson deal different from Theresa May's one would have to grapple with the Irish conundrum. The new government spared no effort to bad-mouth and to demolish the backstop deal but gave not the slightest hint of what it proposed to put in its place. This was only to emerge after a meeting between Boris Johnson and the Irish Taoiseach, Leo Varadkar, after which it gradually became evident that

Johnson was preparing to accept a solution which effectively left Northern Ireland inside the regulatory framework of the Single Market and, to some extent also, the Customs Union, thus necessitating checks and controls on trade across the Irish Sea between Northern Ireland and Great Britain - a solution which had been tentatively explored at a much earlier stage in the negotiations by the Commission and which had at that time been characterised by Theresa May as one which no British Prime Minister could ever accept. It was also, of course, unacceptable to the DUP since it would give a powerful boost to a "united Ireland" concept, which could easily, over time, spread from the trade to the political arena. In the meantime, and before this pretty fundamental surrender took place, I wrote an article for InFacts on 12th August, 2019 bringing the Irish dimension once again into focus, since it was certain to figure prominently in any end -game deal:

PM calls backstop undemocratic: he has odd idea of democracy.

N° 10's spokesman has taken to metronomically calling the Irish backstop "undemocratic". Is it in any way justified?

Well, there is no doubt at all that the people of Northern Ireland voted by a substantial majority in 2016 to remain in the EU. So the backstop, which is merely designed to ensure that the economic relationship between Northern Ireland and the rest of Ireland remains the same until alternative arrangements, which do not currently exist, are put in place to avoid any new border controls replacing those removed by the Good Friday Agreement. So the only thing undemocratic in Northern Ireland terms is the Democratic Unionist Party's insistence on removing the backstop.

What about the UK as a whole, which did vote to leave the EU in 2016? Well the Good Friday Agreement is part of the constitutional order of the UK, and maintaining it by avoiding any new border controls was entrenched in the 2018 EU Withdrawal Act. So that can hardly be said to be undemocratic.

If the UK leaves the EU without a deal, it is not the EU which will necessitate the levying of tariffs on goods crossing the border between the two parts of Ireland. It will be the obligations which both the UK and the EU have entered into democratically under their membership of the WTO which will require that.

So, where is the claim of a lack of democracy in the Irish backstop coming from? Presumably it lies in the determination of a majority of the Conservative party to reject that part of an agreement freely entered into with the EU by the previous Prime Minister - ignoring the fact that the current Prime Minister signed up to the core principles in December 2017 when he was Foreign Secretary (see Para 49 of the "Joint Report")? That is a pretty odd definition of democracy.

One result of the Supreme Court's judgement on the illegality of the July prorogation was that Parliament found itself unexpectedly in session in early September. Those short September sessions, sandwiched between the end of the summer holidays and the party conference season in

294

late September/early October, had, over the years become widely discredited as being too short for the transaction of any serious parliamentary business. That was not to be the case in 2019. It became clear to the cross-party majorities in both Houses which were determined to rule out the option of leaving the EU at the end of October without a deal that legislative action would be needed in September if that objective was to be achieved. So a short bill was brought forward in the Commons which required the government to ask for another Article 50 extension beyond the end of October unless Parliament had by then approved a deal or had approved leaving without one. This Bill, later to be known as the Benn Act (named after Hilary Benn, the Labour chair of the Commons Brexit negotiations oversight committee and a neighbour of mine in Bedford Park - son of the fiercely anti-European warrior, Tony Benn, and memorably self-described as "a Benn but not a Bennite"), squeaked through the Commons, after many procedural shenanigans, by a wafer-thin majority.

The Bill reached the Lords late in the first week of the September mini-session, thus leaving very few parliamentary days for the completion of its legislative progress and no room at all for its passage if any amendments to it were to necessitate its return to the Commons. The ultra-Brexiters in the Lords, led by Michael Forsyth, a former Conservative Secretary of State for Scotland, and consisting almost exclusively of back-bench Conservatives (joined by a couple of Labour peers and a small minority of cross-benchers) set out with the determination to filibuster the Bill and thus to wreck it. More than 70 amendments were tabled; and the House had to sit through time-wasting speeches of more than half an hour, one after the other on each amendment. We slogged through seven hours of this agony, at intervals moving successfully that the debate on a particular amendment first be terminated and the amendment then be rejected. Each of these manoeuvres required two divisions which took up twenty minutes or so. In the early hours of the following morning it became clear that this laborious process would not suffice to get the Bill through in time, so the prospect loomed of the need for a guillotine motion on further debate, an unprecedented procedure in the Lords (although the Commons did it all the time). At that point the government front bench threw in the towel, persuaded those filibustering to desist and gave their support for the further stages of the Bill to be completed early the following week. In the words of the poem "It was a famous victory". And the Benn Act was given Royal Assent before the September mini-session was over.

With the Benn Act on the statute book, offering some protection against the Johnson government's still daily reiterated determination to ensure that the UK left the EU on 31st October, with or without a deal, attention in October switched back to Brussels where the new government returned to the negotiating table in a last ditch attempt to get a deal which was somehow sufficiently different from Theresa May's deal to win majority support for its approval in the Commons. But the government's attention was already focused on an alternative parliamentary strategy of abandoning hope of getting approval from the House of Commons as currently constituted and calling a general election to be fought on the platform of the people against parliament.

Their problem was that the Fixed Term Parliament Act, which had been pushed through by the coalition government in 2010 to protect the Liberal Democrats against a snap election at a moment of the Conservatives' choosing, required substantial opposition support before an early election could be called. And early attempts by the government failed, faced with virtually across the board abstentions by the opposition parties and some rebel Conservatives.

The tricky issue of sequencing between an early election (the normal timetable did not necessitate one until 2022) and a decisive push for a People's Vote, which could be linked to any parliamentary approval of a deal reached in Brussels, was present in many people's minds but was possibly too little raised in public and not discussed with sufficient rigour and frankness by the cross-party alliance pressing for another referendum. To some of us, like John Kerr and I, it was of capital importance to play out the full referendum scenario before an election was held but, as non-party individuals, we had no say in the matter. The breakaway members from both main parties in the Commons were in no doubt either; and held the same view. The bottom line position of the main opposition parties was less clear. Labour was still struggling to define a clear position on the desirability of holding another referendum at all, although it moved a few more baby steps towards support for a referendum at its annual conference in late September. But Jeremy Corbyn, misled by his relative success at the 2017 general election (effectively more a failure for May than a success for Corbyn) and by the not too bad outcome for Labour in the June European election, and ignoring his own very poor scores in opinion polls on voters' preference for Prime Minister, remained personally wedded to the attractions of an early election. Plenty in his party did not share that view and I recall Angela Smith, the Labour leader in the Lords, telling me in colourful language that an early election would be a disaster for her party - she proved to be right. The Liberal Democrats, under the new and untried leadership of Jo Swinson, had already shifted their position by embracing the policy of revoking Article 50 without holding another referendum (although they remained supportive of such a referendum) and were grossly over-interpreting the national implications of their success in the European election. The Scottish National Party were tempted by their chances of winning back in an early election a number of the Westminster seats they had lost to the Conservatives in 2017; they could not therefore be relied upon to resist such an election in all circumstances.

So the battlefield, both in Brussels and in London remained blanketed in fog. And then the fog rolled back on 17th October when a UK/EU deal was announced in Brussels and was immediately submitted to Parliament for approval (all 500+ pages of the legally binding Withdrawal Agreement and 25+ pages of the Political Declaration which was not legally binding). One of the most astonishing features of that deal was that the Johnson government was able to present it to the public as a negotiating triumph, a tribute to British grit and perseverance, when on any objective analysis it was nothing of the sort, but was in fact a surrender deal. Why so? Well the divorce settlement and the treatment of EU citizens in the UK remained as in Theresa May's deal; the Political Declaration had been tinkered with a bit, modestly weakened and made more obscure (but not sufficiently so to avoid it being comprehensively dumped when the new, post-election Johnson government opened post-Brexit negotiations with the EU in February 2020). The only real differences were the provisions related to Northern Ireland, where Johnson swallowed an idea earlier put forward by the Commission and at the time described by Theresa May as one no British prime minister could accept, which involved Northern Ireland remaining in the regulatory framework of the Single Market and which necessitated checks and controls on trade across the Irish Sea between Great Britain and Northern Ireland to ensure the latter did not become a back door entrance into the EU's Customs Union. My own analysis of the deal was set out in an InFacts article on 18th October, 2019 before the matter went to a vote in the Commons:

Johnson treats UK like a banana republic.

If you just stop to think about it, the attempt by the government to bounce through Parliament tomorrow a momentous decision determining many aspects of our lives is pretty outrageous. The deal they struck has not even been reported to Parliament by the Prime Minister and will only be so at the beginning of tomorrow's debates in both Houses. The urgency is artificially created by the government's own refusal to ask for an extension of the Article 50 timetable, a request mandated by Parliament in the Benn Act. This is the politics of a banana republic not of the mother of parliaments.

Has it not struck you that supporters of the deal seem to have identified no real advantage to it other than that it exists? Although the Chancellor of the Exchequer is, shamefully, refusing to produce an impact assessment of the consequences of this deal on our economy, there are plenty of well-resourced analyses which do so. And every one is negative, worse even than Theresa May's deal which Parliament, including some of those in the present government, rejected.

And then there are some dirty tricks tucked away in those many pages of legal prose. Most significant probably is the switch from a legally binding commitment in the Withdrawal Treaty to maintaining a level playing field on environmental standards, labour laws and much else, to a merely aspirational text in the Political Declaration which has no legal force. Cold comfort there for those who have come to rely on them in their daily lives.

The government's claim to have abolished the hated Irish backstop is as empty as it is misleading because they have in fact substituted for it a front stop in the form of the new deal, and "consent" provisions which bear no resemblance to the ones they proposed themselves a mere two weeks ago.

To those who agree with Theresa May that the union of the United Kingdom is indeed precious, the way in which her own government, and even more so the present government, put that at risk - not just in Northern Ireland but in Scotland and Wales too - is a cause for despair. Does anyone seriously doubt now that the best way to consolidate our own Union is to remain in the EU?

The arguments for Parliament to reject this deal are therefore compelling. It is not a case of this deal or no deal. If Parliament does reject the deal, then the provisions of the Benn Act will be triggered that day and a request for an extension of Article 50 will be presented. Will the EU 27 agree? Well, fed up as they may be with all the twists and turns of the Brexit debate in this country, there is no evidence at all that they would reject such a request, particularly if it was to hold a referendum or a general election. That is surely the best course for Parliament to set.

And I followed this with another InFacts article on 23ʳᵈ October, 2019 reviewing the implications of the deal for the unity of the United Kingdom:

PM is shaking the UK to its foundations.

Few aspects of the Brexit saga are more counter-intuitive than the way three successive leaders of the Conservative and Unionist Party have acted in a manner which is shaking the union to its foundations.

David Cameron, by holding a referendum so soon after a narrow escape in the Scottish referendum vote, which was certain, whatever the overall outcome, to pit the four nations of our union against one another;

Theresa May by deciding at the outset, and without any prior consultation with the devolved institutions to quit the EU's customs union and single market, thus greatly accentuating the damage that would be caused by Brexit in any case; and now Boris Johnson by doing a deal which would involve installing customs border arrangements between Great Britain and Northern Ireland of a kind which both his predecessor and he himself had said could not be contemplated by any British Prime Minister.

Bad enough, you might think, but worse still when you look at the detail. Northern Ireland is to be saddled with an import regime of extraordinary complexity for goods coming from Great Britain or from other countries outside the EU, with tariffs having to be paid upfront and not reimbursed until it was certain they were not going through a duty free backdoor into the EU (and all this controlled by European institutions in which they would have no representation). This will inevitably impose substantial costs on businesses in the province. It is hard to believe that these new arrangements will not, as Jonathan Powell who played a key role in negotiating the Good Friday Agreement has pointed out, act as a steadily increasing incentive for the province to become part of, and not just a quasi-colony of, the EU, in which they voted to remain in the first place.

For Scotland the equation is even worse, despite the fact that they voted to remain in the EU by an even larger majority than Northern Ireland. They will have access to none of the provisions thrashed out for Northern Ireland and will, in terms of their future trade access to the EU, be entirely dependent on whatever future deal the government in London may negotiate with the EU - and that government could well turn out to value regulatory independence higher than frictionless trade. Is it surprising that support for Scottish independence was on the rise even before the terms of Johnson's deal were known?

And Wales, which did vote, narrowly, to leave, is equally, like Scotland being discriminated against when you compare their position with the Northern Ireland deal.

This really is a topsy-turvy outcome which the Parliament of our union is being pressed to accept. If that union is, as Theresa May so frequently said, precious, as it certainly is to many of us, then the simplest way to strengthen it is to decide to remain in the EU or, less conclusively, at least to negotiate a customs union with the rest of the EU.

To no one's great surprise the October deal failed to win approval in the Commons - the DUP, on whose votes earlier in the 2017 parliament the government's majority depended, voted against it, since they had been comprehensively betrayed by their erstwhile allies. The scenario laid down in the Benn Act then played out in Parliament, necessitating as it did a change in the 31st October exit date and the right to accept a new date after agreement was reached in Brussels. The necessary legislation to shift the date passed in both Houses, although not without another failed filibuster attempt in the Lords. And the world was then treated to some bizarre and humiliating comings and goings between N° 10 and my old mission in Brussels designed to spare Boris Johnson the personal ignominy of having to put his name to this request for a further extension of the Article 50 cut-off which he had earlier said he would rather die in a ditch than ever request. The request was made; he did not die in a ditch; and a further extension, to 31st January, 2020, was agreed by all 28 member states. The choice of date was certainly not ideal since, while it did provide enough time to hold an election it did not provide sufficient time to legislate for and to hold a referendum on the deal. But, since the deadline had by then already been extended three times and since it had always been assumed that, however great their frustration, the EU 27 would be certain to agree to a further extension to allow the UK to hold a referendum, this did not, at the time, look too big a problem.

However, having successfully avoided shipwreck on the Scylla of a no deal exit at the end of October, within days the ship of state was steered onto the Charybdis of an early general election, with no solution to the key issue of approval of the October deal, with or without a confirmatory referendum, in sight. How did this, as it turned out disastrous, error of judgement come about? The government's position was clear. It wanted the earliest possible election to be fought on the slogan "Get Brexit done"; and it wanted that election to take place in the narrowing window of opportunity before the Christmas and New Year holidays supervened. The SNP and the Liberal Democrats now swung into support of that option. A glance at the glum faces of the Liberal Democrat benches in the House of Lords told its own story - that this was not a choice with which they concurred. But the new leader of their party, Jo Swinson, had the bit firmly between her teeth and her colleagues in the Lords were given no say in the matter (ultimately the decision was to cost her the leadership of the party and the loss of her own seat in Parliament). This left the Labour Party isolated and in an impossible position to continue their resistance to an early election, particularly in the light of their own leader's constantly reiterated calls for an early opportunity to turn out the government. So, the die was cast; and the necessary majority under the Fixed Term Parliament Act required to stage an election on 12th December was achieved. To make matters worse all this played out against the backdrop of a messy and unpleasant bout of infighting in the People's Vote campaign, triggered by an attempt by Roland Rudd, one of its leaders, to get rid of the principal officials managing the campaign for a confirmatory referendum. It really was a script written in hell.

The election campaign itself, which then ensued, and in which, as an independent cross - bencher, I, as usual, played no direct role, was a pretty dispiriting one. It was clear from the outset, and from all the opinion polls, that there was no realistic chance of the Labour Party, now at last committed to a confirmatory referendum on any deal, winning an overall majority - clear that is to everyone except the leader of the party. So the best realistic outcome from the point of view of supporters of a referendum was another hung parliament and one in which the SNP would have a powerful influence. For the general public, mentally exhausted by several years of parliamentary infighting and deadlock, this was hardly an appealing prospect. Whereas a referendum ahead of any election would have decisively settled the outcome of Brexit and would have meant that any subsequent election campaign could focus on the many other important domestic issues which had been neglected for too long, holding an election ahead of a referendum enabled the Conservatives to appeal not only to their own core voters but to Labour-inclined Brexiters, and to play on the weariness with Brexit - and of course also on Jeremy Corbyn's poor rating as a possible prime minister. All that was entirely predictable and it is odd, to say the least, that so many of the key players failed to predict it.

I continued writing for InFacts throughout the election period, concentrating as far as possible on the positive aspects of the choice the electorate would have in any confirmatory referendum. Thus, following a peculiarly horrifying episode of human trafficking, terminating in the deaths of a large number of Vietnamese illegal immigrants in the back of a refrigerated lorry, I returned to the issue of the benefits derived from European cooperation over security and law enforcement matters in an article on 31st October, 2019:

European cooperation needed to stop human traffickers.

There is nothing like a real-life, real-time tragedy such as the discovery of those 39 victims of people trafficking in a container lorry in Purfleet to shine a harsh and unforgiving light on the potential implications of leaving the EU.

Here was an example of a burgeoning branch of international criminal activity which can only be successfully combatted by the sort of enforcement machinery which the EU has laboriously put together over the last twenty years.

The government announced today the setting up of a Joint Investigation Team (JIT) drawn from the member states touched by this crime - that is an essential piece of EU law enforcement machinery, along with others such as Europol and Eurojust which are already involved in dealing with cases of human trafficking. We may well need to use European Arrest Warrants (EAW) if all those involved in this appalling incident are to be brought to justice and if others involved in trafficking are to be deterred.

And yet, if the government's relaxed attitude to the UK leaving the EU without a deal this Thursday had actually come to pass, all this machinery would have become non - operative that same day. A narrow escape, indeed, you might think. As long as the risk of our leaving without a deal exists - on 31 January or at some later date - then that kind of damage to our internal security will continue to be a real one.

Nor does Boris Johnson's deal avoid plenty of collateral damage of this nature. The truncated transitional period up to the end of 2020 will not leave the UK in the same position as if we were still a member state. We will be out of Europol and Eurojust, unable to rely on the European Arrest Warrant, deprived of access to all of the EU's criminal data exchange systems. And beyond the transitional period? The non-binding Political Declaration is full of the sort of good intentions which often pave the way to hell. Much about "considering" this and "examining" that, but no certainty that it will prove possible to construct the sort of load-bearing cooperative systems without which effective action against international crime will not be possible. Do not forget that the EU has never done this sort of thing before with a third country. It has taken almost a decade to get Norway close to being able to benefit from the EAW system.

In a way, Purfleet is a wake-up call to remind us of how much of our security has come to depend on our EU membership. What we are talking about here is not the exchange of sensitive intelligence, which will no doubt continue since it does not depend on EU channels, but working, effective law enforcement systems to deal with the scourge of international crime.

On 12th November, 2019 with the election campaign just getting under way I wrote an article for InFacts on ways in which the UK would be a stronger global player if we remained in the EU than if we left:

5 ways we'll be a stronger global player if we stay in the EU.

Theresa May used to boast about how Brexit would turn us into "Global Britain". One doesn't hear so much of that rhetoric under her successor - perhaps because Brexiters have become embarrassed by how a Trump trade deal could lead to things like maggots in our orange juice and rat hairs in our paprika.

We will be stronger and more effective on the global stage if we stay in the EU. We will be working together with 27 other countries with whom we share values and interests - rather than flying solo and being bullied by bigger powers.

Here are five of the main ways we can advance our national interests and contribute to a more effective European voice in the world.

Climate Crisis.

The EU is an essential player in the efforts to implement and to enhance the Paris accords, particularly now that Donald Trump's America is withdrawing from them. There will be plenty of tensions within the EU over how best to fulfil that role. The UK should be in there influencing that debate in an ambitious direction. EU rules will not stop us from going even further ourselves if that is what we decide.

Trade policy.

While we have been agonising over Brexit, the EU has been getting on with negotiating freer and fairer trade agreements with many of the most promising trading partners - South Korea, Japan, Vietnam, the main countries of Latin America (Mexico, Chile and now Mercosur). More such agreements, for example with Australia and New Zealand, are in the pipeline. We could be on the inside pushing that agenda , not on the outside competing with it. We could also be working to sustain the World Trade Organisation against the damage being inflicted on it by Trump's trade wars.

Security.

Europe needs to pull its weight more effectively in NATO and make a greater contribution to its collective security. The UK has always been a key player on European security issues and is more likely to be so again if we are shaping European policy from the inside. The EU has just made a serious mistake in refusing to open accession negotiations with North Macedonia and Albania, a decision which risks undermining European security and over which we had no influence because we were on the way out.

Regulating and taxing multinationals.

We need to get to grips with giant companies that use their power to bully consumers and don't pay enough tax. Are we more likely to do that if we are supporting the European Commission's vigorous efforts? Or will we achieve more if we are on our own, and open to pressure and blackmail, when other countries such as China and the US do not like what we are doing?

Human Rights.

The challenges to human rights are, if anything, increasing. Integrating a human rights dimension into foreign policy is always a high-risk undertaking. Will we be more effective at doing so as part of the EU which broadly shares our values and interests, or acting on our own, and so liable to be buffeted by threats of retaliation and discrimination?

All this will be on the line on December 12, put there by a government which is desperate to take us out of the EU on January 31, come what may.

And on 18th November, 2019 I returned too to the sensitive issue of immigration and why the Brexiter promises in this respect had no solid foundation and were unlikely to be honoured:

This is no way to "take back control" of immigration.

Anyone following the debate over immigration in the first two weeks of the election campaign could be forgiven for thinking they had been invited into a Mad Hatters' Tea Party.

The party which is advocating the Brexit-at-any-cost solution of Boris Johnson's October deal is proposing (belatedly) to drop its unrealistic and unrealised target of limiting net migration to "the tens of thousands". Instead it vows to introduce what is rather vaguely described as an Australian-style, points-based system - apparently ignorant of the fact that it's application in Australia has resulted in a steady and substantial increase in legal immigration.

For the Conservatives reducing immigration is now to be achieved not by reducing immigration from third countries, over which we have always had control even as a member state of the EU, but by clamping down on freedom of movement from the rest of the EU, which currently only represents just over a quarter of the overall immigration total. The approach is summed up in Michael Gove's insidious question: "Why should we treat a Slovenian better than a Bangladeshi"?

The other main party is struggling to handle its hesitations over the positive reference to "freedom of movement" backed by its September party conference. This is despite the fact that it's commitment to hold a confirmatory referendum on any Brexit deal necessarily involves the possibility of continued compliance with the EU obligation on freedom of movement between its member states.

Meanwhile debate over the May government's White Paper on immigration has revealed plenty of defects in those proposals and given rise to any amount of misleading rhetoric. To take a few examples:

- The £30,000 income guideline for immigrants is clearly far too high and risks inflicting serious damage on many sectors of the economy, as the CBI and other business representatives have pointed out;

- The government's current mantra of only admitting "the brightest and the best" is fatuous in the extreme. Clearly seasonal agricultural workers and relatively low-paid social carers are never going to fall into that category. But they are needed if the NHS and British farming are not to be in real trouble. With unemployment at historic lows, our own citizens show no sign of taking up the slack;

- The need for more trained medical professionals to help staff the NHS is so obvious that the government is already planning to create a loophole in any new rules to exempt them;

- Admitting students and researchers who have offers of places at our universities is equally desirable if we are to sustain our second place world-wide in the higher education market. This is, after all, one of the few sectors of our economy which is now a world leader and has the potential to remain so. The shift in government policy to allow two years of post-study access to the labour market is welcome but insufficient.

We can draw two broad conclusions from all this. First, our politicians are nowhere near identifying an evidence-based, economically viable and humane immigration policy. Trying to hammer one out in the next few weeks of election campaigning will lead to substantial self-inflicted harm.

A second broad conclusion is that it was utterly wrong to make immigration from Europe a touchstone of whether we should stay in the EU or leave, and it is foolish to make reducing immigration from the EU an object of policy post-Brexit. If we cannot work out a rational policy for immigration from third countries, what on earth is the meaning of that dishonest slogan "Take back control"?

No one, and no political party, doubts that the December election will have decisive implications for Brexit. That indeed is the thrust of the speech being made today by Boris Johnson.

In that case, why is it that so many of the contributions on the subject in the first week of campaigning have been so trite, so misleading and even downright untrue?

Take, for example, the interview given by Sajid Javid, Chancellor of the Exchequer, to the BBC economics editor on November 11. Javid told Faisal Islam that ratifying the Johnson deal would end the risk of a no deal Brexit. That is simply not true. It merely delays the evil day.

Both Boris Johnson and Michael Gove have ruled out any possibility of extending the transitional period beyond the end of 2020. Yet no one with any knowledge of the EU and other trade talks believes that the sort of future partnership deal sketched out in the Political Declaration, which goes far beyond matters of trade policy, can be negotiated and ratified in the eleven months between the end of January and the end of December 2020. So the risk of a no deal Brexit is merely postponed until the end of 2020, not ended. That is certainly the view of David Gauke, former Justice Secretary, and he was sitting at the cabinet table until four months ago. Now he is running to be elected as an independent, against the Conservative party which expelled him for voting to block a no deal Brexit.

Back in his BBC interview, Javid does admit that there will be "some changes" to customs procedures for British businesses trading with the EU as a result of any trade deal. He could have added there would inevitably be new rules and red tape for trade between Great Britain and Northern Ireland as a result of the new checks down the Irish Sea. Yet Johnson himself seems unclear about having accepted that in the deal he struck in October.

There is no hope of the frictionless trade we currently have with the EU, thanks to the Single Market; no mention of the position of services, which make up four-fifths of our economy; and no clear picture for Britain's businesses of the likely cost to them and to the wider economy of these changes.

Why not? Because Javid refused to allow the Treasury to produce an impact assessment of Johnson's deal when it was struck in October and before it was put to Parliament.

Is there any silver lining? Javid did give a rub or two to the jewel in the crown of Brexiter rhetoric - the prospect of free trade agreements around the world. But all the economic analyses carried out have made it clear that such agreements take a long time to negotiate and cannot possibly compensate fully for the loss of our frictionless trade with the EU, which accounts for 45% of our global business. The biggest prize, an agreement with the US, does not look particularly promising. That is not just because of the terms the US would be likely to demand for access to agricultural and other exports. It is also because the greatest Brexit champion in the US, Donald Trump, recently cast doubt on whether any agreement at all could be reached if the UK went ahead with its current deal with the EU.

There really does need to be a lot more plain-speaking and honest analysis about Johnson's deal, which the electorate is, in effect, being asked to endorse in the election. Not least, every aspect of it needs to be compared with the deal we already have as a member of the EU.

Finally on 28th November, 2019 I set out a five-point agenda for Project Hope:

Five ways we can make the EU's single market even better.

The EU's single market isn't frozen in time. We can shape it in our interests - if only we stop Brexit. Here are five important opportunities we'll miss out on if we quit.

Research and Innovation.
The UK has been at the forefront in developing the EU's steadily expanding projects and programmes for research and innovation. Out universities and research establishments have regularly been among the top two member states, and have benefited from the international cooperative networks so established.

We have been a substantial net beneficiary from the EU budget spending on research and innovation. The EU's next seven-year budget cycle is set to increase that spending. The government's aim is to find some way of retaining links with those EU programmes after Brexit. But we would have no role in shaping these, as we do now. And, in all probability, our return from any such involvement would be limited to the amount we contributed.

Data protection.

It is pretty well unthinkable to British business that we should try to operate different data protection rules from the rest of Europe. That too has been the view taken by the government which hastened to sign up last May to the EU's new regulation (GDPR). Over time the EU is likely to adapt these rules; but we will have no say over those changes and will have little choice but to follow suit.

Capital markets.

London has been, and is likely to remain, Europe's biggest market in financial services. But it will lose an EU "passport" giving it the right to offer services seamlessly across the single market. The "equivalence" regime which will take its place will leave the City in a precarious position with respect to rulings by the European Commission. We will also lose any direct role in shaping EU policies, especially the gradually emerging Capital Markets Union.

Services.

The single market in services is far from complete. But for British businesses which rely on the freedom of establishment everywhere in Europe - and for architects, lawyers, accountants, doctors and many others who benefit from the mutual recognition of qualifications - it is a reality and a valuable one. So too for our creative industries which are European leaders. Progress in completing the single market in services will certainly be slower when we are no longer at the table. We won't

317

*have any say over how it develops and won't get full
access to it either.*

Competition policy.
*The UK has been, throughout our membership, a
firm supporter of the Commission's role in enforcing fair
competition rules and limiting state aids. Both these
functions have protected our businesses against unfair
competition.*
*There is now pressure from within the EU (from
France and Germany in particular) to constrain the
Commission's powers and encourage the emergence of
European "champions". Outside the EU, we will no
longer be able to push back against these developments.
But we will still, almost certainly be on the receiving end
of the Commission's powers as a part of any trade deal.*

When election night came on 12th December I joined Hugo
Dixon, his mother and brother and a few members of the
InFacts team, at a supper party in Hugo's mews house just
across the motorway from the macabre, shrouded skeleton
of Grenfell Tower. Our mood was sombre from the outset,
since the hopes of another hung parliament had been
fading for several days. When the exit poll prediction of a
Conservative overall majority of around 80 seats was
followed by constituency results bearing that out, we all
knew the Brexit game was up; and that parliamentary
endorsement of the October deal and the UK leaving the
European Union on 31st January 2020 was a certainty. The
conclusion, endorsed around the table, that InFacts no
longer had a viable purpose was acted on by Hugo the

following day. My career as a part-time journalist and commentator was over. I drove home to Bedford Park as depressed as I had been on the referendum night in June 2016, contemplating the wreckage of the project to which I had devoted much time and energy since setting out for Brussels in September 1965.

The epilogue was as we predicted that night. Parliament approved the October deal and the domestic legislation needed to implement it in January; and the UK left the EU on 31st January, 2020.

Chapter 14

Look back in anger

My choice of title for this final chapter of my book on Brexit is both risky and contentious. Anger is not an appealing or attractive emotion. Yet, as I look back over the period of thirty years covered by the narrative in the preceding chapters, and indeed over the last fifty-five years since I first set off to Brussels in 1965 to take up a junior post in the UK's Delegation to the European Communities, it would be disingenuous to pretend that the emotion does not come through quite strongly, although I hope not to the exclusion or distortion of rational observation and argument, which has been my stock in trade throughout my professional career.

The anger I feel is rooted in the sheer unnecessariness of the process that culminated in the 2016 in/out referendum, the four and a half years of chaotic parliamentary infighting that followed, and Britain's departure from the European Union at the end of January 2020. The nature and scope of European integration has often been a matter of dispute in other member states, leading in some cases to hard fought referendums on particular treaties designed to carry that process forward - most notably when Giscard d'Estaing's Constitutional Treaty was voted down in 2005 in referendums in France and the Netherlands. But in no other member state has the issue of continued membership ever been the focus of debate and in none of them has a mainstream political party embraced the cause of leaving; only in Britain have both the largest parties, one after the other, first Labour in the 1970s and 1980s, then the Conservatives from the 1990s onwards, fallen prey to that unnecessary existential debate and been devoured by it.

Why unnecessary? Because, by the time the issue of our membership was put to the vote in 2016, British exceptionalism within the EU had reached its apogee and was firmly entrenched in the European treaties, only capable of being altered to the smallest degree with our own agreement, endorsed by the approval of our own, sovereign parliament. In the 1980s, following nearly five years of negotiation, the inequity of the impact of the EU's budgetary system on the UK was recognised and redressed by Margaret Thatcher's rebate instrument; and, by 2015, Britain's per capita contribution to the European budget was ninth among the member states, almost as low in fact as that of Norway which was not a member at all. In the 1990s Britain's omission from the Schengen area of passport-free travel was recognised; as was our right to decide unilaterally whether and, if so, when to join the Euro. And in 2014, almost unnoticed, the handling of Britain's opt-in/opt-out choice for Justice and Home Affairs legislation was regularised. Hence my despair when David Cameron made such a meal in the 2015/16 re-negotiation over the preambular treaty reference to "ever closer union" which had never, and never could, compel us to go further than we were willing to go in any future treaty changes.

Unnecessary too because, over the previous decades, the European Union had developed in a way that owed much to British initiatives and priorities. The establishment of a Single Market was the most notable example of this evolution; but enlargement to include the countries of Central, Eastern and Southern Europe, freed from fascism and communism, was another; as was the European Union's trade policy, steadily moving towards freer and fairer trade; and its environmental policies based on implementing the Paris accord on climate change. And the idea that the EU was set on a course ineluctably leading towards the creation of a federal United States of Europe, a view that had purchase not just on the wilder shores of Euroscepticism but right across the leadership of the Conservative party when it returned to office in 2010, flew in the face of all those involved right across Europe in the process of permanent negotiation of which the governance of the EU consists.

My own views on all these matters, for what they are worth - and I was never a decision-taker in the full sense of the word - can be glimpsed in that valedictory despatch I sent from Brussels when I left my job as the UK's Permanent Representative to the European Communities in the summer of 1990 and which are set out in one of the early chapters of this book. I certainly am not, and never have been, a believer in a federal concept of Europe, let alone a United States of Europe in which its nation states would have merged the exercise of their sovereignty. I have always believed that British exceptionalism needed to find its place in the European Union if our continued membership was to be consolidated - hence the time and effort I devoted to the negotiation of our budget rebate and of our untrammelled right to decide whether or not to join the Euro. And I was an early supporter, and remain one, of the concept of variable geometry which enables some considerable degree of variation between member states when applying European integration to specific sectors, such as membership of the Euro and of the Schengen area. My guess is that variable geometry is going to remain a durable feature of the EU, even now that one of its leading protagonists, the UK has left. How long will some of the countries which are not members of the Euro remain that way? A long time, I would suspect. So, even if much of what I have written in recent years and much of the content of my all too frequent speeches and interjections in the House of Lords may have convinced some that I am an uncritical, maximalist supporter of the EU and all its works, that is not what the record of my professional life actually shows. I would describe myself rather as a pragmatist who is convinced that Britain's national interests were best promoted through membership of the EU and who worked for a succession of governments from Macmillan to Blair whose overall view was precisely that. I do not regard the result of the 2016 referendum as having invalidated that view, merely as having, tragically in my view, rendered it inoperable.

In the rest of this concluding chapter I will give answers to a number of the more testing questions posed by what I have written over the years:

1. Was Britain's EU membership doomed from the outset, merely coming to a pre-ordained conclusion in 2020?

No, I do not think so. It is no use denying that Britain's route into the European Communities was fraught with setbacks and miscalculations. First the miscalculation in the 1950s which resulted in a failure to appreciate just how significant a project the European Coal and Steel Community, the European Economic Community and EURATOM were, and thus in Britain standing aside from the creation of these organisations even when it was made clear by the founding fathers how welcome its participation would have been. And then General de Gaulle's two humiliating vetoes in the 1960s. Underlying all this were the cultural, economic and political differences between the twentieth century experiences of the six original member states - what Michael Charlton, in his brilliant series of interviews with those in London principally responsible for that original miscalculation called "The Price of Victory"; my 1990 despatch from Brussels describes those differences and their consequences for our EU membership in extenso and I will not repeat them here. Suffice it to say that I do not think those differences were incapable of being managed and overcome - as they were in many instances such as remedying the inequitable budgetary burden. I have no doubt that many future commentators will treat Britain's exit as inevitable. It is always easier to write history when you know the outcome; and to forget that those who shape the events that become history are often like drivers in foggy conditions who cannot see very far ahead and are not always aware of the consequences of the policy choices they make. So, beware predestination. It can be a cop-out from accepting responsibility for what actually happened. What can be said is that Britain's EU membership status was, from the outset, more fragile than that of any other member state.

2. Who should bear the major responsibility for the slide towards the exit in 2020?

The question could be re-phrased more simply and less personally by asking how a 2:1 majority in 1975 in favour of staying in the European Communities on the terms re-negotiated turned into a 52%/48% majority in favour of leaving the EU in 2016. But the answer cannot possibly be a simple one, nor can the responsibility be attributed to one person, one group or even one party. It was complex and cumulative.

The choice on both occasions to take the responsibility to decide on Britain's European status away from Parliament and submit it to a national referendum was a deeply flawed one, even though the contradictory outcomes make 1975 a date to be air-brushed out of history by Brexiters and 2016 a date to be mourned by those who wanted Britain to remain a member. On both occasions the choice was made not as a matter of constitutional principle but by prime ministers (Harold Wilson and David Cameron) in an ultimately mistaken gamble that this would heal deep divides within their own parties. That the referendums failed utterly in that objective is a matter of historical record. Asking the public to decide on a matter of great complexity, even assuming that their votes would be cast on the basis of the question posed rather than being influenced by many extraneous issues, was to play Russian roulette with an important national asset. Neither Wilson nor Cameron have so far received many marks from historians, nor did they get any political rewards from those failed gambles - quite the contrary.

More widely, politicians of both of Britain's main parties, which alternated in office during the forty-five years of our membership, failed comprehensively to incorporate that membership into a convincing part of the national narrative which gets politicians elected in the first place. Instead they either dissembled over it or tried to pretend it was not a matter of great importance. Negotiations in Brussels were treated as if they were fixtures in some rarefied European Cup competition, scored like a game of football, with any concept of collective benefit from the decisions taken lost in the melee. And while Labour gradually rid itself of the anti-European isolationism of the 1980s, it was only fitfully replaced by a desire to shape European decision-making. Just look at how few of Tony Blair's European speeches were made to a British audience. On the other side of politics, the influence of the groups of elderly retirees, whose views weighed so heavily in the choice of candidates for safe parliamentary seats, was exercised in an increasingly anti-European direction, thus changing the balance in the parliamentary party. I once asked a Conservative MP friend if he ever talked about European issues to his constituents. "Oh no" he replied "it only causes trouble". It was in this vacuum that Euroscepticism thrived.

There were some prominent British politicians who did indeed play a major role in creating the conditions which made the outcome of the 2016 vote more likely. Margaret Thatcher, despite the fact that, even in her moments of greatest irritation and antagonism towards the EU, she never, while in office, contemplated the idea of Britain leaving, was one of them. Her negotiating modus operandi was to whip up those feelings of irritation and antagonism, which brought short term benefits both in negotiating terms in Brussels and in domestic political terms at home. But it also sowed the dragon's teeth of the virulent Euroscepticism of succeeding generations of Conservative politicians and it reduced the willingness of Britain's partners in the EU to cut the deals which are a daily part of European decision-making. Nigel Farage, first as leader of the UK Independence Party and then of the Brexit Party, purveyed a particular brand of saloon bar bragging and bluster which enabled him to put to effective use his membership of the European Parliament, even if it never managed to win him a seat at Westminster. And Boris Johnson, a Pied Piper type of political operator, who was still weighing up the pros and cons for his own political career of campaigning for Leave or for Remain on the day the national debate was engaged, suffered no pain travelling in a battle bus emblazoned with a figure for the money sent weekly to Brussels which bore no relation to the truth - after straight bananas that was child's play. Not to mention Dominic Cummings, Johnson's Svengali, not even a Conservative and (like me) never elected to any post, but who clearly played an important role at two stages in the Brexit saga - during the 2016 referendum campaign and during the 2019 general election which resulted in the UK actually leaving the EU in January 2020. Ideologically motivated or just driven by a desire to disrupt, a competitive instinct to win at any price? Certainly arrogant and completely unfazed by the falsehood of the assertions he was making.

3. What role did the media, the printed press in particular, play in the shift of opinion between 1975 and 2016?

This is hard to quantify but it cannot be dismissed as a figment of Remainer hand-wringing. In the 1970s the balance of reporting and commentary in the British press was pro-European - even the Daily Telegraph was in that camp. But gradually the pendulum swung and the printed press became overwhelmingly negative towards the EU in general and towards Britain's membership of it. Several of the main newspaper proprietors - Rupert Murdoch and Conrad Black figured prominently in this shift; as did editors like Paul Dacre of the Daily Mail. And some individual journalists, among them Boris Johnson, then the Daily Telegraph correspondent in Brussels and now Prime Minister, made their living, their reputations and their future political careers out of a stream of "straight banana" stories, quite deliberately designed to provoke derision and antagonism towards Brussels and all its works. Brussels did not help, however, becoming increasingly paranoiac about the British press and never finding an effective way of presenting, not just in the UK but right across the EU, the process-driven, acronym-riddled daily work of the European institutions.

4. Should the cross-party alliance in Parliament against Theresa May's deal have accepted it as being better than nothing and less damaging than the sequence of events which followed its rejection?

It really is doubtful whether that option was ever seriously on offer once a massive number of Conservative back-benchers had voted against May's deal in January 2019. Admittedly that number was whittled down in subsequent votes on the deal but never to a size that made approval likely. In theory too, a deal could have been struck in the talks between the government and the Labour opposition in May 2019; but that would have required the government to agree to remaining in a customs union with the EU and, given that it and most of its supporters were determined to pursue the mirage of an independent trade policy capable of more than compensating for the trade benefits lost by leaving the EU's Single Market and Customs Union, that course was never on offer either. Moreover the fate meted out to the contents of the non-legally binding Political Declaration, which was comprehensively junked by the Johnson government within three days of the UK leaving the EU, when the post-Brexit negotiations for a UK/EU trade deal began in February 2020, demonstrated that the Brexiters never contemplated honouring that declaration and that changes to it conceded during the government/Labour talks would have been worthless. The hard fact was that every aspect of the May deal (and of the Johnson deal that followed it) was less advantageous to the UK than continued EU membership. So insisting on the need for a confirmatory referendum before any deal could enter into force, and insisting too that the option of remaining in the EU should be one of the choices in any such referendum, was fully justified in the eyes of the cross-party alliance; and failure to achieve that objective did not discredit its strategic validity.

5. Should the cross-party alliance have embraced the Liberal Democrat and Scottish National Party preference for revoking Britain's Article 50 notification of withdrawal without the need for another referendum?

No one who has followed the evolution of my own thinking about referendums, described earlier in this book, can doubt my opposition to any recourse to plebiscitary democracy to resolve the European issue, whether in 1975 or 2016. But, once the vote had taken place in 2016, I simply could not see the political viability of reversing that vote without another referendum. For one thing there was no majority for doing that in the 2017 Parliament, and much less support for it than there was for subjecting any deal to another referendum; and the outcome of the December 2019 general election demonstrated that it was not a vote winner in the country. In addition it seemed to me inconceivable that the Brexiters would have accepted that outcome, even if a majority could have been found for it in Parliament. The demand for another referendum would then have become their battle cry; and the polarisation between Leavers and Remainers would have continued to divide the country to the detriment of addressing other policy priorities. I was often asked why I was so sure that Remain would win another referendum. I was not. I thought it quite possible we would lose. But it seemed to me that a referendum was the best way of settling the matter definitively, which was why I favoured making the result of any further referendum legally binding and was glad that the People's Vote campaign accepted that and made it part of their platform.

6. Does not the whole Brexit saga - and indeed the whole troubled history of Britain's relationship with the EU from the 1950s onwards - demonstrate an obsession by the political class with a set of policy issues which were a distraction from more important policy choices?

The first senior politician I came across who held that view was Tony Crosland, then President of the Board of Trade, when he visited Brussels in 1967 during our second, initially ill-fated, bid for membership. A few others crossed my path, but not many. Most British politicians I advised simply accepted it as a fact of life that they had to trudge through a European quagmire, imposed on them principally by the politics of their own party, first Labour and then the Conservatives. But they did so without enthusiasm and without asking themselves if there was any alternative. It was in my view a correct judgement that Britain could not duck the hard choices to be made about the country's relationship with the rest of Europe. Britain had from time to time flirted with an isolationist foreign policy so far as continental Europe was concerned - in the second half of the nineteenth century when it even acquired the label of "splendid isolation" and in the 1930s when a Prime Minister could call Czechoslovakia "a faraway country of which we know little". But these brief flirtations had all ended in tears and in much deeper involvement with European developments. Once it became clear that the European project and the institutions established by the Six were here to stay and were capable of navigating through crises and of bringing prosperity and stability to their citizens, it was inevitable that Britain would have to swallow its pride and work out a close relationship with the then European Communities. A first attempt to limit this to a free trade area - an approach which bears an uncanny resemblance to the sort of trade agreement the post-Brexit Johnson government is now seeking with the EU - ended in failure. And successive prime ministers (Macmillan, Wilson, Heath, Thatcher, Major, Blair, Brown) set about getting into the club and, once in, establishing Britain as a significant player in shaping the EU's policies which regulated an ever more interdependent Europe and much else besides.

Nevertheless there is a grain of truth in the critical question I am trying to answer. Other member states' domestic policies were much less disturbed by European issues than Britain's were. From time to time major European issues caused controversy in one or another member state - over the UK's and other countries' accessions, over the foundation of a Single Market and of an Economic and Monetary Union, over the Constitutional Treaty - but the debates on those issues were invariably conducted within an unwritten code, accepted by all main political parties, that their country's membership was not at stake. Only in Britain did such debates lead quickly into a kind of existential polarisation, ending in our exit in 2020. So the visceral and obsessive nature that discussion of European issues brought to British politics was purely self-inflicted, and one can only speculate that, if our politicians had conducted them within the same unwritten code as our continental neighbours did, we could have avoided much of the displacement of domestic priorities and the miserable denouement in 2020.

7. Why stop the story now, with the UK negotiating to define its post-Brexit relationship with the EU?

Well you have to stop somewhere and the end of our EU membership in January 2020 marks a brutally clear caesura. The evolution of our relationship with the rest of Europe will not, of course, stop there. Indeed, if history is any guide, it will never stop. Even if the transitional period ends in December 2020 without a deal on our future relationship that will not be the end of the story. In those circumstances it is perfectly possible, indeed probable, that negotiations on a future relationship would resume under a different government and at a later date. The same could happen even if a shrunken, minimalist deal is struck. But all such negotiations will be conducted on a different basis and within a different framework than when we were still a member. And a Britain which, in my view, will be less prosperous, less secure and less influential as a result of leaving will get a less good deal than it ever did as a member. So, rather than trail off into an open-ended epilogue, I decided to close the story as we left.

8. Has my own personal experience skewed this account to an unreasonable extent?

I was compelled to face up to this question at a very early stage, as I sat over tea in my son Philip's and my daughter-in-law Ghislaine's garden in Agon-Coutainville in the Cotentin region of Normandy in August 2016 chatting to a French senator friend of Ghislaine's family. "Was I not personally affronted and horrified by the recent course of events - wrecking much of my life's work?" was the gist of the question put to me by the senator. My response at the time was, and remains, that it is important not to personalise events of such fundamental importance. As someone who had worked on European issues for fifty years I believed I had a stock of knowledge and experience which could help in navigating the difficult course on which we were now setting out as a result of the 23rd June vote to leave; and, as a minor figure in public life, that was what I intended to do.

That said it would be idle to deny that I was personally deeply depressed by the outcome of the referendum, a feeling of depression which only intensified when, following Donald Trump's election as President of the United States in November of that year, he set about disrupting and dismantling the rules-based international order, to whose construction I had devoted those parts of my professional life which were not spent labouring in the Brussels vineyard. I feel profoundly that those two developments are leading Britain and the rest of the world in quite the wrong direction, one fraught with risk and one haunted by the ghosts of the first half of the twentieth century, when the international community tried twice and twice failed to handle the rivalries and shifting great power relationships which are an unavoidable feature of the world we live in. My temperament as an incurable optimist has been pretty badly shaken; and it has yet to be restored.

9. Will Britain ever re-join the EU?

It is with some pain that I give a negative reply to that question, although I have been around the diplomatic circuit for too long to use a word like "never". But I find it hard to envisage the circumstances in which either of the main parties which continue to dominate our politics would embark on such a high-risk venture. And I also find it hard to see Britain, from the outside, being able to negotiate again those features of British exceptionalism which were such an essential part of our EU membership by the time we left. Some of them, perhaps, but not all. And without them the chances of any re-negotiated terms being approved in a confirmatory referendum, which would be hard to avoid, could be slim indeed. The British Empire may have been acquired in a fit of absence of mind but our membership of the EU was cast off in a fit of pique and of ignorance as to the consequences. So, having made our bed, we are going to have to sleep in it; and I fear it will not be very comfortable.